POSTMODERNISM
AND THE
REVOLUTION
IN RELIGIOUS
THEORY

STUDIES IN RELIGION AND CULTURE

John D. Barbour and Gary L. Ebersole,
Editors

POSTMODERNISM
AND THE
REVOLUTION
IN RELIGIOUS
THEORY

■

Toward a Semiotics
of the Event

■

CARL RASCHKE

UNIVERSITY OF VIRGINIA PRESS

CHARLOTTESVILLE AND LONDON

UNIVERSITY OF VIRGINIA PRESS
Printed in the United States of America on acid-free paper

First published 2012

1 3 5 7 9 8 6 4 2

Library of Congress Cataloging-in-Publication Data

Raschke, Carl A.
  Postmodernism and the revolution in religious theory : toward a semiotics of the event / Carl Raschke.
       p.   cm. — (Studies in religion and culture)
  Includes bibliographical references (p.   ) and index.
  ISBN 978-0-8139-3306-1 (cloth : alk. paper) — ISBN 978-0-8139-3307-8 (pbk. : alk. paper) —
ISBN 978-0-8139-3308-5 (e-book)
  1. Postmodernism—Religious aspects. 2. Semiotics—Religious aspects. 3. Derrida, Jacques.
4. Badiou, Alain. 5. Žižek, Slavoj. I. Title.
  BL65.P73R37 2012
  210—dc23

                                                                                    2012009485

To my family—Sunny, Erik, Kes, Casjen

CONTENTS

■

ACKNOWLEDGMENTS

■

IN THE evolution of this manuscript I have been blessed with many assistants and contributing "theorists" who have played both crucial and occasional roles. In particular, I would like to acknowledge the following: the Department of Religious Studies at Rice University, which hosted me as a visiting scholar, and where I began this particular venture over a decade ago; the University of Denver, which afforded me a sabbatical to take time to launch the project; Dr. Victor Taylor, at York College of Pennsylvania and the *Journal for Cultural and Religious Theory*, for his support and suggestions for the development of the concept of the book; Dr. David Hale, former doctoral advisee and currently on the faculty at Colorado Mesa University, for opening my eyes to the significance of Deleuze's work; Rachel Tillman, at present a doctoral candidate in philosophy, for her close reading of an earlier version of the manuscript; Tyler Akers and Heidi Rhodes, my doctoral students, for similar readings of a later version; Joshua Ramos, also a PhD student, for his thorough and scrupulous proofreading and copyediting; Jason Alvis, for his reading and observations; my wife, Sunny, for her deep love and devotion to me and encouragement of my work.

The book has incorporated both excerpts and major portions, along with various emendations and extensive revisions, of a number of previously published articles in other books and journals. They include "Paratheology: The Study of Religion and the Science of the Negative," *Journal for Cultural and Religious Theory*, December 2000; "The Deposition of the Sign," *Journal for Cultural and Religious Theory*, December 2001; "From Religion to Faith: Levinasian Ethics and the Grammar of Address," *Journal for Cultural and Religious Theory*, December 2002; "Bataille's Gift," *Journal for Cultural and Religious Theory*, December 2003; "The Monstrosity of Žižek's Christianity," *Journal for Cultural and Religious Theory*, Spring 2011;

"Rending the Veil of the Temple: The Death of God as Sacrificium Representationis," in *Thinking Through the Death of God: A Critical Companion to Thomas J. J. Altizer*, ed. Lissa McCullough and Brian Schroeder (Albany: State University of New York Press, 2004), 1–10. Thanks to these sources for permission to rework or reprint earlier published portions of this book.

POSTMODERNISM
AND THE
REVOLUTION
IN RELIGIOUS
THEORY

INTRODUCTION

■

The Question of the "Religious"

THE QUESTION of the "religious" today continues concomitantly to haunt, fascinate, and discomfit us. Ever since Jacques Derrida and Gianni Vattimo announced the "return of religion" as an "auto-immune" reaction to secularism in the early 1990s, scholars have wallowed in their own confusion, not only about whether it is really happening, but also about whether it is a good thing. In the immediate wake of September 11, 2001, much of the Western academic world for a short period tended to give Derrida and Vattimo the benefit of the doubt. During the same period we witnessed, as a result of various culturally complex factors (but largely due to the interests of leading Continental thinkers), the so-called religious turn or theological turn in philosophy. Lately, the wheel has turned once more, and the "auto-immunity" of the secular, academic mind has become just as pronounced. The meteoric and broad popularity of the writings of the so-called new atheists has been shadowed in the academic context by the trendiness of the so-called new materialists and speculative realists, all of whom have a not-so-subtle antireligious, or antitheological, agenda.

The problem is, however, that few of those who constantly chatter about religion and its putative revival have much of an idea of what in general they are really talking about. Multiculturalism, anthropological relativism, ethnographic descriptivism, and a colorful selection of socioreligious identitarianisms have all combined with a certain political correctness to choke off the rise of what the current interest in religion desperately requires—a more encompassing, *theoretical architecture* in accordance with which the varieties of the world's prevalent and more exotic species can be accounted for. At the same time, the would-be "religious" or "theological turn" in philosophy has not offered much help for understanding the question of religion in general. What amounts to relatively arcane questions of standard Christian theology, framed solely within the argot of contemporary Continental philosophy, have dominated the discourse.

The explosive growth of the field of religious studies, virtually nonexistent only half a century ago, has mirrored these trends, which really run as far back as the late 1960s. The academic study of religion has succeeded in naming, profiling, explicating, and often functioning as an apologetics for hundreds, if not thousands, of forms of belief, ritual, and cultic practice that a hundred years ago were dismissed as archaisms or superstitions. It has been responsible in many ways for fostering attitudes of acceptance and tolerance while enlarging considerably the spectrum of recognized "religious diversity," sometimes even to the point of absurdity. At the same time, the rise of religious studies as a field would have been impossible were it not for two major, perduring factors: (1) the great, richly seasoned "stewpot" of American spiritual experimentation and innovation, as opposed to the old homogenizing "melting pot" metaphor, and (2) the even more powerful agency of cultural comingling and interpenetration that goes by the somewhat murky designation of "globalization." Without globalization, religious studies would be unimaginable.

But the blessing has been mixed, to say the least. As the prominent social philosopher and theorist Olivier Roy, whose work on the contemporary interactions between Islam and the West has been acclaimed in recent years, points out, the "return of religion" in the minds of the Western intelligentsia has not been an organic, historical process. It consists essentially in a trick of the eye when viewing the phantasmagoria we see in the world today of religious incidents, expressions, and symbolic actions. We have been "bewitched" (if we may use Wittgenstein's famous term for the confusion of words with concepts) by a *culturalist* fallacy. The culturalist fallacy (not exactly Roy's term, but mine) consists in the misidentification of semiotic tokens, or effervescent sign-functions, as underlying cultural realities—or, to put it in shopworn Marxist terms, mistaking the "substructure" for the "superstructure." As Roy observes laconically in his latest book, *Holy Ignorance*, "In this sense, religious 'comeback' is merely an optical illusion; it would be more appropriate to speak of transformation. Religion is both more visible and at the same time frequently in decline. We are witnessing a reformulation of religion rather than a return to ancestral practices abandoned during the secularist hiatus."[1]

This reformulation—or "reformatting," as he prefers to call it—has more to do with the market-driven and milieu-conditioned performance of religious life in the new global cosmopolis than with any kind of set of texts or "traditions" which religious studies scholars tend to specialize in. The global marketplace has made "culture" a vast supermarket aisle of customized consumer items, a set of symbolic codes and accepted practices that eventuate from both competitive and often commercial efforts to "locate" and domesticate a person or a group within the global emporium of ideologies and life options. No longer is there such a thing as a Buddhist or a Muslim in the "authentic" cultural sense, if there ever was one, especially when the latter adopts the postmodern American and European invention of "worship bands," or the former exports what was already a highly modernized set of meditation practices that can be accommodated to any relatively affluent American style as a form of "New Age" self-realization.

One of the reasons "theory" has been largely clueless in acknowledging the kind of transformation Roy describes is that in most respects it is still peering through the lenses of either nineteenth-century essentialism, in keeping with the legacy of Continental scholarship and *Religionswissenschaft* (which in turn was heavily dependent on German idealism) and of early twentieth-century sociological functionalism inaugurated by Emile Durkehim. Theory has also been beholden to late twentieth-century cultural Marxism, with its perpetual engines of "cultural critique," together with its numerous derivatives and permutations.

These two persistent paradigms of "theory" still remain rampant and are fed routinely by an insatiable fascination on the part of Anglophone academics for the latest "runway" intellectual fashions from Paris, regardless of whether anything is really added to the conversation. Often the latter has little to say about the theory of religion, only about using the question of religion as a barbed wedge to advance other agendas. Ubiquitous expressions such as "secular theology," "weak theology," or "religion without religion" are good cases in point. These words have entered the discourse not as genuine theoretical terms but as casual markers, or quasi shibboleths, for rather vague philosophical pursuits that have no serious grounding in the real discourse of the philosophical movements from which they have been lifted. The notion of a "religion without religion," for example, taken from Derrida's seminal essay "Faith and Knowledge," which in itself is an idiosyncratic reading of Kant's *Religion within the Limits of Reason Alone,* where the expression first occurs, has often been used as a designator for what to the innocent reader might come across as a "theoretical" attitude. But it is not. The same holds as well for the so-called new phenomenology, inspired by Marion's takeoff from Derrida.

The Age of the Sign

There is, as Gotthold Lessing might have said, a "big, ugly ditch" that separates the deep-veined mother lode of Derrida's intricate, extensive, and still not yet transparent body of writings and the kind of cheap "Derridism" (of various brands and denominations) that dominated American academia for almost three decades. Now that the interest in Derrida seems to be fading because he is no longer au courant, it is probably time to ask the question adopted from the old fifties game show *What's My Line?*: will the real Derrida please stand up? But that is not our task here. The real Derrida was always in marvelous and inventive ways what he appeared not to be in his later years—*a philosopher of the sign*, or an emissary of the *semiotic revolution*, to which the broad movement known as "postmodernism" really amounts. Derrida himself announced the semiotic revolution in 1963—in fact, he described his time as the "age of the sign"—long before he announced "deconstruction," which he saw as a technical prosthesis of his radical revision of structuralist linguistics and phenomenology, amounting to virtually everything he wrote before 1980. The revolution has arisen, he wrote in 1963, as the more enduring symptom of the postwar era's "anxiety about language." Yet "whatever the poverty of our knowledge in this respect," Derrida added, "it is certain the question of the sign is itself . . . something other than a sign of the times. To dream of reducing it to a sign of the times is to dream of violence."[2]

The semiotic revolution in both Continental philosophy and the humanities as a whole, which Derrida himself launched, has been betrayed repeatedly by partisans of various ideological persuasions, not least of which are the sundry self-proclaimed "theologians," who utterly confuse the deconstructive project with some kind of constructive critique of long-held or normative positions. Or they conflate it with certain well-known ideological stances, such as "radical orthodoxy," garden-variety Protestant liberalism, or even the curious construct of a "secular theology." This confusion is in many ways as chronic and egregious as the "culturalist" fallacy concerning religion, on which Roy focuses. The American addiction to idealist pleasantries and saccharinities, much like its addiction to fast food or silver-tongued politicians, is not a small segment of the problem. But the revolution Derrida himself helped set in motion can be belatedly set right if we begin to examine closely what he has wrought in terms of postmodern philosophy as a whole, which can serve also as the launchpad for a *revolution in religious theory as a whole.*

In order to set things right, we will go back over many of the major figures associated with philosophical "postmodernism"—Nietzsche, Heidegger, Derrida, Deleuze, Levinas, Badiou, Žižek, among others—and examine how each of them has contributed in his own manner to the semiotic revolution in religious theory and how they have can be appropriated consistently to think more profoundly and anew about what we mean by the "religious." We will then, we hope, look through different eyes at what is meant by the phrase "the return of religion."

In doing so we will call to attention and scrutinize the implications of several key terms that populate and lower at the forefront of the discourse in philosophical postmodernism—*sign, singularity,* and *event.* Religion is not a "form" or "cultural formation"; it is neither an "essence" nor a generic characteristic of phenomena. It is a singularity around which the signs of language and culture, which include the semiotic markets of theological discourse, as well as the *events* that constitute our historicity, *swarm and circulate.*

In religious theory we must begin to *theorize from the sign to the singular, and theorize from the singularity to the signs that constitute culture and history,* Derrida's "signs of the times." As with Piet Mondrian's efforts to reconstitute art as art theory from art's zero point—black lines, white shapes, and the primary colors—so we must redo the idea of religion as religious theory, beginning with its own kind of "ground zero," or what we term its "singularity" or "event horizon," drawing on the metaphoricity of these terms as used in theoretical physics.

Finally, we need to excise once and for all the pervasive academic notion that religion is a "phenomenon" like thunderstorms, cricket infestations, or sexual dimorphism. Phenomenon-talk, even if it is couched within the more recondite vocabulary of "phenomenology," or inscribed within the inductive prototype of the "empirical sciences," overlooks a most obvious factor that, ironically, "faith-based" theologians for generations took for granted. That factor is the *transphenomenal* character of the religious (which is why Immanuel Kant over two hundred years ago had to invent the expression "noumenal" to give some account of it). We can no longer rehabilitate the old theological, or metaphysical, nomenclature to do the work of theory today. But we can recognize that the assertion of trans-empirical realities that can be adduced from formal patterns of inference are a regular feature of scientific theorizing these days. These realities are not so much "constructs," implying a mere hypothesis or a voluntaristic fabrication of certain ideas that can be easily dissembled once the "data" come in. They are pure *semiotic formalisms* that are necessitated by the signifying patternings and operations which our inquiry has undertaken. These formalisms never "materialize," even in our theoretical gaze. But they are eminently real.

Kant's notion of the "postulate," a mathematical term in its own right, to characterize a necessary conjunctive piece in our structuring of cognition or the imagination carries more of this sense than the familiar language today of "constructivism" or "constructionism," which connotes an arbitrary undertaking of some kind. Like Thomas Kuhn's new "paradigms," these formalisms account convincingly for inconsistencies or anomalies in the prevalent field of argumentation, investigation, and discovery. We may be able, if we develop the proper devices, to "see" them as what we would name *entities.* But their entitative status is uniquely bound up with what C. S. Peirce, the founder of semiotics, identified as their "abductive" quality, the kind of inference we can draw—or choice of language we can make—from a significant, or even infinite, extension of samples or instances, a process postmodern philosophy refers to as the "play of signifiers." What we end up with is not the identification of an object, but the *detection of an event* that seems to be "postulated" as part of this semiotic chain. There are indeed religious events. But these events, arising from an "ensembling" of signs and sign-processes, circle around a "horizon" that our observation, or our determinate naming, cannot traverse. This particular *event horizon*—or "singularity"—of the semiotic universe as a whole is what we mean by the "religious."

The religious is indeed Blake's tiger that we find "burning bright" with its "fearful symmetry" in the "forests of the night." But in the era of "poststructuralism" its "symmetry" is actually an *a-symmetry,* although it is indeed a fearful one. It is Rainier Marie Rilke's "terrifying angel," as the poet calls it in *The Duino Elegies,* that can easily discomfit us in our own comfortable house, where we routinely cannot see out of our one-way mirrored windows made up of so many undeconstructed, substantialist, or essentialist constructs.

But the religious also can be "located" in our "globalized" worldspace where which horrors abound, boundaries fray, and distinctions dissolve. If the religious has always been about what seeks to globalize its inner force and fire—we can think of Jesus's Great Commission, Mohammed's "seal of prophecy," Gautma's journey to the "far shore"—globalization is truly about the religious in a much deeper sense than we grasp. We now live in what we might term a "Deleuzian" world-space that is no longer simply "deconstructible," because it has set its entire structure in frenetic motion. That world is a religious world. From Darfur to Sri Lanka to the transformation of China and Africa by a strange, indigenous sort of subtle "Christianization," the globalization of the world proceeds in tandem with its *religionization*. In such a Deleuzian world there is constant "deterritorialization," if by territory we mean a terrain that is comfortably circumscribable and habitable. But this movement of deterritorialization and reterritorialization has its own "zero" plane, or *plan* (the actual French word used by Deleuze), of immanence. It is a "territory" that is not a territory, a peculiar territory that amounts to what Deleuze labels an "absolutely deterritorialized" territory—the territory we understand as the "religious." Briefly tracing the shadowed history and ironic index of site, or *place*, this name conveys, the following book constitutes a quest for a new "place" or "territory" that is beyond all territorialization, so far as theory is concerned.

The Question of the Event

But there are other metaphoric strings that are equally useful in communicating a sense of what we have in mind here. To communicate this sense we must adopt Deleuze's own "sense" of the term *sense*. For Deleuze, sense is a kind of singularity in its own right, containing both the "expressed and the expressible," what he elsewhere terms the "virtual" and the "actual," or the "boundary between propositions and things." Sense is the "event," which compasses this very duality. Deleuze goes on to say that "the event belongs essentially to language; it has an essential relationship to language." Yet the event "is not [to be] confused with its spatio-temporal realization in a state of affairs."[3] In other words, the event, which both *inheres in* and *coheres with* the intricacy of what it signifies *in actu*, is not visible as event per se. Nor is it strictly a "transcendental" condition (in Kant's usage) of the event itself, insofar as such a condition is necessary for something to cohere but has nothing to do with its inherence. Deleuze's curious idea of a "transcendental empiricism," a concept to be explicated later in the book, captures this sense of *coherence within inherence*, and *inherence within coherence*.

In short, the event is both "immanent" and inherent, for Deleuze, though not in any obvious manner. It has a horizon, what in scientific parlance is known as an "event horizon." An event horizon is, theoretically speaking, an indiscernible boundary that separates the possibility of light reaching an observer from the impossibility of it ever yielding an "observation." Broadly conceived, the event horizon bounds off the virtual from the actual. The "virtual" in both physics and philosophy often means that which has the properties of the "real" but is not technically real itself—as in "virtual particle," "virtual number," or "virtual reality"; it is not to be confused with the Aristotelian "potentiality." Neither the virtual nor the "event" is observable.

Yet everything that remains meaningful or signifiable depends on this *sur-reality* of the virtual. The virtual is not comparable in any way to Baudrillard's *hyperreal* ("more real than real"), but in fact can be considered *hyporeal* (what Deleuze refers to as "the minimum of being that befits inherences"). The virtual is thus the *hypo-thesis* of the real. It is a singularity (as are "black holes," not to mention their theorized correlates "white holes," which constitute singularities that remain prior, not posterior, to all events themselves). Event horizons should also be distinguished from *eventualities*. Eventualities are specifically distinguishable and locatable; they can be "placed" in sequences, or marked on multidimensional gridlines. Eventualities can be *signified*; events have no signifiable traits in themselves, only in their actual effects, or ramifications.

Today the talk of "events" has overspread the lexicon of postmodern religious thought. Largely because of the prestige and influence of Badiou, an increasingly formalistic type of *event-talk* has inhibited us from exploring the fecund suggestions behind the notion of the event as *generative singularity*, something that can be approached in the spirit of Deleuze's transcendental empiricism.

Our thesis—or more specifically our *hypo-thesis*—is that postmodern religious thought, broadly stipulated, in this age of the event has systematically and bizarrely failed to consider the singularity behind the event from which it claims to speak—the *religious* per se. We, therefore, deliberately seek to avoid any routine resort to the generic term "religion," which suggests a generic assemblage, an "essentiality." We prefer the adjectival substantive "the religious" to remind us of the "horizon-tal" character of what we are theorizing. We do not attempt to theorize religion as a peculiar type of signification, but as *the singularity* around which the infinity of such significations tend to swirl and mobilize.

The event, as well as the language of the event, *contains* nothing. It only directs us beyond our own horizon. It points us in the direction of the singularity for which language is our horizon, indeed the horizon of all language, which cannot be totalized even as a language of presence and absence, concealing and revealing, the hide-and-seek of all metaphysical legerdemain. We stand in awe of this singularity. That is the import of the religious as religious. Only postmodern philosophy, the significance of which we have barely yet absorbed or adjudicated, through its radical exposition of the sign, and its understanding of the sign as proliferation and expression of the signifying singularity, can be of any genuine philosophical value in this moment of crisis. Ironically, postmodern philosophy can only be of real assistance when its endless procession of innovations and "procedures," as Badiou calls them, has exhausted itself. Postmodern philosophy can perhaps only be useful *after postmodernism*. Hegel was right when he noted that the Owl of Minerva can only take flight in the gray twilight of "theory."

One question that keeps coming up as friends have looked over this manuscript is, "If you are going so far as to talk about a theory of the religious, why don't you give us lots of examples?" Though well-meaning, the question is fundamentally *mis-placed*, and *mistaken*. Here, we follow the actual procedures of the *science of singularities* (in the sense that theoretical physics employs such nomenclature). No one has ever "observed" singularities; they have only predicted them as well as *placed* them through the observation of other celestial events and phenomena. It is the elegance of theory that *gives them place* in the first place. For all the "data" of religion that are out there, few find themselves able to theorize the religious. As a "phenomenal" presence—the subject matter of a standard "phenomenology of religion"—the religious is irremediably untheorizable. Only an essentialist phenomenology or a theology, which presupposes the "identity" of the presence of the religious, can offer such a pretense.

Heidegger once said that if the philosophical question were framed right, one no longer was obliged to continue asking the question. Similarly, if the theory of religion is posed in the proper philosophical fashion, one no longer has to scrape up all the data to "demonstrate" the theory. It will locate the religious, as the theory of "black holes" may locate one within the vast regions of outer space visible to our telescopes, among the limitless galaxies and nebulae of our languages, performances, and everyday comings and goings. I leave it to religious scholars in the strict sense to carry forward this endeavor. But religious theoreticians dare to sally forth on a different venture. Charting this venture is the purpose of the following book.

Part I

.

THE REVOLUTION OF
THE SIGN

1

RELIGION AND THE SEMIOTIC
REVOLUTION

∎

> The content of consciousness, the entire manifestation of mind,
> is a sign resulting from inference.
>
> —C. S. Peirce, "Some Consequences of Four Incapacities"

AFTER THE postmodern turn seems to have come full circle and we
find ourselves yearning to know what "comes next," we continue
to be confronted foursquare with the aporia of the *religious*. Postmodern philosophy has exfoliated in hundreds of different directions,
and "postmodern theology" has leveraged this development to pose a
variety of questions and a profusion of *problemata* that both challenge
and reaffirm the historical arcs for its trajectories of thinking. But
postmodernism as a movement has skirted the question of "religion,"
or the "religious," even while it has constantly called attention to it.
This avoidance may stem from the reluctance of Jacques Derrida, who
at his death was truly the movement's grand old man, to confront the
religious *as* religious, even while in his later years he made the religious an operative theme in his writings and infused the vocabulary of
postmodernism with various words and phrases that hint at the "mysteries" of religion—faith, the messianic, the secret, the gift—without
actually going there. Religion must be avoided because it is at once
"the clearest and most obscure," as Derrida says, of subject matters.
It cannot really be amenable to any "phenomenology" of religion,
because it does not "appear" as phenomena are supposed to do along

any surfaces or in any guises. The religious is a curious "alliance" of the "calculable and incalculable."

While the ubiquity of religious faith and praxis is evident world-wide, a burgeoning population of ordinary believers, particularly in third world nations, defies decades-old expectations of triumphal sec-ularity. In addition, as a metastasis of religious violence somewhat tendentiously characterized as "terrorism" spreads fatally and unpre-dictably, religion as a theoretical challenge becomes ever elusive and murky. At the same time that theological conversation has paled into political and ideological wrangles posing as substantive theory, aca-demic research in the area has shattered into a muddle of sociocul-tural methodologies with no common thread except a vague interest in *res religiosa*, or "matters religious."

The Deposition of the Sign

Although "religious studies" as a field has sought for several genera-tions to become a *Religionswissenschaft*, or "science of religion," the outcome has been something disturbingly to the contrary. The nineteenth-century concept of "religion" in the grand sense flowered from the assumption that wherever the venerable term occurred, a shared *situs* for speech could be located, and the "phenomenon" itself mapped and assessed. The "classical theories" of religion, elaborated by such intellectual giants as Weber, Levi-Bruhl, Durkheim, Otto, van der Leuw, and Robertson-Smith, were launched from this very proposition. The establishment of the academic field and intellectual pursuit of "religious studies," deriving historically from the merger of liberal Protestant theology and comparative religions, carried this trend further under a rising regime of the social sciences.

Yet in the past generation the search for what might be consid-ered a general consensus concerning the meaning of such words as "God," "the sacred," the "divine," and even the "religious" itself has petered away. "Theological" inquiry, which at one time focused on the meaning of the word "God" (Greek *theos*), has been undercut by the strident contention that such an undertaking is inherently sectar-ian and incapable of comprehending the limitless diversity of reli-gious experiences and faith stances. Inquiry into religion as a whole, which a generation ago ignited endless discussion and the writing of monographs, has for the most part given up the ghost. In contrast, academic attention has been concentrated on enlarging the gamut and complexity of what are conventionally called "area studies," on outlining perspectives on familiar religious or cultural motifs without asking the uncomfortable question of why these topics matter in the first place. It is as if medieval historians were to deliberate constantly on arcane concerns about papal legitimacy, feudal sovereignty, guild practices, and mercantile economies without ever seeking to understand what the phrase "Middle Ages" connotes, or what "history" itself might signify. The theory of *theos* has been reduced to a surface grammar of banal rubrics of classification.

Much blame for this dissipation of research, at least by cultural conservatives, has been hastily heaped on "postmodernism." The cultural and institutional sources of this changeover are complex and probably await a new "sociology of knowledge" that charts twentieth- and twenty-first-century ideology as a function of the nascent knowledge economy. Postmodernism in many ways has simply served as a convenient descriptor for the intellectual trends of the last thirty or forty years, and whatever worth, or lack of worth, one may attribute to the movement reflects the attitudes one already had toward these events anyway. Nonetheless, postmodernism, whether one protests or not, is the full firmament for intellectual inquiry nowadays. It is not one alternative among many, any more than a dedication to inductive science was merely an option at its height in the nineteenth century.

The preponderance of the cultural debate on postmodernism, however, has ignored the philosophical, and by extension the theological, imperatives that have brought about the demolition of the modernistic template. The common image of postmodernism has been created by certain eccentricities of style and sloganeering adopted by its most prolific proponents. The most visible envoy of postmodernist belles lettres, of course, is Derrida. But Derrida has only carried forth a special program in late modern philosophy that has its genesis in the writings of Nietzsche. The project itself germinates in Husserlian phenomenology, finds a pragmatic outlet in "structural" and "poststructural" linguistics, and comes to fruition in both the later Heidegger and the work of Gilles Deleuze. This venture may be characterized as the *deposition of the sign*. And it is the "deposition of the sign" that, contrary to all the characterizations or profilings that suffuse the endless literature on postmodernism, expresses the "revolution" in religious theory that has been underway for some time.

To "depose" means to remove from a certain place or position, particularly a "high position." It also connotes a "written testimony." It was Derrida who discovered that writing alters all vectors in the act of signification. The grapheme, or "grammatological" reference, is severed from the pristine presence of the spoken utterance, or phoneme. In writing, the unity of signifier and signified is broken. Writing opens up a terrain of difference that cannot be sublated by reflective thought. The text and the name have entirely different genealogies. However, it was not the theory of inscription, from which derives the view that textualization amounts to a "deconstruction" of the idealistic architecture of modern philosophy, that brought to light the possibility of a new thinking about the sign apart from the act of denotation.

The antecedents to deconstruction can be discerned in both C. S. Peirce's doctrine of "thirdness" and Husserl's concept of intentionality. Peirce launched the "science" of semiotics by characterizing the sign as "a third mediating between the mind addressed and object represented."[1] The sign interrupts the pure continuity of word and thing and raises the problem of the "other" to which an expression is directed. Because language is not "representational" but social or intersubjective, the *semiotic model* of the sign challenges the centuries-old principle that "what is" somehow always coordinates with whatever mirrors or "represents" it. Most accounts of signification in philosophy from Descartes to the mid-twentieth century are simply sophisticated variations on Plato's doctrine of *mimesis.* Although he had no relationship with Peirce, Husserl in his own tortuous elaboration of the "phenomenological method" argued that what the former called the "trichotomic" nature of sign operations actually can be considered tetradic. Husserlian phenomenology showed how signification has a fourfold constituency—the subjective or agential relationship to the object supplemented by the action and the scenario.

Thus in Husserl the "structure" of a constellation of meanings always varies with the aim and outcome of a semantic undertaking. This undertaking remains independent of any logical nexus between the sign and the signified. The realization that, when one is thinking or speaking, one is also in the presence of "other minds" with whom it becomes vital to communicate has crystallized many of the philosophical perplexities pursued, often obscurely, by such figures as Jean-Paul Sartre and Maurice Merleau-Ponty. Derrida would later stress that writing is the premier system of communication and thus makes us aware that the sign has been jarred from its original socket of reference, that it has been *deposed.* The deposition of the sign is the root of what postmodernists have in mind when they engage in a critique of "correlative" doctrines of signification, or what Heidegger and Derrida have termed "ontotheology."

Consequences for Religious Thought

The deposition of the sign in postmodernism has intricate consequences for both religious thought and religious studies. The impact on theological research has already been extensive. But the effect on the study of religion as a whole has been negligible. The study of religion as a whole for generations remained beholden to both functionalist anthropology and a kind of descriptivist, or literary-textual, idealism most obviously evinced in the work of Eliade. In recent years the study of religion has become more vaguely polymethodological, and has incorporated the varieties of cultural critique and methodologies that have risen and fallen as fashions within the academy. Yet the failure to appropriate in any easily recognizable way the postmodernist revolution in philosophy and letters—other than the sundry "theologians" and philosophers of religion who are not really doing any theory of religion—is still quite pronounced.

Increasingly, descriptivism wears a trendier and more ideologically correct mask, particularly what we call "identity theory." The descriptivism of religious studies has a long "colonial" history, as critics such as Jonathan Z. Smith have argued. The descriptivist bias stems from the origin of "comparative religions" in the exotic narratives, ethnographies, and travelogues of missionaries and explorers, and has been reinforced in recent years by polemics of the "new historicists," who extol cultural particularities over the universalizing statements of earlier, Eurocentric writers.

But the hegemony of the descriptivist hermeneutic in the study of religion, according to Smith, also masks a kind of cultural imperialism that secretly privileges the Greco-Christian metaphysical outlook while purporting to delegitimate it. Cultural radicalism turns out to be simply the program of a new generation scrabbling for the unclaimed perquisites of the ancien régime. The contemporary study of religion as a mythic terrain invested with numinous qualities "welcomes the foreign if only to show, by some allegorizing or rationalizing procedure, that it is, in fact, the 'same.'"[2] A similar point applies to the profusion of present-day articles and essays that touch on the "social" and "political" import of familiar, or bizarre, types of religious belief and practice. Inside the planetary curiosity shop that merchandises the religious life of the human race we find the persistent prejudices of the West's intellectual elites. It is colonialism with a compassionate face. The ever-fashionable narratives of exploitation and victimization are increasingly crafted neither to "raise consciousness" in the classic, Marxist manner nor to propound a strategy of liberation. Too often the exemplary topics are either recondite or historically inconsequential.

The true aim is to flaunt the hermeneutical privileges of the particular religious scholar by demonstrating his or her eye for the other, and by displaying the vast archipelago of social powers and influences that render all religious matters as comparable manifestations of one's own critique. The same point has already been made by Jean Baudrillard in his acid commentary on the anthropological imagination in postwar Europe. The multicultural sentimentality is "rivaled only by the profound contempt it is designed to conceal. For 'We respect the fact that you are different' read: 'You people who are underdeveloped would do well to hang on to this distinction because it is all you have left.' Nothing could be more contemptuous—or more contemptible—than this attitude."[3]

If the deposition of the sign in the realm of theory constitutes an insurrection against the totalizing scepter of the metaphysical, it likewise becomes apparent that a criticism of the current "metanarrative" of the sacred is absolutely necessary. Such a criticism would expose the constraints of the "celebration" of difference and would unmask the real game that is played in such a casino of constructivism and contrarian accounts of the religious world in which we are immersed. The scholarly academy fears such a move because it would call into court its hidden, sectarian, and *antitheoretical* agendas. The political hermeneutic of religion is perennially tempting, because it offers a semblance of the theoretical without doing the hard work of excavating the phenomenon that the study of religion poses as a question. The study of religion can only be approached as a foray into the phenomenon of religiosity, and such a foray is impossible without mobilizing the instrumentalities of theory. Such theory invariably entails a transaction within the matrix of signification we call *interpretation*. And every theory must be germane to its topic area. It must be more than merely reading one set of signs as something thoroughly alien.

Thus a biology of politics—what is fashionably now after Michel Foucault known as *biopolitics*—is conceivable, but a politics of biology does not really attain to what the "life sciences" are all about. Any biopolitics remains a type of politics and answers none of the pertinent questions about the "biological" per se. The same can be said for a political investigation of the religious. It has little in fact to do with the religious. It is not accidental that in all previous cultural epochs the academic study of religion is tantamount to what we call "theology," or that it is intertwined with what we loosely comprehend as the "philosophical." This observation holds not only in the "Christian West" but in the Islamic and "Oriental" worlds as well. Theological speculation may take somewhat different paths with a variety of emphases, but in every instance it is tantamount to a "scientific" attempt to make sense out of what the particular culture considers worthy of unqualified devotion. An Islamic jurist seeking a determination on an item of the sharia, for instance, is not by any stretch of the imagination endeavoring to make some kind of covert "social statement." That perspective is radically secularist and belies not only his intent but his "intentionality" in the phenomenological sense. The critique requires a rereading of postmodern literature not simply as differentialism but as *deposition*.

The deposition is not a confusion of predicative specifications, as positivists and rationalists of all stripes protest; nor is it simply a dislocation of syntax, as deconstructionists insist. The deposition amounts to a disjunction in the virtual dyad of presence and representation, at once warranting the trace that can be pronounced as the "other" (*das Andere, l'autre*). Gavin Hyman contends that the warranting of the trace serves also to warrant theology. Theology after all, according to Hyman, is the discourse that enfolds the trace and alchemizes it from what is strange to what becomes intelligible as divinity. But this line of analysis, while provocative, is misleading. Hyman, who seems more sympathetic to radical orthodoxy than he wants to admit, lets the trace suffice as kind of incarnational episode within a curious sort of *para-ontology.* A grammar of traces, while rhetorically defensible, is philosophically inconceivable. The explanation is straightforward. The very notion of the "trace" requires a kind of double coding that theology in its traditional format is incapable of assimilating. The philosophical construct of the trace, which appears in the early Derrida, suggests a duplicity of language while generating the very paradox that necessitates the transcendence of metaphysics, so far as postmodernism itself is concerned.

Such a paradox arises from the logic of representation itself. To be is *to be doubled,* supplemented, overdetermined, encoded, *inscribed.* The doubling posits the perdition of what has been duplicated. The trace, for Derrida, is a sepulcher—marbled on its facade, but hollow inwardly. In the work of Emmanuel Levinas, who I will argue later can lead us out of Derrida's labyrinth of recursive cryptograms, the trace takes on a different kind of dimensionality.[4] The trace performs as a kind of "fourthness," if we are to unpack what Peirce had in mind and what Husserl perhaps intimated with his concept of the sign's "intention." Otherness, for Levinas, is neither an absent "thereness" or a present absence, as it has been delineated in so much postmodernist writing. To be other is to be that space of engagement toward which one struggles for expression. The other that is signified is the *l'autre* with which one seeks to communicate.

But this other must remain *totaliter aliter,* insofar as it is a horizon that recedes as the transaction we call speech advances. The other of course is not merely a horizon, a distantiated and ephemeral presence. The other responds to every act of saying, thus traversing language and authorizing dialogue. It is the other as interlocutor, rather than as a vanishing point of representation, that makes possible the deposition of the sign. The sign is *assigned* within the functions of language to what it can, or shall, signify. But the visibility of the other as other is what causes contention within this structure. The "wholly other," the trace that shows itself as God's "face," is comprehensible to the extent that speech goes forth in search of a who, rather than a "what," that can *talk back.*

It is in this setting where we can begin to talk of "faith" in a postmodern parlance. The fiduciary character of speaking to another is what unsettles all signification. It is also what concretizes the otherness of the other. Both theology and philosophy from the modern, let alone the postmodern, standpoint have been unable to take any kind of "theoretical" account of faith because of the way in which the intentionality of all religious conversation, whether one is talking to one's neighbor or to one's Maker, savages any descriptivist bias. The deposition of the sign is both a viral infection of contemporary semantics, what Baudrillard terms the "negative intensity" of the nameless surface grammars and simulacra that have proliferated at the closure of the modern conversation, and a blast that reveals an openness to a new *grammar of address.* This new grammar of address requires an understanding of the orthogonality of speech, as opposed to the linearity of discourse. If Nietzsche seeded the postmodernist revolution with his assault on the grammar of identity, we must now go beyond the revolution itself by breaking the totalizing stranglehold of differentialism—not the metaphysics of identity in difference, but the new metalogic of *difference as identity,* the kind of "bad boy dialectic" for which Deleuze became infamous.

The Default of Theory

The rise of religious studies as a "discipline," or so it has been misnamed, in the last generation was propelled largely by theologians and philosophers, who sought to traverse the shifting boundaries between

"sectarian" approaches to religion, comparativism, and classical anthropology. In this particular venture religious studies has stumbled
grievously. It has produced homologies rather than heterologies, iso-
topes instead of a table of elements. The genesis of the field in a nut-
shell can be described as an opportune merger of interests among the
legacies of the theologian Paul Tillich and the narrativist anthropologist Clifford Geertz. The growth of a pop, post-Christian spirituality
among the baby boomers—later incarnated as the curious, contemporary syncretism we know as the New Age movement—initially
fueled student interest. Religious studies from its emergence was a
consortium of disparate intellectual impulses reacting to a historically contingent set of market conditions. The inherent conservatism
and glacial rate of change within traditional postsecondary learning
has sustained these consortial relations now for several decades. Yet,
in the same way that once-vibrant neighborhoods reach a point of
decline where they cannot be resuscitated without a plan of sweeping redevelopment, so the academic study of religion cannot survive
much longer under the present circumstances.

    While a commitment to cultural and religious pluralism has be-
come the established norm within the field, defining once and for
all the scope of what we mean by "the study of religion," the polymethodological character of its scholarly work has become a severe,
and onerous, liability. Polymethodology, or methodological pluralism, is by no means unheard of, or even unusual, within the social
sciences and humanities. Academic psychology, for example, runs
the gamut from the "hard science" of neuropsychiatry to the pastoral
and quasi-religious forms of clinical and counseling therapies. Even
philosophy spans the interminable, and seemingly unbridgeable, divide between Anglo-American empiricism and Continental phenomenology. But the latitudinarianism native to well-established modes
of inquiry such as psychology, sociology, or literary criticism differs
from the fragmentation of perspectives and purposes that afflicts religious studies. There is a much wider gulf between the mythography
of a Jungian analyst and the ethnography of a "South Asian religions"
specialist than between, say, a cultural anthropologist and an archae-
ologist. A loose thread of coherence binds the various strategies of
"empirical" inquiry into the realm that constitutes "anthropological"
subject matter. The existence of these affiliate structures of investigation is tacitly acknowledged by the suffix "-ology," as in the word
anthropology.

    The founding of the field of religious studies was in actuality, even
if it was not so recognized by its adherents, an attempt to pluralize

the dominantly Christian—and by and large Protestant Christian—
confessional community by introducing competing types of "sec-
tarianism" masquerading as the study of "alternative altars." From
the beginning, religious studies was a strategy of "deregulating" and
opening up to global competition the praxis of theological espousal.
Religious studies never aimed to be a "science" in the sense that
even the "human sciences" could be regarded as such, that is, as a
focused and unified means of finding commonality amid heterogeneity. Religious studies was in itself a semiconscious, deconstructive
move against Protestant thinking, all the while remaining bound to
the Protestant, pietistic, and antihegemonic norms of its Protestant
predecessors. In short, what religious studies, in contrast to most humanities "disciplines," excluding so-called area studies, has decidedly
lacked is *theory.*

The shyness of religious studies researchers toward elaborating
sweeping theoretical discourses that might somehow explicate what
religion is all about can be accounted for in part as the consequence of
the passing in the last generation of what was known as "philosophical theology." The animus toward "theological" statements by the
positivist social sciences has also been a critical factor. But the fre-
quent pretense of religious scholars that they are offering some kind
of "neutral" account of the beliefs and praxes they have entertained
is routinely belied by their refusal to generalize beyond the swatch of
cultural materials in question. In other fields even the narrowest trajectories of historicist investigation have drawn upon operative theories. Finally, it could be argued that the refusal to generalize ensues
simply from the tendency within a youthful discipline to play it safe
politically, and that religious scholars are a notoriously timid lot.
However, even this straightforward observation misses the mark, inasmuch as the field in its early phases had a rich reserve of "theoretical" resources that were neither Christian nor theological on which
to bank.

As it turned out, the movement toward an "anthropology" of religions, which overtook the field in the early 1970s and was inspired by
Clifford Geertz's writings, never really gained currency. Nor has the
fashion of "cultural and critical studies" in the humanities as a whole
made much headway to date among religious specialists, of which
the general demographic still consists of historians, ethnographers,
and linguists. The rejection of theory by the religious academy stems
from the field's still hidden confessional curriculum. Most scholars of
religion are not self-consciously immersed in the business of prosely-
tizing. Nor would the majority of them admit that their insistence on

defining their pursuits in terms of a spectrum of competencies in specific "religions" or "traditions" really conceals a calculated system of political "checks and balances" for a preponderance of faith-based promotions. Yet that is the effective calculus in most "departments of religious studies."

The tragedy in recent years has been the almost total eclipse of any serious deployment of the new philosophical tools provided by the postmodernist revolution in the study of religion per se. Certainly there have been innumerable variants on what has been dubbed the "theological turn" in Continental philosophy of religion—"deconstructive theology," the "new phenomenology," the rarified subspecies of scholasticism that nowadays have adopted the label "radical orthodoxy." But these twists and turns have for the most part scrupulously avoided the very questions that gave rise to the field of "religious studies" in the first place—namely, what is religion, what do we mean by the word "religion," how do we theorize about religion? Raising "religious" questions and asking the question of religion itself are two entirely different breeds of animal. Religious theory itself is reviving slowly, but it has parceled itself into numerous schools, approaches, methods, and legacies, each of which claims the superiority of its own particularized "operating system" over the other. Such partisans have only a minimal *self-consciousness* concerning the philosophical—and hence the *deep theoretical*—matrix in which it has been constituted. Even though religion is almost by definition what Jürgen Habermas would term a system of "communicative action," no effort has been made to deploy, for instance, the exploding genre of communication theory in the analysis of religious phenomena.

Theory is disturbing for many researchers in the field because it offers unsettling questions about what religious people actually think and do, and how these modalities of signifying praxis compete and challenge one another. As both Marxists and the sociologists of knowledge discovered a century ago, the passion of religious belief can be an upsetting and destabilizing force in the world. Whether we are talking about the millennial visions of the Diggers during the Puritan Revolution of the seventeenth century or the Islamically configured tribalism of Chechnyan fighters in the present Russia, the capacity of religious fervor to unravel the pragmatic governing arrangements of the politically privileged is substantial. Theory, therefore, poses embarrassing considerations of how religious ideologies might in certain instances cast a violent, or troubling, shadow over the peaceful *imperium* of the global market in ideas as well as commodities.

The Collapse of Grand Narratives and
the Possibilities of Theory

The major shortfall in the theoretical analysis of culture in general, and religious culture in particular, has been the loss of a credible strategy of critique with the death of "grand narratives" (Lyotard). The collapse of Marxism worldwide as both a form of revolutionary consciousness and a type of post-Christian theodicy has been more significant than many "theoreticians" care to admit. So much of the burden of theory in the last twenty years has been carried by so-called cultural Marxists who take their cue not only from Lyotard but from the writings of Fredric Jameson. It was Jameson who recognized that the key to postmodernity, and postmodernism as a movement in philosophy, the arts, literary criticism, and theological inquiry, lay in what Perry Anderson has called the "de-differentiation of cultural spheres."[5] In the modern period, and regarding modernism itself as a kind of broad, conceptual *Bild* of the strands of that epoch's culture (what Max Horkheimer and Theodor Adorno in their manifesto of the Frankfurt school termed "Enlightenment"), the trend was always toward totalization and the varieties of explicit as well as covert fascism—the subsumption of cultural forms by the state, the immanentization of religious life and the spiritualization of both the materiality of labor and the law of exchange. Culture is concealed within the general forms of political theory and historical reflection. As the authors of *Dialectic of Enlightenment* wrote in the 1940s, "Culture is a paradoxical commodity. It is so completely subject to the law of exchange that it is no longer exchanged; it is so blindly equated with use that it can no longer be used."[6] It has become a kind of fatality.

Ironically, the sudden implosion of Marxism signaled the liberation of the "cultural principle" from its former prison house of ideology. Whereas Marxism as a modernist strategy of interpretation had always circumscribed its understanding of culture within the dialectics of capital, postmodernism as a type of "post-Marxism" not only delineated cultural theory as separate from political economy but made it overarching and central. As most observers have pointed out in recent scholarship on the rise of postmodern thinking, the catalyst for the reconceptualization of Marxism was Baudrillard. While the transition among European Marxist theorists during the 1960s and 1970s from the "negative dialectics" of Sartre to the full-blown cultural materialism of Althusser and Gramsci is a complicated story of the failure to comprehend contemporary history adequately, it was Baudrillard who first grasped clearly that the force of capital had mysteriously morphed into the power of the sign.

Similarly, for Baudrillard, what Marx had termed the "relations of production" had now been transformed into the semiotics of desire and consumption. Even while the so-called consumer capitalism of the postwar era had been exhaustively analyzed by economists, the changeover from nineteenth-century modes of social and political reflection had barely penetrated the "humanistic" disciplines. Baudrillard saw, and identified in terms that were far less tendentious and jargonistic than Jameson could have mustered, the symmetry between late capitalism and the explosion of the communications industry. The "cultural logic of late capitalism," if we may borrow Jameson's phraseology, is not a logic at all. It is a process whereby the rationality of cultural expressions and subdivisions gives place to what Baudrillard terms the "excrescence" of images and representations in an expanding orgy of signification.

At one level, of course, it is possible to read Baudrillard merely as a philosopher who discovered a language to account for commercial advertising, the cult of media celebrities, and the Dionysian topology of pop culture. But Baudrillard's insights are not to be trivialized. In the post-Marxist age the practice of "theory" per se is on the verge of achieving a new currency through the comprehension of all that is "cultural" in its myriad and diverse guises. The explanation is not all that opaque. The "de-differentiation" of the realm of culture itself means the terrain that was heretofore a kind of "plantation" for certain specific ecologies of inquiry has now become common ground for all the "disciplines." That de-differentiation has had an especially strong impact on the study of religion. Were it not for the methodological "warlordism"—narrow and inherently self-legitimating foci of scholarship—that dominates the field today, religious studies would be frolicking in the sunlit fields of cultural analysis. Paul Tillich's insight that religion is the "form" of culture is more pertinent at the turn of the millennium than it was in the early postwar era.

The efflorescence of what is gradually coming to be known as "postmodern faith"—the syncretic, experiential, individualistic, and media-dominated modalities of spirituality that have assumed the somewhat misleading labels of "New Age" religion or "postdenominational" Christianity—fulfills Baudrillard's dicta. Postmodern religion is a vast, and de-differentiated, circuit of cultural signs and metaphors that do not add up to anything resembling what religious studies scholars in the past have identified as "movements" or "traditions." Postmodern religion is the motivational underlay of postmodern culture as a whole. Whether we are talking about metaphysical seekers who chant to the "ascended masters" using quartz crystals, or urban Pentecostals who find "gold dust" on themselves after having received "miraculous healings," or Christian rock singers who can hardly be distinguished in their demeanor or music from other pop musicians, we are no longer entering into some arcane, academic discourse about "dialogue" among Buddhists, Hindus, Jews, and Christians. We are no longer even talking about "religion" as conventionally construed.

The discourse of religion under postmodern conditions adds up to what Richard Murphy terms a "counterdiscourse" that constitutes a whole new theoretical strategy.[7] Such a counterdiscourse is no longer about the "disciplinary object" we know as religion. It is not "about" anything at all, in fact, but amounts to a second order of simulation—the retextualizing, or developing, of an interpretative code for the play of performances and iconic showings that make up "religious culture." If, as Baudrillard stresses, a simulacrum is distinguishable from an entity by the fact that its "reality" can be discerned in its replication, then religious studies amounts *to a simulation of the simulacra* that precess autonomically and "chaotically" within the circulatory system of signs that is culture. The study of religion has no "subject matter"—only a sweeping and undemarcated topography over which the theoretical eye may wander. Our theory is what Gary Genosko calls "undisciplined theory," that is, *semiotics*.[8] But this approach is also something that conventional "religious scholars" have not even begun to fathom.

A Semiotic Turn

What exactly is semiotics? Semiotics, which its founder Charles Sander Peirce termed "semiology," is—simply put—the "science" of signs and sign-functions. Only in the past generation has semiotics matured as a serious area of theoretical endeavor, and its influence to date has been largely felt within interdisciplinary undertakings, such as film studies, media philosophy, marketing research, and art criticism. In order to understand the importance of what could well be characterized as the "semiotic turn" within the theoretical pursuits of the humanities, we must take a look at the way in which French poststructuralism, particularly the "deconstructionism" of Derrida and his imitators, has set a new course not only for the philosophy of religion but for the study of religion in its entirety.

The importance of Derrida as a philosopher, historically, is that he fell like an anvil blow on the smug world of Anglo-American analytical philosophy. While Derrida's early attacks on "logocentrism" have usually been construed as a critique of the later Heidegger, his arguments ironically slashed through the empire of logico-realism that had swaggered in the philosophical academy since Bertrand Russell. "Deconstruction" was never, even by Derrida's testament or reckoning, a philosophical method. It is those scholars who have made it a kind of method, if not an actual ontology, that have given "deconstruction" a bad name. Deconstruction aimed to demonstrate once and for all, by drawing on the new "science" of linguistics, that referentiality is a conceit, and the grand philosophical narratives of reference constitute a kind of imperial poison pen. Unmasking this conceit was only the beginning of a longer and more encompassing theoretical project of which even Derrida, unfortunately, has lost sight.

Within the ambit of epistemology, the dissolution and dissemination of the referent could only ensue as the liberation of the signifier. Once the signifier is loosed from it phantasmal "object" or representation, it is free to become migratory, and hence "semiotic." The concept of semiosis, which is integral to semiotics per se, implies nothing more than a mapping of the dynamic interoperability of multiple sign agencies. Insofar as deconstruction turns the tables on the method of "logic" by denying that grammatical constraints *contra* Wittgenstein are the boundaries of signification and that philosophical statements of "meaning" are the perimeter of discourse, so semiotics surpasses all attempts at "deconstructive" countertheorizing by demonstrating that the erasure of presence in the motion of the sign is, in fact, the revelation of the power of the sign itself. If deconstruction is the negation of the ontological, semiotics is, rather than a negation of the negation, a "letting go," as both releasing and unleashing (in Heidegger's sense of *Gelassenheit*) of the *power of the negative differential*. The saying of the "semiotic" is what indeed Derrida claimed Heidegger cannot say. Heidegger's talk about that which is "coming to presence" in language merely consists in a Teutonic mystification of what semiotic science tells us in plainer speech. The *logos* of the new onto-logy, or "theory of being"—is not logic; it is the *swarm of significations.*

"We scholars," as Nietzsche would say, must realize that the way we frame our questions and inferences in "doing what we do" is not some arbitrary choice we make, or some happenstance of personal history whereby we choose to become a "sociologist of religion" as opposed to, say, an intellectual historian. The pervasive problem with the study of religion as a field is that it has resolutely and consistently engaged in the "grand refusal"—a refusal to be even minimally theoretical. The hermeticism of a Carl Jung or a Huston Smith, the crypto-sacramentalism of a Eliade, the anthropologism of a Jonathan Z. Smith—these slants have all conveyed a sense of strategically explaining religious matters for academic curiosity seekers. But at the same stroke they have proven unable to do what the study of religion with its inherent "ethnographical" proclivities could have done from the outset. They have failed to make manifest the integral and conceptual relationships among the windings and trail ways of anthropological findings to such a degree that religious phenomena can be "understood" at a global level rather than simply browsed from a privileged, political vantage point.

If "theory," as the classical meaning of the word intends, signifies the gaze of the theatergoer, the critical viewing eye toward a "performance," then every "theoretical" statement concerning religion must amount to something far more compelling and discerning than a mere abstract proposition about the "sacred," the "numinous," or the "spiritual." There can be no theory without a conversation with the signs themselves. And there can be no round dance of the signs without the engagement of the theoretician. In the same way that quantum physics revolutionized our notions about scientific "objectivity" almost a century ago by positing the "observer-dependent" character of theory, so a semiotics of religion can overhaul our now historically obsolete habits of taking religion either as something private and confessional or as a phantasmal castle of Durkheimian "social facts."

Both models are, in truth, empty idealizations. As Peirce first recognized in proposing the "triadic" structure of the sign, as Heidegger discovered at an early stage in the development of the phenomenological method, and as Merleau-Ponty refined in his later sketches for an analytic of the body, "theory," that is, the philosophical means of seeing, arises from the act of interpretation at that moment of self-revelation when the interpretation of the system of signifying relationships discloses the very "sign" of the interpretant itself.[9] Theory is the signifying probe or "position" (in Derrida's ironical sense) that distributes the events of signifying praxis which make up the "phenomenal" order of things. Religion does not, or cannot, stand alone; it is inextricably semiotic in its texture and weave. It is "theory-dependent."

A justification, interestingly, for the study of religion as a kind of *higher semiotics* can be found in the critical method pioneered by the classical form of religious theory that went by the name of "theology." We, of course, do not have anything resembling "systematic" or "dogmatic" theology, "Christian theology" or "Hindu theology."

The idea that theological thinking can be partitioned off as indications of specific religious traditions makes no more sense than the view that biology can be divided methodologically according to the different species under scrutiny. "Theology," stripped of its ecclesial, doctrinal, or even ethnological trappings, simply betokens the *science of the divine,* and that in a broad sense is what religious theory must strive toward. If one examines the different "religions," one finds that each "tradition" in its own right is theology-laden. Though the origins of both science and mathematics are shrouded within their own cultural conditionedness, their theoretical means and aims have been unflaggingly independent of the cultural formations within which they were incubated.

Theoretical thinking within the sphere of inquiry we call "religion," therefore, of necessity must be a *semiotic way of thinking.* What do we mean by semiotic thinking? Semiotic investigation is a venture into thinking through the *theatrical* (hence, the implicitly "theoretical") character of human experience. What do we mean by "theatrical" in this context? As Jack Goody notes in his examination of "theatrical" or "theoretical" languages, including the language of religion, the concept *au fond* merely implies the broader strategy of mimetic patterning.[10] Mimetic patterning has nothing to do with replication, or copying, as Plato thought, and is not related to the representational or correspondence theory of knowledge that has dominated philosophy prior to the postmodern era. The "mimetic" is not at any level a reduplication of the real. Instead it a "redrawing," which in fact brings about a disfigurement at the site of depiction. It is *an act of reference that exceeds and overcomes the referent.* The "presentation" of the real invariably establishes a synecdochal style of sign-connectivity between the representation of the real and the real that is represented.[11] And it is that sort of *archaeo-semiosis* which constitutes the theatrical/theoretical nature of all language and cognition, a fact that Kant understood quite well.

The study of religion is semiotic at its core, because it is not about "words" and "things" as philosophy and logic conveniently regard them. It is not about "mirroring" nature according to the canon of "clear and distinct ideas," as Descartes and the epistemology of modernism has held. The study of religion is about the way in which the typological and replicative constraints of mimesis are bracketed, yet remain *significant* at the same time. As Genosko observes in his overview of the recent cycle of scholarship in both semiotics and cultural studies, the pursuit of the humanities at large is a wandering in the "theater" of mimesis.[12] And all mimesis is "theological, a matter of filling gaps."[13] When one begins to frame the "theory" of religion as a theory of semiosis, or how mimetics functions in extremis, then one can do philosophy of religion, if not "philosophical theology," in a whole new manner—as *religious theory*. Religion itself is a lattice-work of sign-operations and signifying processes that transcend the grammatics of common sense. These signifying elements do not co-alesce into some kind of metaphysical object, as Durkheim and others have always believed. The mysterious, yet theoretically inconsequen-tial, construct of "the sacred" belies this means of misconstruing the subject regions to which we append the label of religion.

The "sacred" has no entitative status, nor does it consist in some kind of affective or "extra-sensory" overlay to ordinary experience. The sacred implies a movement, or even a mutation, of signs whereby the mimetic relationship between the different signifying constitu-ents is entirely asymmetrical. It is this unique asymmetry of religious semiosis, wherein the "object" signified is neither visible nor recog-nizable in terms of the signifier, that produces the mythical, or the numinous. The performative character of religious action accentuates this movement. When Eliade talks of religious ritual as a reenactment of sacral events that took place *in illo tempore,* he is speaking in a metaphysical vein of the asymmetry of religious mimesis. Derrida's original insight that representation is an erasure, not a repetition, of presence can be translated into this scheme of reference. If origin can never be recovered after the act of signification, then the *archaeo-semiosis* that distinguishes religious language is such a complete rupture within the "deconstruction" of the sign that only the dis-course of *wholly otherness* is possible. Religious theory is an exten-sion of cultural theory in the measure that it opens up the hinterland of all those representations and signs that can be counted as part of human "anthropology." To reduce the study of religion to a descrip-tive anthropology, as has happened largely in the last generation, is not only intellectual cowardice, it is methodological malpractice.

It was initially Aristotle, and ultimately Plotinus, who understood that any account or "explication" of phenomena resides in the articu-lation of the relationship between terms, not as a predicative relation-ship, but in the ambivalent sense of what Aristotle called *proto ti,* as an aesthetic configuration that evades every logic of equivalency. Plotinus used an expression that, Stephen Gersh argues, is the anchor of semiotic procedure itself—*logos tes scheseos,* a "rationality of re-lation [of difference]."[14] This rationality of the relationship between what is otherwise perceived as a "disfigured" form of mimesis, as a drawing of strange maps and impossible terrains, is the "theological" charter of religious theory. It is a rationality that is ultimately "hetero-logical" in Georges Bataille's sense. But it is a rationality nonetheless. Semiology requires the incongruity of "the other." So-called scientific anthropology, on which the study of religion has slavishly modeled itself, has surpassed itself in this generation by recognizing that *to heteron* is not a datum of science, only an affectation. It only becomes "scientific" when it becomes *heteronymous,* a naming of impossible names. Religious scholars can celebrate the disparate and the diverse until a dark sun rises on the ruins of an exhausted millennialism.

But the vocation of theoreticians is far different. The call of theory constitutes a demand for accountability in both method and content. Theory after postmodernism is not merely an exchange of philosophi-cal reference groups and rhetorics, of which so much "postmodern theology" is pronounced guilty. Theory after postmodernism is an invitation and response to the kaleidoscopic "scene" of the globo-roiling and the globo-convergent; it is the loosing and comprehen-sion of the signifying festiveness of multicultural and multireligious expressivity, the indiscretion inherent in a carnival of the linguis-tic, the esthetic, and the electro-virtual. It is the wild dance of Nietzsche's Zarathustra, who teaches the "overcoming" not just of our *Allzumenschlichkeit* but of our obsession with predicative logic and the negative semantics we have raised to the level of theology under the banner of apophaticism.

But before we move to religious theory as a plotted and well-disciplined *flight of sacral signifiers* we must understand more fully its tutelary genius, its resident genius who did not turn structural semiotics on its head but pulled the platform out from under its very feet. We must let go of any infantile and infatuated "Derridism" and embrace Deleuze's vision.

What Derrida actually discovered in broad compass, if not at a "globo-theoretical" level, is the pervasive role of the paradoxical quality—in Kiekergaard's sense—of *faith as the de-constituting and de-posing* signification of all sign-movements, as the grand *de-sign* within the economy of every "world religion." In other words, Derrida, through his deconstruction of the texts of religion as the interiority of faith, introduces the power of the "semiotic" into any future reli-gious theorizing. Derrida's own strategy of what we shall designate a *dynamic, deconstructive semiotics* derived from the mimetic, or duplex, processes inherent in the signifying activity of all reading, writing, and thought—a second-order process that belies the illusory conviction of an originary moment in all discourse, a process to which "deconstruction" essentially is tantamount.[15]

In the 1980s Derrida, in responding to the controversy over Heidegger's Nazism and cognizant of his own debt to Heidegger, seemed to have realized that deconstruction is inconceivable without this duplex moment. Out of this "duplicity"—or as we have said, the "depositional" function of the sign—arises all "deconstructive" readings of the text. Writing requires reading, reading requires interpretation, dissemination of the micro-meanings forged by each hermeneutical intervention, re-*assign*ing the threads of reaction and response, and so forth. Derrida was always keen on dispelling—unfortunately to this day not with much success—the popular as well as academic misconception that deconstruction connotes some sort of head-on critique of monolithic beliefs, or hegemonic systems. The work of deconstruction is always at work within the literary work itself. It is the *auto-deposition* of apparent signifying totalities that engender the defense "auto-immunity" of the sort of religious fundamentalism to which Derrida called attention in the 1990s.

The key to this transition is his notion of the *khōra,* a term adopted from Plato's *Timaeus* which Derrida introduces around the same time. Derrida's *khōra* is a transitional term in the movement from the "negative theology" of deconstructionism to his dynamic semiotics, which drives his later writings. It is also quite relevant to the semiotic theory of religion. Following Genosko's suggestion of the semiotics of the theoretical/theatrical, we can see how Derrida appropriated his insight regarding the semiotic doublet in revisioning the entirety of Western philosophy through a rethinking of what is meant by deconstruction. In his essay "Khōra," Derrida writes: "Platonism" serves to "command this *whole history* [of philosophy]. A philosophy as such would henceforth always be 'Platonic.' Hence the necessity to continue to try to think what takes place in Plato, with Plato, what is shown there, what is hidden."[16] Furthermore, it is Platonism that fosters the idolatry of the text as a repository, that "is," that endures in itself and for itself as the essence of what is meant, what is the "tradition." "Platonism" itself emanates from this idolatry. "'Platonism' is thus certainly one of the effects of the text signed by Plato, for a long time, and for necessary reasons, the dominant effect, but this effect is always turned back against the text."[17] What is "turned back" is the doubling of the semiotic doubling, the "gap" or "absence" of the mimetic interval in signification itself. This gap Derrida previously understood, perhaps following Lacan, as a "lack." But with "Khōra" it becomes pregnant and productive, as it was strangely for Plato. The "pregnancy" of the *khōra* is the productive power of the sign.

Heretofore Derrida was limited by Lacanian semiotics, and Lacanian semiotics was always limited in turn by its self-defined psychoanalytical application. Slavoj Žižek's cultural Lacanianism, which has sparked its own kind of mild "theoretical" revolution, has always been tethered to a not-so-concealed political as well as polemical agenda. *After postmodernism religious theory must convert the logistics of difference into a global analysis of sign-distinctions, sign-functions, sign-dynamics, sign-relations, and full-scale sign-movements and sign-transpositions.* The semiotic enterprise is not at all new. In the context of cultural theory it has reached an impasse because of its inability to disclose the fecundity and mobility of the signifying complexes and domains of culture with the same precision and consistency that, starting with Peirce and evolving through Saussure and Hjelmslev, it translated formal or mathematical logic into syntactical substitutions and correlations.

But the semiotic imperative can, and must, gain new life with the opening of the new "territory" of religious theory. Religious theory in the future will be viewed in deference to "religious studies" and "religious thought" as what psychoanalysis in the twentieth century was to philosophical psychology and earlier genres of empirical psychology. In short, it will map what Deleuze names a "geophilosophy" of the signifying terrain—the "semioscape" of metaphors, terms, tropes, figurations, collocations, implications, paradigms, and syntagms (the flora and fauna of semiotic theory) that include broad-scale codings of written tradition and observed moral, ritual, and other symbolic practices as well as the interpenetration of these singular tokens by cultural wave forms that can be identified and schematized, if not ultimately resolved conceptually. The "postmodern condition" is not really a mode of historicity; it is but a gaudy carnival of multicultural and polymodal ways of rhetorically scoping and visualizing the virtual rondo of transient, global artifactualities and viralities, of media and communications, and of their distinctive signifying processes and intensities with accelerating events around the planet.

After postmodernism, and after the death of Derrida, religious theory must begin to move with the same compass. But first we must ask the question of what is implied in such a theory of carnivalesque signifiers and the ubiquitous negative spaces—what Derrida identifies as Plato's perplexing *khōrai*—which roam throughout the madding crowd.

2

THEORY AND THE *DEUS EVANESCENS*

CAN THERE TRULY BE A "SCIENCE" OF RELIGION?

■

The god-stuff roars eternally, like the sea, with too vast a sound
to be heard.

—D. H. Lawrence

POSTMODERN PHILOSOPHY has tirelessly and for way too long been
accused of being reckless and contrary to the "rational," including
the various templates of rationality that often go by the name of "science." It might be assumed that the postmodernist movement has
ground to rubble once and for all the idea of a *Religionswissenschaft,*
a *science de religions,* or a "science of religion," for which the nineteenth century yearned. But such a concept of science was entrapped
by the Enlightenment notion of a pure method buttressed through
universalizing propositions, or covering laws, that could explain in
some observer-neutral and subject-independent fashion what could
once-and-for-all be indicated as the "religious" in all possible circumstances. Such a venture proved impossible, largely because the
method of description and generalization demanded by empirical scientific protocol turned out to be awkward and complex. It became
completely impractical to disentangle the ideal of observer neutrality
from certain theological or antitheological presuppositions. Scientism
in the study of religion found its default in a taxonomical *essentialism*
that later came to be named the "phenomenology" of religion, which
rarely had anything to do with the supposedly "rigorous" philosophical approach invented by Husserl.

With postmodernism we have moved way beyond essentialism, but we have substituted for it an uncritical and *weakly theoretical* descriptivism, combined with a methodological particularism, that seeks to preserve the innocence of the immediate evidence gathered rather than foster conceptual innovations that might challenge the self-referentiality of the academic practices themselves. The persistence of the nomenclature of religious inquiry as "religious studies" telegraphs this means of "playing it safe" when it comes to theorizing about religion. But we must ask ourselves at this point: can there indeed be a bona fide *Religionswissenschaft* that compasses and comprehends the whole of what the ancient Romans first identified as the *religiones*? The problem of the *religiones* for the Romans, who provided a name for the peculiar phenomenon we now call "religion," derived from the unique character of their own practices and rites.

Religion and the Paralogical

As has been observed by ancient scholars, Roman religion was neither monotheistic nor imaginatively polytheistic as its Greek counterpart had been. Roman republican religion was centered on networks of family loyalties and bonds as well as contractual exchanges between mortals and deities. With the coming of empire this focus on reciprocal obligations morphed into the notorious system of Caesar worship along with a centralized state polity. Rome, famous for its emphasis on religious "tolerance," viewed religious belief and commitment in much the same way as Rousseau did almost two millennia later. Religion was always a form of "civil religion" that was principally ethical and social with the key function of ensuring the responsiveness and political fidelity of the republic's citizens. If on occasion the Romans did construe the content of religious beliefs and observances other than in pragmatic terms, they were constantly confronted with the *force of religion,* those sorts of "fanaticisms" such as they encountered in Judea, when they encountered or subdued certain peoples that did not buy into the idea that loyalty to God and loyalty to the *imperium* itself should be indistinguishable. There were those *religiones,* such as the monotheistic and separatist passions that sparked the Jewish revolts of the first two centuries or the dark and secretive human sacrificial rites they attributed to the Celts.

Roman piety was self-consciously public, not private. And it was this "civic" anxiety about the dangers of secret practices and convictions that compelled Roman emperors from the second century onward to suppress, or even ban, the "mysteries" which were very popular among the people, especially those immigrants from the East. Roman suspicion and hatred of early Christianity can be explained by simple but widespread perceptions of it as a strange "cult" from the East, which mostly reflected their inability to comprehend anything that did not fit their model of civil religion. Christianity was considered fanatical largely because of its Jewish origins and was identified in the popular Roman mind as a barbaric and conspiratorial type of secret society. This attitude gave rise to the canard that the early Christians were "cannibals" because of the Eucharistic ceremony of "eating" the body and blood of the savior. The Roman mind had little sympathy for mystical insight and passion. It feared the *upsurgence* of private religious fervor as much as the hostility of those peoples, inside and outside the empire, who for whatever inexplicable reason did not welcome the identification of political subjugation and conquest with the humanizing and "civilizing" blessings of *Romanitas*. The Enlightenment had a perspective similar to that of the Romans. The cultural ideal of *Romanitas*, intimately associated with *humanitas*, could easily be translated into Kant's *Aufklärung*, where "educating" and "civilizing" meant the necessity of expanding moral and cultural European influence through gunboat diplomacy and colonialism.

The ancient Roman penchant for viewing religion as politically indispensable yet spiritually and psychologically shallow, with the actual substance of religious attitudes far less important than their behavioral effect, has left a long-term imprint on religious studies. This outlook directly influenced the Enlightenment picture of religion, enunciated by leading figures of the period from Rousseau to Kant and brought into the nineteenth century through such theories as those of Émile Durkheim and Will Herberg; and it has been the primary source of inspiration for the vast variety of modern liberal attitudes about the virtues of religious pluralism in a democratic context. Only a few modern philosophers, such as Kierkegaard and—ironically—Nietzsche, who has been on the main regarded wrongly as simply a polemically antireligious thinker, have truly penetrated into the distinctive constitution of religious faith, inspiration, and motivation. It has always been easy for scholars to have a "scientific" take on the religious by inspecting only the outward expressions or the ordered externals of such a complex phenomenon. The other gambit has been to pursue something superficially akin to "science" by elaborating various types of taxonomy, misleadingly termed "phenomenology." Eliade's pioneering work in establishing religious studies as a discrete field in its own right by adopting this latter strategy easily comes to mind.

But a science of religion should be more compelling and sophisticated than botany. Such a science would need to take into account
the portmanteau sense of the Roman word *religio*, which classical and
even some current etymologies trace to the word *ligare*, to "bind" or
to "bind tightly." The meaning of this "binding" has to be sought at
two different levels, not only at the level of social cohesion and ethical
consistency, but at the level where human cognition and agency can
be understood as "bound" to something deeper and far more compelling than contractual obligations. The Roman/Enlightenment paradigm is crucial to understanding the connection between religion and
public life, but useless when it comes to making sense of the *origin*
of the religious as a form of motivation and persuasion. Kierkegaard
came closest to articulating the conundrum in his formulation of
faith as a movement toward the "infinite" by virtue of the "absurd."

But Kierkegaard's famous "existentialist" solution, domesticated
in Tillich's language of "ultimate concern" and Derrida's use of the
phrase "the impossible," only starts to do the job, because it relies on
the tension of nineteenth-century Romantic thought, which played
on the paradox of the limited and limitless, the Kantian transcendental and transcendent, the strictly *nonrepresentable* as well as the
boundlessness of the sublime. The perpendicular probing of the religious in this "vertical," nonsyntactical manner demands its own
kind of progressive "unlayering," similar to Nietzsche's genealogy or
Foucault's archaeology. A genealogy of the religious, however, would
amount to something far more than a depth probe into the concentrics
of the phenomenon, unmasking the progressively descending strata
of hierarchy until one rests in the bosom of truthfulness. Nietzsche
himself warned that the "will to truth" (*Wille zur Wahrheit*), especially foundational, metaphysical, or religious truth, itself must be
unmasked as a form of the *Wille zur Macht*. The will to truth is often
an "inversion" (*Umkehrung*) of the will to power, a subterfuge of life
turning upon itself in the kind of autoimmunity that Derrida identifies as the outgrowth of the strange nuptials of postsecular religion
and science cum technology.

Genealogy is not about truth but about demonstrating the intensive assemblages of signifying connections that spiral both upward
and downward in relationship to the impenetrable singularity that
sets them in motion and imparts to them a unique force. Nietzsche
had no other name for this singularity than "will," a misappropriation
of a term from German idealism for which Heidegger ruthlessly faults
him. Genealogy is historical in its overview, but it refuses the tempta-
tion to *historicism*. It does not allow us to understand history, only

to set it free for a bolder and more adventurous effort at theorizing. Genealogy is a "science" only in the sense of a *gaya scienzia*, a "joyful" science (*fröhliche Wissenschaft*) that does not buckle under the weight of its own gray and bloodless generalizing, which Nietzsche associated with the ascetic ideal, the inverted will to power, the will to truth that turns into the powerful lie.

What would, then, a real science of religion involve? Can there ever be a "religiology" in the same sense there has been for some time a sociology, or an anthropology, or a psychology? If there could be, should there be? Does the subject matter that goes by the name of *religio* offer itself to the same sort of discursive expansion and methodological execution as the *bios* of biology? If a "religiology" were practicable, how would it actually be presented, or pushed forward?

Contrary to the positivism of the "social sciences" that has dominated in religious studies during the last half century, an integral science of religion would require that any theoretical assessment of the *religiones* be anchored in a formal structure of inquiry. Such a formalism has always seemed alien to the study of religion. Ever since Roman classical authors profiled the *religiones* as "cultic responsibilities," as dark and disquieting mysteries impenetrable to the gaze of reason, the idea of a "scientific" resolution of the issue has remain essentially problematic.[1] Yet such "scientific" considerations are becoming almost inescapable. In recent years "religious studies" as a field ballasted by any common aim has slowly and unremittingly imploded, largely because ethnographical and taxonomical concerns have replaced any gesture toward general theory. A mounting, pathological suspicion of theory itself has made the development of religious studies as a *discipline* well-nigh impossible. Because theory must of itself be comprehensive, it is routinely disparaged as monolithic and "hegemonic" at a political level. A science of religion would of course demand some kind of ontological commitment.

Is it possible to undertake a "scientific" study of religion that presupposes at the same the "deontological" method of the postmodern without succumbing to the rage for the antitheoretical and the vogue of cultural relativism? The task appears formidable, if not futile. Yet there is a "way" open before us that has seemed barred in the past. For the sake of rigor we may describe this way as the *via paralogica*. Any "religiology," as we shall see, turns out to be a strange and interesting sort of "paralogy." What do we mean by the "para/logical," so far as it touches on a theory of religion? A paralogism is defined in the *Random House Dictionary of the English Language* as "an argument violating principles of valid reasoning" or "a conclusion reached through such argument." But this standard definition misses the "deconstructive" role of all paralogies within language itself. The concept of the paralogical pertains to whatever disinhabits the logical. The paralogical is a kind of discursive "catachresis," inasmuch as it bends and disfigures the syntactical relationships within a textual formation until a whole new semiotic moment arises. More precisely, the paralogical eludes the *ratio* of all syntactical elements, teasing them beyond their boundaries into the hazy region of "paratheory." Paratheory, or what Victor Taylor has called "para/inquiry," ensues from the "disinheritance" of theory. "Linguistic disinheritance is an event in which philosophical and literary meaning are cut off from absolute presence, absolute center."[2]

Disinheritance is suggested by the Greek prefix *para-* itself. The prefix means "beyond," "aside," "amiss," as well as anything connoting "alteration" or "change." Taylor observes: "'Para' is the dangerous prefix (much more dangerous than 'post') which defies the rule of identity, the rule of linkage. 'Para' suspends the condensation of the syllogistic rule by first instigating the erring thought and second linking the error to the word or action. The prefix 'para' draws attention to the repressed excessiveness of the word—its negative instantiation. The paralogical is a logical necessity, just as the paramedic is a medical necessity."[3]

In what way does the study of religion constitute a form of paralogy? What do we really have in mind when we refer to inquiry into the "religious" as a paralogical venture? From a linguistic standpoint the paralogical emerges out of a vacuity of the metaphysical content of rationality itself. It is the *kenosis* of the sign. The kenotic sign-function is the key to the deconstruction of the text and the moment of semiosis. In deconstruction the moment of signification is simultaneously a *deconstitution* of the act of reference. In standard reference theory the dyadic relationship between subject and other, between intention and object, is the architecture for signification. According to the Scholastic dictum *aliquid stat pro aliquid*, "something stands for something (else)." But in the movement of deconstruction this bipolar configuration is annulled in one sweep. The *aliquid* at both ends of the continuum "de-substantializes." The evanescence of both the referent and the referendum is intimated in both Heidegger's critique of ontotheology and Derrida's "marginalization" of predicative discourse. To signify is to dis-seminate, to "sow the seeds" of further signification along the furrow of syntax. The plenitude of signifying presence—the Hegelian *Begriff*—is exposed as lack, as lesion.

Making this point lyrically, we can say that being is everywhere cracked and fissured. *The whole is full of holes*, holes that are not fixed

but transient, doorways that manifest and vanish, wounds that tragically open and are miraculously healed. This insight, driven home for
a generation now through Derrida's poststructuralist revisionism of
reading, has become our new postmodernist "Archimedean point," a
point that is actually a promontory jutting out into the stormy ocean
and constantly absorbed by the wave motions.

Religion as "Dark Matter"

The *religiones* are this vast ocean. They are a capacious and unten-
anted sign-space, which gives more precision to Žižek's post-Lacanian
cultural productivity of the Real. The sign-spatiality of the religious
crops up on our "scientific" map as an abysmal, watery sector. It is
where the "topics"—or *topoi* in the cartographic sense—of religious
theory can be seen as oppositional to the space of inferential discourse,
much in the same way that the study of Japanese gardens is attentive,
not to discrete botanical speciation and design artifacts, but to the
emptiness that suffuses the landscape. Religious theory examines this
"negative" yet mobile terrain of signification. It generates its own
"narrative" by charting this space as a flux of discursive relations that
do not necessarily satisfy the formalistic calculus of "natural" science,
yet somehow exhibit a "recursive" functionality—as in the generation of complex, "jagged" patterns through fractal geometry—that is
intelligible and describable. Like any fractal configuration, the language of religious theory is deformed, that is, "paralogical." But such
a paralogy can become meaningful or "significant" only if it somehow says what has hitherto been evanescent—Derrida's "spectral"
and Žižek's "parallax" differentialism.

In a misplaced move toward becoming "empirical," the study of
religion over the last three decades has preoccupied itself with the
positivity of linguistic and cultural data, tallying up a massive geography of symbolic artifacts and practices distinguished only by their
anthropological peculiarities and ethnomethodological idiosyncrasies. But this triumph has come at the expense of understanding the
"deep grammar," as Wittgenstein put it, of religious discourse in toto.
The deep grammar of religion is a darkness. More precisely, it is a
"semiotic" opaqueness, an opaqueness enveloping the very construct
of "grammar" itself. It is a darkness that can only be construed topo-
logically, as a kind of *parasubstantiality,* a simulated alterity urgently
intruding into signifying relations that make up all denominations of
"descriptive" science.

This alterity is part of the process of semiosis itself. Like the "dark matter" of astrophysics, which cannot be seen with a telescope, yet serves as a necessary construct in the apportionment of visible stellar phenomena, the notion of the *religiones* underwrites the theory of representation and signification that has dominated Western philosophy since Plato. Remarkably, the discovery that the *religiones* may be the key to resolving the philosophical dilemma of presence and representation can be found in the musings of Derrida himself. The great conceptual failure to reconcile a rupture between the two, the "erasure" arising out of the linearity of *logos,* which Derrida has referred to as the "catastrophe" of Western philosophy and Husserl once named the "crisis," is, of course, what the methodology of deconstruction involves. *Deconstruction addresses the dilemma by acknowledging the default.*

Deconstruction becomes an exegesis of the asymmetry of the linguistic architecture of connotation and reference. Derrida's notion of "dissemination" conveys the entropic movement of signifying praxis, which is never reversible. The postmodern view of signification, according to Derrida, can never truly be assimilated to Heidegger's understanding of *logos* as "gathering" and "recollecting," for what has been distributed can never be put back together. The catastrophe, therefore, says Derrida, is more than a contretemps. It is "apocalyptic." In his essay "Of an Apocalyptic Tone Newly Adopted in Philosophy" (1992), Derrida characterizes the apocalypse of Western philosophy as a "change in tone." Derrida understands this philosophic tonality as a kind of hyperrationality, an excess of systematization that concurrently claims some privileged truth or "secret" (*Geheimnis*). It is not clear in the essay whom precisely Derrida is (his ipsissima verba) "lampooning" here. But the context of the article suggests it could be the culmination of both the Continental and the analytical traditions at once. He also seems to have in mind the present-day American university.

The apocalyptic "tension" in Derrida's perspective results from a latter-day obsession with what philosophy—or theology for that matter—must "speak about." It is the *about* that comes into question. The "about" connotes the *aliquid,* what is "stood for." In its fury to settle the issue of the "about," philosophy turns oracular. *Vernunft* and *Gefühl* become a singular, mixed modality. The outcome is what Derrida dubs a "mystagogy" that succeeds in "perverting the voice of reason, by mixing the two voices of the other in us, the voice of reason and the voice of the oracle."[4] Such a perversion, however, is inevitable insofar as Western thought remains hypnotized by the cult of representation, the apodictic regimentation of sign and signified. The spell is broken by an "apocalypse."

> Whoever takes on the apocalyptic tone comes to signify to, if not tell, you something. What? The truth, of course, and to signify to you that it reveals the truth to you; tone is revelatory of some unveiling in process. Unveiling or truth, apophantics of the imminence of the end, of whatever comes down, finally, to the end of the world. Not only truth as the revealed truth of a secret on the end or of the secret of the end. Truth itself is the end, the destination, and that truth unveils itself is the advent of the end. Truth is the end and the instance of the last judgment. The structure of truth here would be apocalyptic. And that is why there would not be any truth of the apocalypse that is not the truth of truth.[5]

The desire to achieve truth in the paramount sense, the "truth of truth," the inseparability of presence and re-presenting, the primordial realm of signification that somehow is tacit in the structure of the discourse, produces a philosophical "aristocracy," or "priesthood," that is privileged to preserve and to vouchsafe the secret truth of philosophy. But the secrecy of "rational" truth necessitates its obfuscation. *Aufklärung*, which strives toward public disclosure of all that has heretofore remained "religious"—that is, "secretive"—must maintain its preferential argot, and hence circumscribes the "voice of reason" with the mutterings of the mystagogue, the eerie, woodland chants of the custodians of the *religiones*. The myth of "Enlightenment" as the exposition of pure presence generates the canard of the strictly esoteric, the conspiratorial magician, the dark lord of the forest, the *illuminatus*. It is out of this paradox that the apocalypse of Western thinking, for which deconstruction amounts to nothing more than "wars and rumors of war," looms large on the horizon.

In a related essay, titled "Post-Scriptum" and published in the same volume, Derrida contends, as before, that the "apocalyptic tone" of representationalist philosophy masks a refusal of difference. But the difference refused is something more all at once than the "spacing" of signifying disjunctions that hermeneutically defines Derrida's "grammatology." *Différance* is a negative topology within "logical space," as Wittgenstein puts it, that cannot be distinguished from the surface features of the grammatology. Yet in "Post-Scriptum" Derrida unexpectedly calls into question, in a manner that had seemed inconceivable in his earlier writing, the unsurpassability of the *scriptum*.

The "post-scriptum" is Derrida's rendering of "negative theology," which is not theology at all in the conventional manner of speaking. Derrida's postmodernist *via negativa* does not flip over into any kind of strange *via affirmativa*. The "post-scriptum" is "beyond interpretation." Derrida has hit upon the peculiar "grammatical" function of "apophasis," the moment when the negative becomes an act of unconcealment. This revelatory instance, or "apophase" of formal inference, corresponding to the joining of land and sea, raises in itself "the possibility of the impossible." Derrida quotes Angelus Silesius, one of the most famous of "negative theologians": "*Nichts werden ist GOTT werden.* . . . To become Nothing is to become God."[6]

Apophasis

How does something become "nothing." How does the *aliquid* pass over into the *nihil*? That is the "secret" of apophasis, which Derrida describes as "the most thinking, the most exacting, the most intractable experience of the 'essence' of language."[7] Is the "essence of language" this *Nichts werden*? Perhaps we can say that the theory of language itself is "in essence" a negative "theology." But what would that mean exactly? It is to say that *logos* itself is striated. Such a striation is not only the logic of the apocalypse of language but the apocalypse of "logic." This striation denotes the "paralogical." Similarly, it drives to the heart of the matter when we talk of any sort of "ontology." In the final synopsis all ontology is paralogy. The paralogy is "religious" in the sense that it projects itself into the shadows circumambulating the sign, the arcana which it is impossible not to regard whenever we think, as Heidegger would say, the "essence" of the linguistic. To speak of the religious is henceforth to speak in an extended manner of what is read "between the lines" or "on the fly" in the negative interlacings and striations of Enlightenment discourse. It is to speak of *theos*, of the "divine," as these peculiar sorts of negative spatializations.

It is impossible to examine the "religious" from a scientific—that is, a genuinely linguistic or logical standpoint—without engaging in a kind of theological, or *theo-semiological*, reflection. Mark C. Taylor argues that something of this order happens in what he has termed "a/theology." A/theology, he writes, "is not the opposite of theology and must not be identified with atheism. Neither exactly positive nor negative, a/theology draws on the resources of deconstruction to develop a nonnegative negative theology that seeks to think what Western ontotheology leaves unthought."[8] A/theology, however, cannot be differentiated from the formative grammar of the "sacred." The sacred usually is regarded as the *topos* first and foremost in the study of religion, and has generally been segregated from *theos,* the proper "subject area" of theology. However, Taylor characterizes the sacred as "the nothing that appears." And this appearance of the *nihil*—the "phenomenon" that is at once a "show" and a "no-show"—is what is implied in the "construct" of *theos.*

In addition, Taylor pursues the theme of the sacred with respect to the technical, Derridean idea of *dénégation.* Derrida himself adapts the phrase from the French translation of the word *Verneinung,* which is used by Freud. According to Taylor, "denegation" serves to capture "the irresolvable duplicity of *Verneinung* in which affirmation and negation are conjoined without being united or synthesized. *Verneinung* is an affirmation that is a negation and a negation that is an affirmation. To de-negate is to un-negate. Un-negation is, of course, a form of negation. More precisely, denegation is an unnegation that affirms rather than negates negation."[9] This moment of "negative affirmation"—a liminal sort of logical space which Taylor posits as the "deconstructive" correlate to the rule of "negative theology" that *omnia negatio determinatio est* ("all negation is determination")—signifies the connection between "God" and the "sacred." The sacred is "the denegation of God, and God is the denegation of the sacred. As negation without negation, denegation creates the possibility of nonnegative negative theology that nevertheless is not positive. Inscribed along the irrepressible margin of difference, the sacred neither exists nor does it not exist; it is neither being nor nonbeing. Moreover, the sacred is not a 'God beyond God,' for it is neither a God nor the other of God but is an other that is precisely not *of* God."[10]

Taylor regards *dénégation* as a kind of suspension of the Hegelian dialectic. It is intimately related to Blanchot's concept of the *entretien* ("talk" or "conversation") which opens up the space of the "between" (*l'entre-deux*), "which is neither positive nor negative, neither is nor is not, is a difference or an other that cannot be dialectically sublated through the duplicitous positivity of double negation." He names this nondialectical "negativity" inserted into the (logical) space in which the negative negates itself as the "paralogic of the neuter," which constitutes what Taylor calls "paralectics." "A paralectic parodies a dialectic by miming the communication of that which is incommunicable."[11]

Taylor's paralectics, however, amounts to a curious type of reading, as in Derrida's reading as well, of the *entretien.* For the *entretien* is not circumscribed within a logical, or even a rhetorical, space. It is not located, as Taylor assumes, within the linear terrain of the text, but is defined by the orthogonal coordinates of language and what surpasses it. The "in-between" of the *entretien* fosters a puzzlement not about "logic" but about the relationship between the speaker and the one to whom speech is addressed. This intervening space is not "neutral." It is charged with an indescribable presence, the presence of the other that draws and withdraws as one addresses it.

Such a spatial reserve can be delineated as "para-logical," not because some kind of deductive rule has been violated, but because it develops not simply outside, but *alongside*, the circuits of *logos*. The language of the sacred, or "religious language," is discontinuous with the very philosophical paradigm of denotation and instantiation that Derrida has undertaken to deconstruct. That is a fateful "domain of difference" that the metaphysics of difference, whether it be termed "denegation" or "paralectics," has overlooked. The sacred is not simply a form of "paralogy." It is a dis-guise of everything that we term "ontic." It pertains to that order of signification which emulates representational, or "theological," discourse in Heidegger's sense, but is actually of an entirely different order. It is the *Glas*, the "mirror side" of Aristotelian predicative logic. It is what we would dub the *para-theological*.

The para-theological is inseparable from the process of deconstruction itself. Derrida's negational "God" is neither a "theological" nor an "a/theological" construct. It is not a negative posit but a syntagmatic *de-posit*, what we term a "negative differential." It is the only one true "God" that can be found in all religions, because it is what religion itself is "about." Implicit in the study of religion is a generalized *apophantic monotheism* that demands theoretical and philosophical articulation. The para-theological speaks the presencing of the Hebraic "I am that I am," which is at the same time the Vedic *neti neti* ("not this, not that") and the Greco-Christian "dark night of the soul." The para-theological does not say what religion is, but neither it does it say what religion is not. The para-theological speaks of what religion is by the manner in which any given *religio* says "not."

Para-theology

The study of religion, therefore, adopts a "scientific" approach that is at the same time a negative reconnoitering. The science of negative numbers, like the science of negative space-time, is a science nonetheless. Just as the theory of matter can compass the phenomenon of antimatter, so the "science of language" is concerned with the incalculable otherness that we understand as the *religiones*. Before the advent of postmodernist "negative theology," no "science" of religion in the sense of a logico-linguistic argument was really possible. A general theory of religion had to rely on what we might term "weak phenomenology," or the employment of what is nothing more than a classificatory system of idealist tokens that could be designated as "sacred" or "holy." We have in mind the work of Eliade, Rudolf Otto, and Gerhard van der Leeuw. Such tokens by and large amount to "limiting concepts," as Kant would have called them. They serve as representational surrogates for what was almost by definition unrepresentable. Tillich's doctrine of the symbol also functioned in much the same manner. Classical theories of religion, even those of Durkheim and other "social scientists," had the same defect.

The transition in the philosophy of science during the twentieth century from idealism to linguistic analysis has never been complemented within the philosophy of religion. Increasingly, however, various "social scientists" have begun to attack the idealistic, or what Russ McCutcheon has termed the "sui generis," theory of religion.[12] These sorts of attacks, of course, are motivated by an agenda that would underwrite the hegemony in religious studies of functionalist social science and organizational theory, which turns out to be almost as spurious as the idealistic position itself. But their criticism of the sui generis perspective is basically valid. While a "social scientific" approach to religion is more likely to substitute quasi-Marxist political ideology (e.g., so-called labeling theory) for genuine empirical research, a gesture toward a true "scientific study of religion" would require the logico-semiotic framework that a postmodern, or poststructuralist, philosophy of language offers.

Despite the evident frustration of Anglo-American thinkers with the late Derridean style of philosophical writing, the conceptual infrastructure for a linguistic science of alterity is present in the deconstructionist version of "negative theology." By the same token, we would be better advised to talk not about "negative theology," which has a definitive historical cachet, but about the "para-theological." If theology is no longer "queen of the sciences," a para-theological venture into the space of *dénégation* would almost paradoxically fulfill the condition of a "scientific" accounting of the phenomenon that heretofore has never been named except as *l'autre*. We may call this reading of the "philosophy of religion" the science of the negative, if we wish. But we must remember that the negative as a "matter" of religious reflection is far more than the reversal of a mathematical sign. It is a plenitude of significance, the significance of the nameless, the forest that shelters the *religiones*.

The negative plenitude—or perhaps a "paroxysm"—of religious space has been delineated carefully and didactically in the work of J. Z. Smith. Smith insists that the textual, or mytho-grammatical, method of mapping religious sign-sectors is inadequate because it presumes that the sense of "sacrality" is based on narrative, rather than ritual, formulas. The study of myths, according to Smith, was originally a "rationalizing procedure" of both Christian antiquity and the Enlightenment. It constituted an archaeology of the imaginative substrates of tradition and narrative in a quest for the concealed "signs of truth."[13] Myth studies, therefore, rendered the "sacred" as a camouflaged *kerygma,* as an embryonic rationality or "eidetic" form of intelligibility, in Husserlian language. The sacred became the esoteric core, the "occult" *secret,* sequestered within the narrative. This quasi-phenomenological take on what came to be called "the essence of religion" was merely one variant of the metaphysics of presence wrongly applied to the theory of the other. But ritual theory shows that this phantom presence we call the "sacred" is most appropriately construed, says Smith, as a locus of differentiation. "Ritual is, above all, an assertion of difference. . . . [It is] not best understood as congruent with something else—a magical imitation of desired ends, a translation of emotions, a symbolic acting out of ideas, a dramatization of a text, or the like. Ritual gains force where incongruency is perceived or thought about."[14]

Such a "thought of incongruency" is both negative space and what Smith terms "sacred place." Yet sacred places are not delineated by "where" they are, but by how they are "marked" by acts of transposition or "displacement." In other words, sacred place is arbitrary, just as the "sacred" per se cannot be ontologized, but only read as a sign of difference. Smith cites Herodotus's tale of the Egyptian king Amasis. Amasis was a "private person" who became king. On his ascent to the throne Amasis's golden footpan, in which he and his guests washed their feet, was melted down and shaped into an image of a god, which became the center of an important cult. The golden footpan is not an "emblem" of some mysterious or "numinous" entity. In no sense can it even be regarded as "symbolic." The story of Amasis concerns "the arbitrariness of place and of placement and replacement. It comes out of the complex ideology of archaic kingship." For "divine and human, sacred and profane, are transitive categories; they serve as maps and labels, not substances; they are distinctions of office, indices of difference."[15]

Smith points out, as most philologists have reminded us, that the Latin *sacer* (Greek *saos*) connotes the act of separating out, or "cutting off." The sense of sacrality implies radical differentiation, which generates lesser hierarchies of distinctions. Most ritual systems, not to mention "holy places," Smith notes, are built upon a Saussurean semiotic prototype. They constitute complex *codes of difference*—the "holy of holies" that must be always walled off from the outer court or portico, the "clean" animal that serves as the anti-type to the polluted one, and so forth. The sacred is registered in, and only within, these codes. The codes themselves have an apophantic character. They "manifest" the sacred through the interplay of negative sign instruments. Furthermore, these moments of apophasis cannot be divorced from the diachrony of textual studies and analysis. The interstices of the "sacred" always can be discerned as instants—broadly conceived—of "negative theology." In a statement that is probably both surprising and disarming to religious ethnographers, Smith writes: "I have come to believe that a prime object for the historian of religion ought to be the theological tradition, taking the term in the widest sense."[16]

The reason is both obvious and not so obvious. The theological stratum of "religiosity" determines the realm in which the signifying praxis of the "tradition" evolves. It makes no sense to talk about different "religions" as coherent systems of meaning without examining and surveying their complex "exegetical" and "interpretative" bodies of literature—in a word, their devices of canonization and anathematization. All religious scholarship, therefore, amounts to a deciphering of these systematic operations. It is what we term a "null point historicism." Every historian of religion is ipso facto a "historical theologian" in the para-theological sense. A science of religion would be a "science of the negative" that is not only postmodern but postdialectical. It was Wittgenstein who opined that the limits of language are the limits of one's world. Beyond those limits is a terra incognita, the "end" of the world that always appeared far to the west on the maps of medieval mariners. In this region the old cartographers wrote: "Here be monsters." The study of monsters is the preoccupation of those who divide the "world" between the intelligible and the obscure, the philosophical and the psychological, the rational and the uncanny. The "science" of para/theology, however, writes in the margins: "Here be God."

The *Deus Evanescens*

Here we are speaking, however, neither of a *deus revelatus* nor a *deus absconditus*, but a *deus evanescens*, a "now-you-see-it-now-you-don't" sort of "divinity." The "gods" of religious theory have certain curious affinities with the Loch Ness monster. As theorists, we "catch sight" of them, yet we do not "see" them, as the etymology of the word theory (*theorein* = "to view") suggests. There are numerous "witnesses" and viewings, but these particular "sightings" are never recorded or captured. Or those recorded or captured turn out to be problematic. Their signifying capacity—and hence their conveyance of the real in Žižek's sense of the term—turns on their elusiveness and phantasmal, or spectral, irregularity. But it is this spectral irregularity that *reifies* them, gives them a larger-than-life reality as in the so-called urban legend. They in principle function as apparitions, as pure "appearances," as something appearing and returning, the modality of the *revenant*—Derrida's ghost or "specter." Their appearing is not in the form of an "object" for consideration, only as a *signature* of some sort of cognitive anomaly whose value in the final summation is not epistemological but semiotic, Lawrence's "god-stuff."

Žižek offers a variety of metonymical conditions for the way in which we can begin to "sight" at a theoretical level this negative *exclusion* of the garden-variety object that results in semiosis. Žižek has a whole repertoire of expressions to communicate what is connoted by the semiotic. Most telling is his phrase "off space." The *semiotique* of the so-called religious relies on the displacement of logical or rhetorical expectation to *make apparent* an event that is both singular and unique. Such an event in classical religious theory is known as an epiphany, or more exact, a *theophany*. The theophany interrupts time and space by negating the conditions of the normal circumstances for the appearance of the object. But this negation is not so much a violation of those circumstances, as in the case of the miraculous, as it is a sudden and nonrepeatable suspension of the same conditions. No "phenomenology" as rigorous science, as Husserl might have it, can gauge the appearance of the god, as one can a tablecloth or a mountain peak. The god's appearance is always an "apparition." It is always "out of place" and "off schedule."

Divinity—the concern of religious theory—is ineluctably *out of kilter* with established order. The reason we associate God with truth, as Žižek slyly impresses upon us, is not because the divine *certifies* the truthfulness of what is true, but because the truth disrupts. And it disrupts, like the category of the sublime in Romantic aesthetics, the very acceptability and proportionality of universal order. Truth is *monstrous*, according to Žižek. Truth, like fantasy, is "not an idiosyncratic excess that deranges cosmic order, but the violent singular excess that *sustains* every notion of such an order."[17] Žižek derives this notion, as he does many of its metonymical equivalents in his theoretical analysis, from Lacan's postulation of the *objet petit a*. The *objet petit a* is a critical, but pivotal, concept in Lacanian psychoanalysis. It is not the object of desire per se, but the semiotic condensation as object of desire in the return of the real. It is what Lacan calls a "supplement," whence Derrida's own use of the term. It is the "leftover" in language, or symbolic commerce, that cannot be left out and thus allows for the breakage in the armature of discourse and thought that makes possible a recovery of the real. It is a signifier that mobilizes on behalf of the subject the entire domain of fantasy and imagination, crystallizing as something desired that is nonfamiliar and spectral, albeit on a cosmic plane.

Žižek writes that the *objet petit a* is the key to how we might theorize such a "singular excess." It is "pure form; it is the form of an attractor drawing us into chaotic oscillation. The art of the theory of chaos consists in *allowing us to see the very form of chaos*, in allowing us to see a pattern where ordinarily we see nothing but a formless disorder."[18] Such speculations, Žižek adds, permit us to envision a "future science of the real," which might also be a paralogical "science" of the religious qua "monstrosity," or negative disfiguration. Let us consider such a negative disfiguration as the "chaosmotic" (cosmos intermingled with and inextricable from chaos), a word borrowed from Deleuze. Žižek cites the Lacanian "science" of psychosemiotics. "Distortion and/or dissimulation is in itself revealing," inasmuch as unpleasant surprises, traumas, disturbances, warps, rips in the fabric, and so forth suffice as reminders that "things" are never programmed and stable.[19] The cosmos is not merely abuzz with "novelty," as the Whiteheadeans constantly tell us. It is tempestuous and conflicted within itself, sloshing back and forth between what we know as order and what we know as disorder. Things are not stable, "the center cannot hold," because any order of signification is actually a regime of trauma and disruption.

It is in this curious, *unheimlich* order of things that we discover signifying power that emerges from the transgression, from the collapse of footings, from the longing for justice that may turn out to be the universe's poetic justice. A "science of religion" would ultimately be a science of the negative, but such a *scientia* does not depend on inferential stabilization and notional stratification, but on a tableau of breakage, perhaps akin to imaginary numbers in mathematics, although not "imaginary" at all in the philosophical sense of the word. Not a descending order, but an order of vanishing points, of fruitful impossibilities and indeterminacies, perhaps reminding us of

Jean-Luc Nancy's moments of *dis-enclosure,* which we will take up toward the conclusion of these investigations.

Here we have perhaps a *semiotique* that can be understood as a *science of the negative.* But such a science would be entirely different from the Hegelian science of the dialectic, of the negated negation. It would also be quite different from Derrida's discovery of the semiotic pregnancy of *khōra* and of undecidability. The semiotic "negative," our instrument for exploring the religious as the focus of theory rather than any remapping, or *retrocatography,* of its myriad significations, consists in a moment of singularity, a singularity to which the signs direct us without necessarily "deconstructing" all their interlinkages and accentuating their interstices.

In such a singularity we find the possibility of a meaning in what Deleuze terms "absolute deterritorialization" or a "smooth space" of pure globalization. It is not the singularity of a pure or transcendental signified, but of an immanent and historically consequential *Jenseits,* a catachresis, what in Nancy's lexicality serves to "*exceed qua principle principiation itself.*"[20] Such an excess is beyond any principle, yet in its *siting* it also retains no position. It is *de-posed* from all positions. But before we analyze further how the "de-posed" religious signifier (the more technical assessment of what we mean by "deconstructed") works, we need first to examine the much greater context in which the "religious" has come to upend our cherished notions of a world, and of world order, that we have inherited from the Enlightenment. We need to consider in depth what Derrida has named "the return of religion."

3

POSTMODERNISM AND THE RETURN
OF THE "RELIGIOUS"

•

> No theory is good unless it permits, not rest, but the greatest
> work. No theory is good except on condition that one use it to
> go on beyond.
>
> —André Gide

FOR DERRIDA, the religious amounts to the spectral—what is ethe-real and shadowlike. It is a fill-in-the-blank sort of phenomenality. As Richard Kearney observes, Derrida "prefers ghosts to gods." He is more enamored with spacing rather than with holy radiance. He is haunted by wraiths that resist any suggestion of corporeality. His work frames an "eschatology" merely of "the possible God," of the unnamed possibility for naming that surpasses finite names, the pure tetragrammaton of all language. He offers a sense of faith as a "deconstructive belief in the undecidable and unpredictable character of incoming every day events . . . rather than in some special advent of the divine as such."[1] Kearney's criticism may be justifiable, but perhaps Derrida is cannier than we realize. At one level a theory of religion after postmodernism *does in fact* require "spectralization." There has never been a sustainable theory of religion since the nine-teenth century in European literature—and there is only slowly emerging something resembling such a theory in non-European or so-called postcolonial writings—largely because the theory of religion has either worn the latest mask of a seductive essentialism, some-times under the camouflage of what is wrongly termed a "phenomenology of religion," or become an overdetermined, complexified, and rarefied *functionalism*, hygienically sealing itself against the "contamination" of theory out of the anxiety that the multifariousness of religion's semiotic expressivity might be reduced to some vague, universalizing pronouncement.

Specters of Religion

Derrida spectralizes the religious indirectly from his reading of Marx, or what is left of Marx, in regard to the "political." What Derrida calls Marx's specter is an "apparition of the inapparent." It is a concern for "justice," the great undeconstructible, that dominates Derrida's subsequent musings on the messianic and the democratic as well as the religious. "Could one *address oneself in general* if already some ghost did not come back? If he loves justice at least, the 'scholar' of the future, the 'intellectual' of tomorrow, should learn it and from the ghost."[2] The *revenant*, as Derrida calls it, is what spectrally "returns." Religion today returns, but can such a *revenant* be theorized? For Derrida, religion is the colossal *aporia*. An aporia is an "undecidable," an impasse, an unmediated, or *nonmediable*, path of resolution or differentiation. That makes theory impossible in the normal sense of the word. Yet if the *revenant* that returns as an aporia has no embodiment, it still has a history, or at least it can be discerned as a skein of traces within our contemporary history.

The *religious* in Derrida turns out to be its own kind of supplement —not the supplement of writing, but the supplement of "Latinity." What does Derrida mean by the "Latin"? According to Derrida, the "Latin" is the word for the West and its techno-scientific dominion. The Latin is what overreaches with its sumptuous signatures of power and meaning; it is a perfection of the organizational, a vast economy of codings as well as a "reterritorialized"—in Deleuze's sense—system of administration necessary for the expansion of a planetary sociopolitical apparatus. To be "religious" is to participate in an impersonal and invisible strategy of "pacification," toward which the Roman Empire with its brutal politics of deportation and detribalization always strove. Today this detribalization proceeds not so much by the tramp of legions and the force of arms as by commerce, exchange, digital communications, and their affiliated political upheavals and armed conflicts. "Politics" depends on the mobilization of innumerable, private aspirations and patterns of consumer behavior through a manufacture of "virtual" values and identities which, as Baudrillard tells us, are just as "real" and motivating as the old order of ideals.

In his essay "Faith and Knowledge" Derrida of course refers to this "postmodern" world historical movement as "globolatinization," the new "war of religion." "The field of this war or of this pacification is henceforth without limit: all the religions, their centers of authority, the religious cultures, states, nations or ethnic groups that they represent have unequal access, to be sure, but often one that is immediate and potentially without limit, to the same world market."[3] The "production" of religion goes hand in hand with "the pledge of faith, the guarantee of trustworthiness," that is necessary to underwrite the "fiduciary experience presupposed by all production of shared knowledge, the testimonial performativity engaged in all techno-scientific performance as in the entire capitalistic economy indissociable from it."[4]

As in Rome, the notion of "religion" functions as an aggregate signifier for the "re-binding" (re-ligio) together of previously profuse and dissociated particularities of faith and devotion with their own indigenous, or "territorial," characteristics into a grand ideology of "unity in diversity," where the principle of integration is the divinization of the political—"emperor worship." If the term "postmodern" originally meant, as it did for Charles Jencks, who coined the expression, the wild eclecticism and hybridization of architectural styles, it now connotes a market-driven syncretism on a global scale of religious simulacra that have long been stripped of their content, of their original "civic" implications. But what is the agency that "rebinds" the simulacra of the gods in our New Rome, our post-Enlightenment imperium of techno-scientific rationality in which the religious returns?

According to Derrida, "Religion today allies itself with tele-techno-science, to which it reacts with all its forces. It *is, on the one hand*, globalization; it produces, weds, exploits the capital and knowledge of tele-mediatization; neither the trips and global spectacularizing of the Pope, nor the interstate dimensions of the 'Rushdie affair,' nor planetary terrorism would otherwise be possible, at this rhythm—and we could multiply such indications *ad infinitum*." But at the same time religion declares "war against that which gives it this new power only at the cost of dislodging it from all its proper places, *in truth from place itself*, from the *taking-place* of its truth."[5] The new "war of religion" is between the "Enlightenment" force of globalization and "telemediatization" on the one hand and the "reactive" force of faith, which is a singularity and has its own "place of truth," on the other.

The new war of religion is a profound struggle between "faith" and "reason," but not in the classic sense at all. While the classic scuffle was between a doctrinal formulation of religious intuitions and revelations that could not be reconciled with either philosophical or "plain" experience, the new battle is between the techno-rationalizing "war machine" (Deleuze's phrase) that "deterritorializes" all signifi- cations of faith in the service of a global consumer *regnum* and the faith's own reactive violence. Faith defends its own particular "situ- ation" against the encroachments of this *regnum* by fighting for the purity and sanctity of its language and authority—a process that has come to be termed "fundamentalism." These fundamentalisms, which have resisted encroachment—sometimes for generations—by carving out enclaves of belief and practice with entry signs that read "Do not disturb," suddenly under the constant and mounting pres- sure of "globalatinzation" turn militant and aggressive. This kind of "reactivity" has proven especially potent in the *fundamentalization* of Islam, inasmuch as Islam historically, far more than the Church with its ideal of "Christendom," has opposed all "empires" with its own opposing *regnum*, the *dar al-islam*, or "house of Islam."

Although Derrida for whatever reasons seems to avoid using the word "fundamentalism," he is without question calling attention to virtually the same phenomenon. "The same 'religiosity' is obliged to ally the reactivity of the primitive and archaic return . . . *both* to obscurantist dogmatism *and* to hypercritical vigilance. The machines it combats by striving to appropriate them are also machines for de- stroying historical tradition. They can displace the traditional struc- tures of national citizenship, they tend to efface both the borders of the state and the distinctive properties of languages."[6] They are "global" in their universalistic and antihistorical compass without any "Latin" tendency to assimilate and incorporate. Instead they become contrar- ian "war machines" of their own, riding roughshod over all historicity and cultural multiplicity and subtlety. The fundamentalist war ma- chine is quintessentially a jihad of deterritorialized faith-nomads ex- ploding, like the Islamic armies after the death of Mohammed, across the vast and crumbling empire of techno-scientific rationality.

But what causes this war to happen in the first place? What sets off the fundamentalist-nomadic explosion? Derrida makes the point that Marx's thinking of the specter is the question of a *nomado- globalization*. Deterritorialization is the production of spaces where one is not at home, one is ghostly, one is *unheimlich*. "Marx remains an immigrant chez nous, a glorious, sacred, accursed but still a clan- destine immigrant as he was all his life. He belongs to a time of dis- junction . . . in which is inaugurated, laboriously, painfully, tragically, a new thinking of borders, a new experience of the house, the home, and the economy."[7] Religion belongs within an economy, but it is the economy that has no territorial locus. It is a site, but not a place. It is a site not merely of the impossible and the undecidable (the aporetic), as we shall discover, but of the *singularity*. The singularity is a *situation* that even for deconstruction is difficult to handle. Nomadism is a circling of all the "space vehicles" of religious expressivity around the singularity.

Derrida in his own right addresses the difficulty by reviving Henri Bergson, whom we are increasingly beginning to identify as the "deep source" of postmodernism. In his *Two Sources of Morality and Religion* Bergson traces the problem to the dichotomy within the experience of time itself, the spatio-mechanistic, calculable sense of "clock time" (*temps*) and the "mystical," undivided movement of interior consciousness (*durée*). Although Derrida is highly elliptical and frequently confusing in his allusions to Bergson, his citation of *Two Sources* along with Kant's *Religion within the Limits of Reason Alone* as the two works that allow us to still "think religion in the daylight of today without breaking with the philosophical tradition" is extremely instructive.

Both books are incidental and migratory reflections—much like Derrida's own essay on faith and knowledge—on historic philosophers in the mature phase of their careers regarding the "religious." More importantly, they are prospectuses on how to "reflect" on the religious. The return of the religious is the occasion to think religiosity. But the "phenomenon" of the religious—that which *appears* as a task, or conundrum, for thinking—is invariably schizoid; it is a "double stratum" because of its "double source." The religious reveals itself as a "quasi-spontaneous automaticity, as irreflective as a reflex." It "repeats again and again the double movement of abstraction and attraction that *at the same time detaches and reattaches* to the country, the idiom, the literal or to everything confusedly collected today under the terms 'identity' or 'identitarian'; in two words, that which at the same time ex-propriates and re-appropriates, de-racinates and re-enracinates, *ex-appropriates* according to a logic that we will . . . have to formalize."[8]

Derrida's strangely "un-Derridean" discourse in this "inaugural" essay on faith is slyly recrafted, if not directly lifted, from Deleuze, who has bequeathed to us a "nomadological" analysis of philosophical change and the evolution of concepts derived from a metaphorized history of the millennial conflict between sedentary civilizations and wandering pastoral peoples. The "logic" Derrida references here is the same Deleuze sets forth in *A Thousand Plateaus*. Religion "returns" only because it is "rhizomic"; it is a constant pressure beneath the surface of the deep; its double sourcing becomes the *double sentencing* of what Deleuze understands as "territorialized" self-identity and "deterritorialized"—mobile or "nomadic"—signifiers that are in "flight" toward unexplored destinations in the history of thought. Deterritorialization is what Derrida characterizes as "de-racination." The modern era of "Enlightenment" constitutes a progressive deterritorialization of the existential locus of faith, beginning with the eighteenth-century critique of Christianity but enlarging itself through the colonial predations of Europe during the nineteenth century and culminating in the grand subsumption of all the world's "sacred" texts and traditions under the rubric of the "scientific study of religion" (*Religionswissenschaft*).

The compression of "religiosity" within the "limits of reason alone" generates a reactivity that Kant himself grasped, but did not think through, as "radical evil." Radical evil, for Derrida as well as for Kant, is the pure disclosure of difference within the Enlightenment project. Yet this disclosure is only made possible by the de-recination of the faith-act and its mobilization of the elements of signification, by its "reterritorialization" as a conceptual problem, or as a datum for "global theology." All "interfaith" initiatives, or global theological agendas, are efforts to smooth over the sharp edges of religious difference, to domesticate them and make them susceptible to techno-rational intervention. Our so-called fundamentalisms thus are not conservative, but genuinely revolutionary in their intention and thrust; altogether they constitute something much more than a collective, quasi-Freudian "return of the repressed" within the economy of global consciousness. All "fundamentalisms" are anathema to the partisans of Enlightenment because they connote a "deterritorialization" of those faith codings that had already been reterritorialized as the general concept of the "religious." They disclose the differencing that is ineradicable for the situation of faith. Their deterritorialization is at once a *de-Latinization*, a barbarian incursion across the borders of empire, a breaching of the *limina*, the invisible boundaries of *Romanitas* from which we derive the word "liminal."

The "Impossibility" of Theory

A "postmodern theory" of religion is capable of accounting for our many-toned fundamentalisms, not to mention our barbarisms. But such a theory itself would be impossible, if only because the religious on Derrida's terms amounts to the undecidable and the impossible. However, such a theory appears impossible because the theory of the postmodern is impossible, as Hans Bertens has shown.[9] But if a postmodern theory of religion is impossible, a theory of religion in the aftermath of postmodernism is altogether conceivable. It is only "after postmodernism" that religious theory can be envisaged, even if a prospectus for such a theory will take many generations to survey and tease out. Religious theory itself requires that we come to locate the "after" of this aftermath, because what has come to be regarded as postmodernist theory has not been able to emancipate itself from the Enlightenment project which both spawned and spurned it. The "after" of postmodernism cannot, and should not, be construed as a postlogue. The hyphen of postmodernism in its own right underscores that something has already elapsed, faded, evanesced. This "epoch" of evanescence has now been recognized and determined, and its effects are at last finally becoming perceptible, while the sense of passage is now for the most part experienced fully.

What comes *after* postmodernism is what was gestating all along in this time of passage, but is only now giving inklings of itself. We cannot speak without being facetious of a "post-postmodernism," because that would belie the force of what has already occurred. Postmodernism is not a calendar event; it is preeminently the final distribution of all the signifying tendencies of what was previously labeled the "modern" combined with a letting go, a true *Gelassenheit*, as Heidegger would say, of the Platonic quest for the manageable signifier. What comes after postmodernism is a bursting of the levees of semiosis, an inundation of the flatlands of predicative logic with new torrents of signification.

Derrida's meditations on religion constitute a kind of prologemenon to a yet unessayed critique of pure philosophy, and of pure theology, that deconstruction of necessity brings onto the playing field. Deconstruction is to this emergent critique what Hume's radical empiricism was to Kant, who was awakened by it from his "dogmatic slumber."

> Now if, today, the "question of religion" actually appears in a new and different light, if there is an unprecedented resurgence, both global and planetary, of this ageless thing, then what is at stake is language, certainly—and more precisely the idiom, literality, writing, that forms the element of all revelation and of all belief, an element that ultimately is irreducible and untranslatable—but an idiom that above all is inseparable from the social nexus, from the political, familial, ethnic, communitarian nexus, from the nation and from the people; from autochthony, blood and soil, and from the ever more problematic relation to citizenship and to the state.[10]

In many respects the era of postmodernism can be seen not as a new dawn, or new era, but as a shimmering and multihued sunset of the modernist period. Bertens ends his searching and detailed account of the emergence of the postmodernist theme by epitomizing it as the full manifestation of the deeper "contradictory" impulses of the Enlightenment. The spirit of the Enlightenment was always both universalistic and antirepresentational. The universalistic thrust turns on the radical ideals of democracy: "liberty, equality, and fraternity"—or "sorority." Political postmodernism, therefore, leveraged this agenda in a multitude of ways, attempting "to make the Enlightenment live up to its promises."[11] A wide swath of ideological critiques with their own revisionist histories—feminism, ethnohistoriography, gay and lesbian studies, postcolonial writing inter alia—served to foster a theoretical framework for social and political "emancipation." Inherent in this method of ideological analysis was a powerful distrust of the classical model of *representationalism*, which political thought after Marx instinctively understood as saturated with the interests of particular classes, groups, or social formations.

Anti-representationalism—what crudely came to be known as "deconstructionism," although the term was always misapplied—was born of the very "hermeneutics of suspicion" that the Enlightenment in its self-reflexive approach to philosophy, inaugurated by Descartes, had engendered. Anti-representationalism was motivated by the emancipatory vision of the eighteenth century. Yet it came to be a two-edged sword that also eviscerated the universalistic claims of reason in which emancipatory politics was originally anchored. The upshot was the emergence of a politics of pure differentiation that could not brook any theoretical perspective that might somehow constitute a subtle hegemonic intrusion of one interest-driven party into the cultural sphere of the other. In the language of Levinas, the sign of same could under no circumstances be drawn across the face of the other. If the universalism of the Enlightenment had already been exposed in numerous instances as "false consciousness," the rough particularism that was the teleological outcome of the insuperable postmodernist *differend* was even more devastating. Postmodern theory, notes Bertens, "became myopically concerned with fragmentation,"[12] and the emancipatory function of postmodernist thought became self-limiting.

The impossibility of religious theory in the "postmodern" epoch according to this template is not yet self-evident, although the difficulties are mounting. The anti-representational critique of all grand theory made its initial impact in the 1960s as the secession of *religious studies* from theological studies. While the separation was also propelled by an increasing tension between the academic as opposed to the "sectarian" approach to religion, the presumed universalism of the Christian faith, on which theology was allegedly founded, met with increasing, and often militant, skepticism.

However, theology has always carried, and in some fashion continues to bear, the theoretical burden of religious studies. While philosophical, psychological, sociological, and anthropological research have all trafficked with the concept of the religious, it is theology alone that has internalized the project of what was once termed the "science of religion," even if its agenda was always preservationist, confessional, or apologetic in seeking to uphold the primacy of a proprietary faith language that might at the same time be clerically sound as well as "objectively" coherent. It is no accident that Kantianism with its idea of the *synthetic a priori,* which the neo-Kantians construed as implying a *religious a priori,* turned out to be the crucial building component throughout the nineteenth century for the academic study of religion. At its outset religious theory was not easily distinguishable from theological thinking. With its notion of the "concrete universal," Hegelianism later gave impetus to the elaboration of both a nondogmatic theological program that extended well into the twentieth century and a more comprehensive program of *Religionswissenschaft,* which functioned as the matrix for the theoretical analysis of religion.

The crisis of theory, on the other hand, can be traced to the collapse of the universalistic construct—and the pretensions of *Wissenschaft*—under the pressures of decolonialization. Charles Long has described the crisis historically with the rise and fall of the "Aryan myth," on which we are finding the justification of colonialism far more dependent than the theology of Christian dominion. So much of religious "theory" harks back to the work of Max Müller, who by Long's reckoning developed an intricate "avowal of the myth" while pushing "his claims concerning the prestige of Sanskrit in general and . . . the Indo-European languages in particular," all the while attempting "to understand myth through an analysis of the history and evolution of language" and his "editing of non-Western 'sacred books.'"[13]

The formalization of the principle of religious alterity through the writing of a "history of religions" over against Christian *Heilsgeschichte*—a stance that "postmodernists" take as a given rather than a dilemma—actually has its beginnings in the colonialist enterprise of discovering a racially and culturally privileged syntax for religious statements that can count as *nontheological*. As Long points out, the earliest forays into the nascent field of "religious studies" were concentrated on philology. The discovery of a *root* language for Europeans led to the premise that beneath the basal syntax of the multifarious Indo-Aryan dialects lurked a hidden ethno-spirituality. The "Romantic *sensus communis* of language and style" ultimately led "to a *sensus numinous*."[14]

During its parturition religious studies signaled, therefore, an "Aryanization" of the universalistic theology of Kant and the *Aufklärung*, which in Long's view represented a counterblow of German Romanticism against the Enlightenment. German culture had been marginalized in eighteenth-century letters, according to Long, and the "Aryan" innovation proved to be a comeuppance. German thought in the nineteenth century transformed Kantian "pure reason" into the historicist, perspectivalist, and ethno-particularist forms of "critical" rationality that are nowadays the benchmarks of stereotypical "postmodernism." Kant's "transcendental categories" become Weber's "ideal types"—empirical constructs regarding religious practices, traditions, and institutions as well as textual corpuses—that seem to differentiate the colonial experience of "cultural diversity" while more covertly managing to subsume them in their entirety as a concealed unity.

This unity was not theological so much as it was *gnosiological*, and it gradually became codified in the deference of the Teutonophiles to the ancient Vedas, composed in the mother Aryan language of Sanskrit. The Vedas were believed to contain the cultural secrets not only of Nietzsche's nomadic "blonde beasts" but of religion as a prelinguistic and archaic pressure within the economy of "civilized" signification, the "strangeness" (*unheimlichkeit*) that had been dispossessed, repressed, and expatriated by the Enlightenment, only to "return"—as Freud and Derrida would later tell us—in some indwelling, yet strictly eschatological or "messianic" sense. The Aryan mystique along with the corollary myth of Vedic profundity, of course, was popularized and "spiritualized" through the theosophical movement, which has generated its own long-held "anxiety of influence" for religious studies. The "Vedic" sign of the aboriginal and its imminent "return" is more than what Foucault would term an artifact of cultural *archaeology*. It is a sign of what Slavoj Žižek—borrowing from Lacan—terms "the real," a real that is perennially "overflowing reality."

The Religious as the Real, and the Real as the Religious

The return of the real is the key to what we envision as the "religious," because it is the fullness of half-forgotten and "repressed" remembrance as well as "ancestral" consciousness. Ancestral worship has multivalent significations, according to Žižek. Although Žižek is not very interested in the religious qua religious, his effort to operationalize Lacan through a psycho-philosophico-exegesis of popular culture draws us intimately into the sphere of what theologically derived theory understands as "religion." Žižek of course only characterizes the religious in an alternative idiom. He speaks not of religion but of the "real." In a curious fashion the real is rendered as the religious through its formation in the Lacanian model as an overdetermined and excessive apparition of the signified. "The ambiguity of the Lacanian real," Žižek remarks, "is not merely a nonsymbolized kernel that makes a sudden appearance in the symbolic order, in the form of traumatic 'returns' and 'answers.' The real is at the same time contained in the very symbolic form: the real is *immediately rendered by this form.*"[15]

Lacan, in his seminar *Encore,* Žižek says, "surprisingly *rehabilitates the notion of the sign,* of the sign conceived precisely in its opposition to the signifier, i.e., as preserving the continuity with the real."[16] The articulation of signifiers lays bare the impossibility of condensing the "real" into that order of articulation. Signifier coalesces into the *sign,* which was heretofore "prediscursive" and its own form of transcendence, a pure *jouissance,* but is now transumuted into "materialized enjoyment."

The sign, as opposed to the hyperbolic Zarathustran dance of signification, and the real are conjugate in this sense with each other. The sign is neither "apophatic" nor "apophantic." It is a sudden unveiling (though in a quite ordinary manner), an *apocalypsis.* The Derridean play of signifiers is in truth merely an elaborate *foreplay* to the desperate consummation of desire in the sighting—or citing—of something bizarre, and completely "non-eidetic," that counts as "phenomenon."

For Žižek, the difference between "modernism" and "postmodernism" is that the former preserves the modesty of philosophy. From Kant onward it refuses to reveal the "thing." "The lesson of modernism is that the structure, the intersubjective machine, works as well if the Thing is lacking, if the machine revolves around an emptiness, the postmodernist reversal shows *the Thing itself as the incarnated, materialized emptiness.*"[17] The thing is the *black hole,* a most formidable *singularity,* in the cosmos of signification, always shadowing and ultimately swallowing up the symbolized objects of desire. *Das Ding* is always a "nondialecticizable, inert presence." It has always been there, but has remained barely noticed, chiefly because the "unconscious" has not properly formatted it. If we are to think "theologically" in a strained, Žižekian fashion, we will realize quickly that the religious with all our God-talk and ontological, or *me-ontological*, patter is what we truly desire. But for Žižek that means a "secularization" of religious theory.

Žižek, who remains as doggedly provocative as he is daunting to read, never lays down the lineaments of what we would ordinarily dub theory. The theory is tacit in his capacious readings of the history of philosophy and contemporary culture. In the same way that one can only extract a theory from Nietzsche's arabesque of aphorisms and polemicisms, one must infer certain theoretical strategies from Žižek's ongoing Lacanian homiletics of film criticism, political asides, Lacanian readings of German idealism, and neo-Marxist evangelicalism. But the theory is undeniably there. For Žižek, a theory of the religious would be digestible within what he names the "new science of appearances."

This "science," according to Žižek, is not derived from Nietzschean perspectivalism, as so much of today's radical subjectivism happens to be, the cheap sort of cognitive, intellectual, and moral libertarianism that is habitually typecast by its critics as the *anomic postmodern* when it is genuinely nothing more than the most decadent form of modernism. We may label it the *pseudo-postmodern*. The pseudo-postmodern is still an effect, or outcome, of the modernist dialectic that begins with Descartes and reaches its grand symphony in Hegel's logic, where any science of appearances is ultimately a science of the self-movement of the unfolding subject into its multitude of predicative entailments, which in turn reinscribe the identity of the subject both in terms of consciousness and as "history." But Hegel's so-called concrete universal is ultimately, as his *Science of Logic* in contrast with his phenomenology—or science of appearances—shows, the temporized identity of the Cartesian subject, now "transcendentalized" through dialectical method rather than as a posture of metaphysics. Žižek's *un-dialectical* theory, in comparison, amounts to what he designates as the "parallax view."

A parallax, as defined by the Merriam-Webster dictionary, is "the apparent displacement or the difference in apparent direction of an object as seen from two different points not on a straight line with the object." The word is originally a technical term from astronomy used to describe measurement of angular difference in a moving object in space from different observation points. But Žižek adopts the technical meaning to his campaign against the obsessive-compulsive character of theoretical discourse, which appears unable to shake the dualism of "appearance" and "reality" introduced by Plato and carried all the way through to Freudian psychoanalysis as well as Marxism with their distinction between the manifest and latent, or superstrate and substrate. "An 'epistemological' shift in the subject's point of view always reflects an 'ontological shift' in the object itself."[18]

An obvious analogy, as Žižek himself cites, is the wave-particle relationship of duality/complementarity in quantum physics. Žižek, faithful to his own neo-Marxism, calls this view "materialism," wherein the subject is included in its own "picture" of itself. But what Žižek truly seems to be striving toward is a *science of difference*, a theory of the *differend*, as Jean-François Lyotard has called it, a theoretical kind of take on the ongoing pageantry of the phenomenal. This differential empiricism, approximating in a less broad-ranging manner what Deleuze calls "transcendental empiricism," constitutes, as in Lacanian analysis, a struggle for a theory that accounts for the irruption of the real amid the conventions of cultural communication and exchange along with the internalization of the laws of language.

In Lacan the "real" returns not as it did for Freud, as the artifactuality of repressed instinct, nor as it seems to do for Derrida, as an "autoimmune" mechanism of pacifying, or "globo-Latinizing," the chaos of virulent archaisms. For Lacan the real returns as a syncopated rhythm involving the neonatal and linguistic—or "symbolic"—registers. It is not the "return of the repressed" but the *resurgence of the real.* The real we will always have with us, to paraphrase Jesus. The real is that which we have within ourselves, which sustains and reproduces "objects" of desire, and which "overflows"—like Nietzsche's *Übermensch,* or "overman"—all linguistic and conceptual structures, or what Lacan dubs the symbolic order. The real is the "exception" to the rules of the symbolic order. This exception does not reside in act of predication or (in a Hegelian sense) of "determination." It is located in the *moment of signification.* As was the case with Peirce, who invented "semiotics" or the theory of signs as opposed to the logic of inference and predication, there can be no "thought," even in the psychoanalytical sense, without the triadic dynamism that we call signification. We shall come back to this thought later on.

Lacan never developed, or attempted to develop, a "theory" of religion. Nor does Žižek as *cultural-theoretical* mouthpiece for Lacan make such inaugural gestures. Yet in blazing this trail we can begin with the Lacanian premise that all our theorizing must flow out of the movement of signifying praxis when language begins to reveal what filters through the screen of language, when the "negative" is disclosed, not as Derrida's formalized "absent presence," but as a rupture on the part of the real by the semiotic process. In this revealing rupture the real continues to "return" as the semiotic codes that erupt in the spaces, singularities, or exceptions within the logic of discourse, that immanently and interminably continue to *signify.* By drawing on the Freudian rule of "free association," Lacanian analysis, as André Patsalides points out, allows the unconscious to be structured progressively as an intricate and eminently fruitful language. "The more we speak inconsistently, the more we express and reveal our own desire."[19]

Lacanian analysis is in actuality a form of couch semiotics, an intersubjective eliciting of the signifying relationships, including the dyads, polarities, symmetries, axes, and "paradigmatic" as well as "syntagmatic" transformations that make the unconscious "objective" to both analyst and analysand. Both structuralism and poststructuralism have rightly recognized that meaning lies in the production of difference, in the generation of a negative or dissociated lo(gi)cal space that becomes the occasion for the play of theory that is never totalizing but always open-textured. Such a redistribution of logical values is analogous to the "dissemination" of aesthetic values, especially luminosity, that began with Rembrandt and gave impetus to modernism in painting. It is the crucial project behind what Derrida later named "deconstruction." But structural analysis—or even the kind of radical historicization and temporalization of structural analysis that characterizes the poststructuralist movement—comes up short when we are confronted with the task of religious theory. The reason is plain. Religious theory on the grander scale we envision requires a *de-textualization* of religion, a departure from the "grammatological" model that Derridism has ironically engraved with invisible ink and to which the classic theological and hermeneutical disciplines have always been joined at the hip. Negative theology remains theology, because even the search for dark windows positioned throughout the text cannot be separated from the text.

De-textualizing Religion

What would a de-textualization of the "concepts" of religion involve? By no means can it amount to a return to the social sciences, particularly the sorts of "anthropological," or typological, studies that sprang up in the late nineteenth century as a way of coding the bureaucratic information and intelligence data of Europe's colonial empires and finally reached a critical mass that jump-started the growth of the field of "religious studies" now over a generation ago. The tension between the empiricism and sociological positivism of the so-called human sciences and the self-regarding and in many respects *self-referential* tendencies of theological inquiry must be overcome, although few have attempted to confront, let alone take on, the challenge. The custom of dismissing "theology" out of hand by specialized scholars of religion has never had the consequences intended. Instead of promoting a habit of theoretical inquiry, it has reinforced a methodological naïveté as well as an extreme crazy quilt of subdisciplinary priorities and topics with hardly any consciousness of the broader and more momentous question of religion in this era of "globo-Latinzation."

One of the major problems with a balkanized field of religious studies is that it proves to be powerless in the face of a planetary "return of religion" in a globo-political sense. In all fairness to Derrida, his efforts to raise the more encompassing "religious" question cannot be construed as any kind of preface to theory. The Capri conversations have been overemphasized by many theological admirers of Derrida starved for some set of cues that will carry them into the realm of religious discourse in a more concrete manner than Jack Caputo offered in his groundbreaking work on Derrida's "spirituality"—his "religion without religion." The issue of whether there was a recognizable "religious turn" in Derrida, which Martin Hägglund savagely attacks in his effort to rehabilitate the earlier assumption of a radically "atheist" Derrida, is beside the point.[20] The impact of Derrida's philosophy on religious thought has been tremendous, even if it has only had weak effects, if at all, on the theory of religion.

Like Deleuze before him and a majority of French poststructuralists, Derrida owes, and acknowledges, a weighty debt to Bergson. Derrida makes the point about Bergson as a *point d'appui* in asking what it would mean to "think religion." "To hold that religion is properly *thinkable,* and even if thinking is neither seeing, nor knowing, nor conceiving, is still to hold it in advance in respect; thus, over short or long, the affair is decided."[21] Derrida goes on to say that his project for "thinking religion" is drawn from the "famous conclusion of the *Two Sources,*" the memorable words that "the essential function of the universe . . . is a machine for the making of gods."[22] Derrida, of course, in his advancement of the metaphor of the religious "machine" is playing on Bergson's intuition of a mystical machine that would overcome all techno-scientific mechanism and defeat all forms of modernist materialism, including dialectical materialism. He is also transposing into the poststructuralist argot the early Heidegger's dictum that in an age of alienation and "dehumanization" along with the absorption of metaphysics by the techno-scientific attitude "only a god can save us." And he is building on Deleuze and Guattari's metaphor of the "desiring machine," which they introduce in a poststructuralist assault on Oedipus as a metonym for the techno-logico-materialist repression of the richness of the imaginal.

Contra Deleuze and Guattari, it is not the instinctual but the religious that implies the ultimate desiring machine. Religion is inherently "machinic," as the phenomenon of a technology-driven, worldwide resurgence of fundamentalism indicates. A machinelike reactivity "to the machine is as automatic (and thus machinal) as life itself. Such an internal splitting, which opens distance, is also peculiar or 'proper' to religion, appropriating religion for the 'proper' . . . , appropriating religious indemnification to all forms of property, from the linguistic idiom in its 'letter,' to blood and soil, to the family and to the nation."[23]

The Capri conversations are maddeningly disjointed and "errant," and they underscore Derrida's attempt to struggle with a subject that in many ways is more daunting than previous efforts to "deconstruct" the discursivity of Western philosophy. He is, in effect, reviving the late Heideggerian project of rethinking the destiny of Being through technology, but in this context the question of ontology becomes the question of religion. Religion's "resurgence" in the world (*déferlement*), Derrida insists, is bound up with the technological transformation and convergence of societies, cultures, nations, and tokens of communication and exchange. It is like a wave that builds and gathers momentum from its resistance. "Religion today allies itself with tele-techno-science, to which it reacts with all its forces. It *is, on the one hand*, globalization; it produces, weds, exploits the capital and knowledge of tele-mediatizaton."[24] The "resurgence" of religion, therefore, is not the same as *retour*, or recurrence. It is neither an archaic revival nor a counterpraxis to the trend toward "secularization." It amounts to a formidable synergy between the power of the "real" and a "globo-Latinized" communications and control system which Derrida describes somewhat unfelicitously as "telemediation." This tele-mediated religiosity is what social theorists have misnamed religious "fundamentalism."

The historical notion of fundamentalism implies a preoccupation with the literality of the sacred text, a concern that only arose in the West from the Enlightenment onward because of the epistemological conflicts generated by the struggle between natural philosophy and dogmatic supernaturalism. As historians of religion are beginning to notice, the *fundamentalisms* that are now springing up in other faith traditions have less to do with their Christian counterparts than meets the eye. Although Derrida's discourse has scant historicist subtlety, it strikes right into the solar plexus of religious theory, inasmuch as it identifies the anomalous affinity of postmodern religiosity for networks and rhizomes of communicative action surpassing the purely textual. For that reason the Capri conversations point toward a whole new modus vivendi for religious theory that is neither textualist nor crypto-textualist. It is ironic that gestation of this approach would come out of Derridean nothing-outside-the-textualism. In putting forth the trope of "resurgence" Derrida is acknowledging the severe limitations of his previous "khōric" meditations as well as the ultimate inconsequentiality of his own theologically popular program of postmodernist apophaticism.

The Capri conversations can, of course, be compared with Derrida's meditations on religion in *The Gift of Death*. While the Capri conversations plot out the curious reciprocity of the symbolical and the real in the genesis of the religious, *The Gift of Death* underscores the incommensurability of finite and infinite through the concept of faith as *responsibility*, a uniquely "European" innovation constituting a tradition "that consists of proposing a nondogmatic doublet of dogma, a philosophical and metaphysical doublet, in any case a *thinking* that 'repeats' the possibility of religion without religion."[25] The origin of such a "religion without religion," which Caputo assigns to Derrida's own distinctive "postmodern" religiosity,[26] is Søren Kierkegaard's "knight of faith," who beards the infinite demand of the *tout autre* to sacrifice his only son, the heir to the promise, in contravention of the ethical universal. The well-known Kierkegaardian leap of faith as a gesture of pure singularity in "fear and trembling"—and hence by Derrida's reckoning as the threshold of categorical responsibility to both God as *mysterium tremendum* and the genuine non-Kantian, and non-Hegelian, "ethical" relationship to the other in Levinas's sense—is at the same time without mediation of any type, including the meditation of history. It is the "logic" of pure interiority, the "secret truth of faith as absolute responsibility and as absolute passion."[27]

The "secret" of faith—an intrinsically "European" innovation as far as Derrida is concerned—contrasts with the pagan mysteries, with orgiastic absorption and rapture, as well as with the "Platonic" codes of representation and their dialectical assize. It is the Christian cipher to what messianically calls us beyond the traditions of theology and philosophy. The unspoken in Western thinking is not the unthought thought of Being, as it is for Heidegger, but what can be adduced by considering the sign of Moriah, Abraham in his inarticulate and unaccountable trek up the mountain. All attempts at deconstructing the texts of Western thought converge upon this sign.

The uniquely theological supplement for all these texts does not inhere in sort of open-ended grammatological intervention or operation, as it does for the early Derrida, but in the *crux* of all representations, in the moment of sacrifice, in the "gift of death" that Nietzsche understood as the reversal, if not the transversal, of the orgiastic—what Derrida terms the "Christian 'repression.'" What Nietzschean and all other overdetermined readings of Christian history miss, according to Derrida, is the recognition that the all-too-familiar metanarrative that might be termed the "history of the faith" is not so much a symptomatology of impotence and rage, or *ressentiment,* as it is a meteor impact creating a grand instability within the grand economy of signs that we call "Western" and "metaphysics."

In the early twenty-first century this instability has had a paradoxical outcome—the fragmentation and dispersal of all self-authenticating metaphysical tokens or *first principles* that previously undergirded religious authority, juxtaposed with the violent return of that very "religion" that *authenticates itself* through its own sheer presence as an active force, as a series of intrusions, as a chain of world-commanding events. The "reality" of religion in this connection is not indicated by any *archaeo-ontological* content that returns. It is the return of the Real in Lacan's sense as a rude awakening from the dream of a simulated rationality, from the skein of signifying codes and indices that allow us to pretend we are mapping, reflecting on, and "explaining" the world with which we have grown so familiar. Religion is the loud noise that shatters our secularist sleep.

4

RADICAL RELIGION IN THE "DESERT OF THE REAL"

.

The desert has its holiness of silence.
— Walter Elliott

SINCE THAT fateful day in September 2001, a vast and tenebrous mist has suddenly spread out over the horizon of Western thinking in general, and the theory of the religious in particular. The sentiment was summarized in the title of Žižek's well-known set of essays published in 2002 as a critique of the terms of the debate after 9/11—"welcome to the desert of the real."[1] The reality of what had undeniably to be denominated as the "religious" brutally and abruptly burst upon the world scene with this "event." The event gave the lie both to the secularist myth of a deftly micromanaged, prosperous, multicultural liberal democracy and to the Baudrillardian version of postmodern culture as a game of substanceless, media-fabricated significations and simulacra, as the sublimation of the real into the "hyperreal" (even though ironically Žižek's choice of the title was inspired from a line in *The Matrix*, the most Baudrillardian of movies from that period). The real not only returned with a vengeance, it was a vast and smoldering wasteland, evident in the rubble of the demolished twin towers.

There is an odd thread that connects the destruction of New York's twin towers, the nightmarish rondo of suicide bombings and military counterstrike that identify the Israeli and Palestinian conflict, the July 7, 2005, bombings in London, other events in Europe, in Iran, and

of course the wars in Iraq and Afghanistan with their ongoing blood-
shed and routine political shocks and aftershocks—not to mention
the more recent mass killings in Norway by a self-proclaimed "Christian." To date, an equally vast "hermeneutics" designed to construe
summarily this specter has gained a head of steam among the Western
intelligentsia, more often than not as a routine rhetorical occasion for
championing the sundry ideological causes of the last half century.
The word "fundamentalist" has become the catchall for naming such
a phenomenon, although the meaning of the term has drifted far afield
from what it has historically connoted, namely, someone who takes
religious texts literally, not someone who acts impulsively, often
violently, and with a self-absorbed grandiosity. Before September 11
"fundamentalists" were considered ignorant, but relatively harmless,
by the liberal secular elites, unless of course they were able to mobilize effectively to attain certain political objectives. After September
11 such literalism was automatically taken as a signal of a lowering
fanaticism that could explode at any moment into random and devastating violence.

The outcome was a Manichaean politics, mirroring the duality of
the Western mind not just "in itself" but also "for itself," as a good
Hegelian might say. The duality has defined all our responses. It is
a duality that, furthermore, happens to be predicated on the West's
own "schizoanalysis" of the religious problem, a problem that even
the most advanced "postmodern" mind is incapable of compassing.
We are all familiar with the well-established academic interest in
"fundamentalism" as a conceptual issue, which might be compared
to the old-style European colonialist's curiosity about body piercing,
or female circumcision. Gianni Vattimo's and Derrida's analogizing
the "return of the religious"—an expression introduced somewhat
ironically by Derrida and Vattimo in their Capri colloquy—to Freud's
recovery of the instinctual is a case in point. Is the religious really
"returning," or has the dismantling of the monolith of post-Comtean
sociologism in cultural theory pried open a serious space where the
obvious can at last be named and successfully theorized? Deconstruction is not theory, as we have seen, and it should never purport
to be theory. But it can begin to make fissures through which can
manifest a signifying of what is otherwise too treacherous to speak.
The return of the religious is ultimately the exodus of signification
from a historicist Egypt. But like the archetypal exodus it is both a
fulfillment and a frustration of an earlier promise. The fulfillment
lies in siting the exodus itself, an escape from an endless bondage
that is ironically the deference of "promise." The deference is the

"sight" of the desert with all its emptiness, horror, and cruelty and the struggle for faith that defines the story of the ensuing, and countless, generations.

Radical Religion and Religious Theory

Radical Islam is this specter one must cite, or site, or sight. Despite efforts to cite the Norway killings as a form of Western cultural "equivalence," the truth is that radical Islam authorizes itself through numerous actual texts, including those concerning jihad, which are of course read selectively but do not contradict in principle the Qur'anic focus on war and military struggle as a central mandate of "faith" itself. The occasional episodes of Christian "fundamentalist" violence, such as the bombing of abortion clinics or even the tragedy in Norway, which was more about asserting European cultural identity than defending any genuine religious principles, do not have such textual backup. So we must ask ourselves: is the present-day outbreak of "fundamentalism" in the postmodern venue really a manifestation of what is *really religious* or religiously real, or is it chiefly a spectral apparition of the "desert" that is revealed when the play of virtual—or "hyperreal"—idealities is suddenly terminated by the shock of the real itself?

We are reminded of Derrida's own meditations on the three "sites," or "aporetical places"—island, promised land, and desert. These sites roughly correspond to Platonic utopian idealism, Judeo-Germanic historicism, and the specter of an *after-modernism*, which may be understood more profoundly with respect to Nietzsche's "specter" of nihilism that stands at the door. It is at this last site where the specter looms larger than ever imagined. Derrida denominates this specter as radical religion's "surge" (*déferlement*). He cautions:

> Never treat as an accident the force of the name in what happens, occurs or is said in the name of religion, here in the name of Islam. For, directly or not, the theologico-political, like all the concepts plastered over these questions, beginning with that of democracy or of secularization, even of the right to literature, is not merely European, but Graeco-Christian, Graeco-Roman. Here we are confronted by the overwhelming questions of the name and of everything "done in the name of": questions of the name or noun "religion," of the names of God, of whether the proper name belongs to the system of language or not, hence, of its untranslatability but also of its iterability (which is to say, of that which makes it a site of repeatability, of idealization).[2]

Radical Islam does not allow for the conceptual "differentiation," in the Greco-Roman or even the "Jew-Greek" sense, of the religious from a multitude of philosophical discourses. Even the twentieth-century totalitarianisms with their death camps, their gulags, and pyramids of sanguinary sacrifice still allowed for the persistence of some circumscribed cultural—and by implication a faintly "spiritual"—sphere of influence. As Lyotard argues, we still have in Auschwitz a strange sort of "differend." But in radical Islam even the differend vanishes. We are no longer dealing with something "religious" in the normal connotation of the word. We fantasize an alterity. The Islamist, we are told, is merely our "Orientalist" shadow that needs to somehow be reintegrated with our overdrawn techno-imperial persona. We must heed Said's warning against "any attempt to force cultures and peoples into separate and distinct breeds or essences"[3]—for example, Huntington's clashing civilizations, or the idiomatic struggle between "the West and the rest."

Even Said, however, a Palestinian, does not conceptualize Islamism, which is a question neither of the West's "demonization" of the collective other nor of the devouring of some irenic Islam by a "chaosmotic" terror monster (in Deleuzian terms), a latter-day Tiamat on whom we have somehow declared "war." The way in which the West historically and metaphysically is forced to "configure" Islam seems to climax in the very kind of *aporism* and mute undecidability that Derrida's meditations on the religious bring to our attention. Derrida, after all, is facing the type of aporia that has dumbstruck those philosophers who seek to entertain the prospect of "naming," a task which the thinker inherited from Adam, the unnameable name. Islam may be the bona fide limiting case for our white mythology.

The recognition that postmodern thought itself has been powerless to wriggle out of this aporia, when it comes to the Islamic call of the minaret, has been brilliantly explored by Ian Almond in his study of what he terms "the new Orientalists." Though they claim to be committed to a postmodernist critique of the reciprocity between modernist claims of epistemological privilege and social formations that sustain strategies of power and dominance, the new Orientalists, among whom Almond numbers Nietzsche and virtually all the major French postmodernists starting with Derrida, have not changed the equation at all when it comes to Islam. They perpetuate what Levinas has designated the "empire of the Same," even if it pretends to valorize the "Other."

Linguistically and rhetorically, the postmodern is still located within this empire. "Postmodernity to a large extent inherits in an altogether subtler way many of the Orientalist/imperialist tropes that had been so prevalent in modernity. When Franz Fanon declared that 'the European game has finally ended,' he was only half-right."[4] Almond's general point, which sometimes becomes obscured in his nuanced unmasking of the pretensions of the secular French left, is that the critique of modernism has consistently utilized the thorough "otherness" of Islam not as an opening for radical engagement and self-reflexivity but as a blunt instrument for their own "progressive" assault on entrenched structures of hegemony in order to assert new privileged constituencies that remain unmistakably Occidental. In Derrida, for example, Islam specifically works "as a kind of *différance*" that succeeds mainly "in giving others identity while forever relinquishing its own." Almond adds that "it is difficult to ignore the political conservatism such a reading of Islam" implies.[5] Islam functions heuristically as an unapproachable Kantian thing-in-itself, or as a wholly otherness that becomes "an utterly unreachable subtext, receding before all our interpretations, while remaining paradoxically the very condition of their possibility."[6]

In radical Islam we are confronting the "sacred," perhaps with its possibilities of "violence," in a way we have never encountered before. What then do we make of Vattimo's argument that we have now all read enough Nietzsche and Heidegger to become apostles of a "weak Christianity" in which we experience "the rebirth of the sacred in its many forms"?[7] What is the difference between the phenomenology of religion and some easygoing, postmetaphysical "animism," the kind against which the Qur'an calls for unending "struggle" (jihad)? A weak Christianity versus a globalized jihadism? An etherized and "pluralistic" hermeneutics versus the totalistic rendering of the Shahadah—"There is no God but God"? We cannot single out the Shahadah as intoned by the Islamists as any kind of "religious" phenomenon. It is a question of neither metaphysical congeniality nor the energistics of the mobile signifier. Radical Islam sets its face against both modernism and postmodernism, against the taken-for-granted sovereignty of the Cartesian subject and the infinite differentialism of the Deleuzian "concept," against the "West" even to the endless extent that the term can somehow be dissembled and disseminated. We are incapable of assessing this challenge on strictly religious, or philosophical, grounds.

Even a decent sort of Derridean *difference/differance/déférence* proves insipid in this context. "The enemy of my enemy is my friend." In the "liberal" West, at least since the late fifteenth century, the "enemy" has been the discourse of the Same with the "enemy's enemy"—the differend. Alterity is glimpsed first in the bourgeois, then the peasant, then the Jew, then the proletariat, then the "second sex," then the wretched of the earth, then the "unconscious," then the ungendered, then all who are somehow silent and forgotten, then identity in and of itself. Hegel understood that alterity must be infinitely generated by the dialectic of the one and the many that begins with Plato's principle of the division and composition of all terminologies. But what if the differend, or not-same, is suddenly and epochally confronted by this differentialism as a strange, "eschatological" movement of nihilation—not "nihilism" in the dumb, "conservative" Christian reading of the term—but active "nullification" of every form and icon envisioned on sea and on land, of every Hegelian "diremption" in the nameless name "there is only"? That is what is really implied by the concept of the "desert of the real."

We are not raising a "political" question here, nor posing the usual problem of religious diversity and "tolerance." The notion of tolerance has its origins in the conviction that there is a proper, if not somehow mutable, "geometry" to the sacred that has its origin in the epoch of *Aufklärung*. It presumes the limitability in a purely Greek manner of *to theos*, the "divine," as opposed to what Derrida dubs the "singularity" that arises when there is no distinction anymore between "desert" and *khōra*, between infinitely expanded and infinitely collapsed, when there is no longer "religion" in the normal sense of the word. *Aufklärung* privileges the subjectivity of "religious freedom" over infinite force. Yet even Derrida in "taking a stand for Algeria" discloses that he is far more comfortable discoursing on the island than in the desert. "Our idea of democracy implies a separation between the state and the religious powers, that is, a radical religious neutrality and a faultless tolerance which would not only set the sense of belonging to religions, cults, and thus also cultures and languages, away from the reach of any terror—whether stemming from the state or not—but also protects the practices of faith and, in this instance, the freedom of discussion and interpretation within each religion."[8]

Metastasized Monotheisms

Today we are witnessing something more profound, more titanic, and far more "perilous" than the religious scholar's planetary *circus maximus* in which the swords and maces of ever more desperate "fundamentalisms" clatter against each other, where dwarves, dancing bears, and exotic exhibitions constantly tempt our craze for novelty. It is certainly not merely religion's "return." It is no coincidence that these metastasized monotheisms have both their scene and origin in the land of the nomad who left Ur for the "no-man's-land" that became a "holy land" in accordance with the strangest of summons. The nomadism of the postmodern mind is not without its incipient drama, as when Abraham wandered into Sodom. The secular academic rage against "theology" is in its very bowels the clamor about "monotheism." But what is monotheism, particularly the kind that has spawned sixteen-year-old suicide bombers and descendants of Holocaust survivors who would easily annihilate the "others" who trace their holy lineage to either Ishmael or Isaac?

We are reminded of Alain Badiou's criticism of Deleuze that his radical differentialism is really nothing more than an immanent neo-Platonism. Have we crossed the Rubicon finally, or transgressed the ultimate threshold of the "theory" of the religious when our differentialism finally encounters the violence of what we might in a kind of Bataillean ecstasy seek to name the *tout autrement*? As has been tirelessly pointed out, there is no dichotomy between the sacred and the secular in radical Islam. Nor does the dichotomy matter any longer. The Romantics laid waste the distinction when they stumbled upon the sublime. Must the entirety of the West, modern and postmodern, now lay waste the differend, particularly as it has been named "religious," when it confronts global jihad?

The global jihad is essentially, as Olivier Roy in his brilliant study of militant Islamism has pointed out, an outgrowth of the postmodern condition. Conventional scholars of religion have regarded Islamism as just another instance of "fundamentalism," which in turn is supposedly the backlash of traditional societies and traditional religious ideologies against the impact of secularization and modernization. While many critics of this model have labeled the expression "fundamentalism" as inherently misleading because it suggests competition between textual literalism and a historicist hermeneutic that Islam, among other religions, decidedly lacks, Roy goes even one step further. He makes the case that Islamic radicalism has nothing at all to do with a defense of some premodern *mythos*. To the contrary, it is a kind of hypermodernization, or *postmodernization*, of the religious factor in age when identity is entirely separate from culture, when religion itself is "de-culturated" and "deterritorialized" (Roy makes liberal use of Deleuze's familiar phrase). What are the chief traits of a deterritorialized religiosity?

Deterritorialized religion is also dehistoricized religion. It has nothing to do with the inviolability, or perceived literalism, of certain texts. Deterritorialized religion requires the evacuation of the indigenous or site-specific content of faith-language and faith-symbols. Ironically, global jihad has the same universal and noncontextualized qualities as McDonald's Golden Arches or Microsoft Windows. Roy ironically dubs this ambiguous trend "neofundamentalism."

> By neofundamentalism I mean a common intellectual matrix that can nevertheless be manifested in various political attitudes. If all radical Islamic groups are indisputably neofundamentalist in religious terms, many fundamentalist elements are simply conservative and law-abiding, even if they explicitly condemn the westernization of Islam. I refer here not to a structured movement articulated around a coherent doctrine, but to a form of religiosity that has spread among different milieus. Neofundamentalists by definition reject the idea that there can be different schools of thought and consider themselves the only true Muslims, refusing to be labeled as one specific group among the others.[9]

According to Roy, neofundamentalists—historically known as "Salafis"—ignore history, philosophy, the arts, and politics. Unlike many contemporary commentators, Roy even distinguishes neofundamentalism from Islamism, which he maintains has political or strategic objectives. Neofundamentalism has no political aims other than the global imposition of sharia, or Islamic law. Neofundamentalism is more interested in making purely "religious" statements about one's personal dedication to God, which often involves passionate and heroic acts of self-sacrifice, including suicide missions. Moreover, neofundamentalism rejects all Western concepts and terminology, viewing them as a violation of the Qur'anic injunction against "innovation," or *bid'a.*

The phenomenon mistakenly labeled "fundamentalism" comes from the "return of religion," but not exactly with the usage that Derrida meant. "Fundamentalism is a means of re-univeralizing religions (whether it be Islam or Christianity)," Roy writes, "that has ended up being closely identified with a given culture."[10] He adds: "The paradox is that the more religions are decoupled from cultures, the more we tend to identify religion and culture. Islamic fundamentalists and many conservative Muslims lobby for Islam to be recognized as a culture in the West, using the common idiom of multiculturalism. This too is a paradox, however, because religion is an expression of universal truth, while culture is relative to other cultures by definition."[11] As faith becomes universalized once again and deterritorialized, its signifying praxis shifts from the concrete, cultural milieu in which post-Enlightenment historicism pursued it as the so-called history of religions toward its own regime of absolute truth.

But this "truth" has little to do with the formal orthodoxies that dominated the historical forms of religion for millennia. The sense of absolute truth coded into the various "fundamentalisms" is less a product of precedent-bound state systems than of the motivational force of the pure signs and icons that have become deracinated from the tradition. Religious terms and shibboleths become sliding signifiers. They have no specificity on the face of it. However, they are at the same time eminently concrete, if not indigenously situated, as Roy stresses, because they serve to personalize and localize religious identity. They are not culturally, only rhetorically, instantiated. They remain susceptible neither to historical, social, cultural, political, or even ideological analysis. They are semiotic performatives for the pure, inward conviction of a special destiny and divine salvation. They are, if we may call on Deleuze's nomenclature, manifestations of the nomadological war machine that deterritorializes the cultural and religious map of the planet.

In that regard the popular images of religious "terrorists" along with fundamentalists are thoroughly misplaced. The terrorist always has some misty social and political objective. The Islamic terrorist, according to Roy, has no objective other than the dramatization of his own fantastic conception of a new, trans-territorial Muslim *ummah*, or "community." The violent performative, such as the brilliant subterfuge on 9/11 of bringing down with planes fashioned as missiles the archetypal symbols of global commerce and finance, merely articulates and reinforces this fantastic idealization. As some pundits have pointed out, the events of 9/11 were more like action art than any calculated military or political gambit. The "return" of the religious in the aftermath of 9/11 is more accurately described as its pure sublimation and *semiotization.*

The development of "fundamentalism" as a distinctively postmodern trend line comes across initially as utterly paradoxical. But it is tacit in all analyses of globalization, or Derrida's "globo-Latinization." Perhaps a better expression would be the *categoricization* of the religious message. Religious expression is no longer variable with respect to time and place. It is both abstract and particular at the same time. It compels adherents to act in a totally and radically self-transcending manner. Strangely, this categoricization follows along with the same "dialectic" of modernism that was captured in Kant's "pure practical reason." The Kantian ethic, epitomized in the principle that the only "good" is a good will, has its religious application in all these "fundamentalisms," which in many ways constitute a genuine return to their prophetic and revelatory origins, even though they remain idiosyncrasies of the present age. There can be no "pragmatic" maxim for the fundamentalist as for the Kantian formalist. One must obey commands as if they were divine commands. Commitment must be complete, and the glorification of God must be total, including even the nihilation of the self. "Fundamentalism" is modern religion that has been "purified" of its historical and cultural particularities, that has been denuded of its multifarious conditions and contingencies, which is why it is uniquely "postmodern" and therefore is not destined to vanish when the forward momentum of global change has transported world civilization beyond a certain juncture.

By and large fundamentalism has been underplayed by religious theory. It is viewed more as some kind of archaism—an episodic revival of what was thought to have passed into oblivion—rather than a gathering of forces that shape the present. Just as Heidegger in his meditations long after the *Kehre* identified the technological transformation of the planet not as a historical peculiarity but as an ontological epoch in its own right, so we must begin to look at fundamentalism as *an unfolding of certain nascent powers prefiguring the reign of the religious*. The future, not the past, is the proper sphere for the study of religion. Only by comprehending the "return of religion," as Derrida does indirectly, as the emergence of an epoch that drives us beyond the modern in a measure that so-called postmodernism is incapable of envisioning can we begin to chart religious theory *after* postmodernism. To devise this chart we must rely on conceptual resources that philosophy or religious thought to date has not provided.

The events of 9/11 have spawned a new academic and government-related industry focused on the analysis of terrorism and "risk assessment." But they have also elevated the importance of the academic investigation of religion across the empirical as well as theoretical disciplines. Before 9/11 inquiries into the nature of religion were often couched as ancillary to various methods of material research. The Marxist hermeneutic of religion as "superstructure" mirroring the historical substrate has persisted in different prominent, or diluted, formats since the late nineteenth century. With the exception of some of the more philosophical French poststructuralists, mainly Derrida and Deleuze, this tacit hermeneutic has persisted through the advent of postmodernism. Religious fundamentalism is designated primarily as a social formation associated with reactionary politics and the resistance to the emancipatory mandate of modernization.

This perspective is most striking in Vattimo's reflections from the late 1990s.

> The return of fundamentalism is, quite obviously, a reaction to the melting away of circumscribed horizons that came about, and comes about, as the (super)market society spreads. That these two phenomena are complementary was something made strikingly clear by the national elections of March 1994 in Italy. The new right-wing bloc that won these elections is an unprecedented ideological blend of consumerism as incarnated by Berlusconi and fundamentalism of the ethnic kind (the Lombard League), the Catholic kind (many members of the Communion and Liberation movement are already allied, or are getting really to ally, with Berlusconi), and the postfascist kind (the various elements, none of them modern or pluralistic, that make up the party of Gianfranco Fini).[12]

Vattimo's postmodernist "hermeneutic" is by his own account a statement of the axial priority of democratic pluralism in a cosmopolitan context.

A suitable postmodernism links the modernist imperative of social and individual liberation to "weak nihilism" in order to complement a "weak Christianity." By "weak Christianity" Vattimo means the refusal of absolute metaphysical or ontological claims of any sort, including the kinds of value claims inherent in religious authoritarianism of diverse stripes. Nietzschean nihilism, which Vattimo does not view with the apocalyptic or cataclysmic magnitude that many of Nietzsche's oracular pronouncements, particularly in his posthumous writings, seem to suggest, is ultimately preferable to an "authoritarian," or metaphysical, revival of any form of transcendentalism. "The end of metaphysics," which postmodernism entails, "has its genuine political parallel in the strengthening of democracy. Philosophy is finding out for its part . . . that reality refused to be confined within a logically tight system, the conclusions of which can be applied to political choice. Politics, for its part, is experiencing the impossibility of adhering to 'the truth.'"[13]

Postmodernism, for Vattimo, is a stalking horse for a "politics without truth." Thus we have in Vattimo a political reinscription of a de-centered ontology—loosely speaking, James's pluralistic universe. Vattimo represents the full turn of the postmodernist wheel back to pragmaticism as a philosophical expression of modern liberalism, as the book's foreword by Rorty indicates. "Weak nihilism" is simply a weasel word for old-fashioned American liberalism with a European face. Neither a weak nihilism nor a garden-variety pragmaticism with pluralistic sentiments can beard the specter of the desert, of an ancient and radical monotheism transformed into a psychological, theological, and political juggernaut aimed at totalizing all language and experience through a "dialectic" that purifies religion of every conceivable magnitude of differentiation, that drives toward absolute unity or what in Islamism, building on the Qur'an, is known as *tawhid*. *Tawhid* is neither Plotinus's nor Eckhard's mystical "oneness" beyond God. It encompasses not only theology but the politics of the state. It is the revenge of the *religio* against every "weak" form of metaphysics, against the ontology of pluralism and the fiction of ethical voluntarism and political multitudinism.

The Clash of Transcendences

The battleground for religious theory is in the final analysis the subtle ground staked out between the opposing semiologies of the *autrement*—the "otherwise than being"—experienced in the intersubjective, the orthogonal/relational, or the face-to-face (Levinas) and of the Shahada, "There is no God but . . ." The mythic "clash of civilizations" is in reality a struggle between the two irreconcilable proclivities within experience that we name the "religious," *a clash of transcendences*. On this battleground a "weak Christianity" cannot survive the initial fusillade. Nor can a weak religious theory that is nothing more than a reinvented liberal theology endure either. Religious theory after postmodernism must leave behind both its colonial heritage of theorizing "religion" as an essential datum about which to generalize and its neocolonial, or "neoliberal," tendencies toward microassessments, to select from the fluctuating and self-liquidating assemblages of sign processes within the terrain we call the "religious" and do some appropriate kind of intervention that can be named *critical or cultural studies*—for example, political hermeneutics, ethnomethodology, or gender analysis.

Neoliberal "methodology," what dominates the field of religious studies nowadays, serves mainly to "slice and dice" what were once various procedures aimed at a totalizing methodology that serves to sustain the intricate micro-order of invisible power relations, which Foucault first diagnosed, in a global knowledge society. The distinction between "study" and "theory" correlates with the classical distinction between cognition (*episteme*) and wisdom (*sophia*). We know too much "about" religion, or the sundry aspects of the religious. We do not have a theoretical language for taking on the question of why we continue to pursue the problem of religion and the kaleidoscopic constellations of "religious" activities and artifacts that interest us. We do not know what we are looking for, which is why we have no theory. We have no vision, or way of seeing except within our own subdisciplinary "reading glasses" for inspecting the small print.

The crisis of religious studies has been archly outlined, and perhaps with no intimation of its irony, by Mark Taylor in his introduction to *Critical Terms for Religious Studies*, one of the more recent "handbooks" to the field.

> The recent obsession with difference in the arts, humanities, and social sciences has obscured the fact that much of the pioneering work in "non-Western" cultural traditions was done in the field of religious studies. As attention shifted from a more or less exclusive focus on Western religions to a broader range of religious beliefs and practices, it quickly became apparent that it was imperative to rethink not only *which* religions were to be investigated but *how* they were to be studied.[14]

The "pioneering work in 'non-Western' cultural traditions" which Taylor references was done largely by colonial administrators in the nineteenth century, who used Christian missionaries as key reporters and informants in their vast intelligence networks designed to provide early warning signals of unrest or insurrection. The administrators understood that religion was a motivating force among the natives. Missionaries, through their journals, written reflections, and communiqués with their home churches, took a crucial and detailed interest in indigenous beliefs so that they could convert the natives and lead them away from "superstition" and "error."

The academic study of religion as a "neutral" science was developed as an essential system of strategic politics for the European, and eventually the American, colonial powers, a point that has been made with varying emphases by scholars as disparate as J. Z. Smith and Edward Said. This colonialist legacy has not been inconsequential. In many ways the tragically chronic refusal of theory in the field can be considered a structural persistence of the "sins of the fathers." Strategies of microsegmentation were invaluable for the maintenance of European domination over subject peoples. As research into colonialist ideology has shown, the Enlightenment universalism that reigned in Western intellectual circles throughout the nineteenth century up until the end of the Second World War had its own built-in semiotics of exclusion and marginalization, both deterritorializing the discourse of indigenous cultures as inchoate significations of the "primitive" while reterritorializing them in the same breath as manifestations of the "sacred" or the "religious." These reterritorialized representations became the building blocks for the new morphology of a colonial era *Religionswissenschaft*, a "science of religion."

In the postcolonial or neoliberal setting the same "divide and conquer" methodology tends to reign supreme, fostering an enlightened despotism of the "human sciences." Every particularity serves as a reciprocal critique of every other "multicultural" particularity, while all these different localizations of the religious contribute to a steel grid of hyperdifferentiated concerns, interests, and specialties. The Holy Roman Empire is a historical analogy that comes to mind. The "soft power" of such empires, which last long beyond their historical importance, in the long run turns out to be more detrimental than the spike-booted oppression of ruthless conquerors. Just as the Holy Roman Empire—fantastically and surrealistically imagined in Kafka's castle—preserved its regime for centuries through complex interdynastic alliances, the affirmation of ethnocultural peculiarities without granting political autonomy, and the subtle cohesion of a bureaucratic and ceremonial state religion, so the "striated space" (Deleuze) of the field is endlessly subsected by means of interdisciplinary groupings and coalitions while collectively organized around the search for an ever more meaningful "diversity" of religious expressions. It is this theme of diversity without an intelligible axis of convergence that fosters the illusion of a field. One cannot have a field without a demand for theory.

Yet pressing on the fringes of this neoliberal "state religion" we call *the study of religion* are the outlaw bands that go by various names— fundamentalists, jihadists, roaming prophets, "Islamofascists," New Age eccentrics, "emergent Christians," spiritual bohemians, seekers, and provocateurs with countless colorings and cross-hatchings. They wander endlessly as nomadic types in Žižek's desert. In contrast with the logocentrism of the field, they are deterritorialized and episodic instances of sheer signification. Their place is "no place." They are errant assemblages of constructed identity that are bonded together by one thing and one thing alone—the singularity of their desires and the singularity of their desideratum. In a postmodern world we confront the reality of these singularities.

The singular is not the differential. The differential is but a means of deconstituting, or de-negating, the conceptual architectures that no longer serve us adequately. The singular is a stopping point beyond which we cannot go any further in our subsecting and subdividing. It is comparable to the limit in mathematics. In physics a singularity is that infinitesimal boundary marker beyond which theory no longer functions. Hence a "theory" of the singular is ipso facto impossible. We have only the "event horizon" beyond which we cannot peer and where nothing is "presentable" or "representable."

If postmodernism is, as Lyotard argues, a "witnessing" to the "unpresentable," then the singularities confronted by our efforts at theorizing call for more than existential gestures. These singularities summon us in their pure otherness, as God does to Moses at the burning bush. A singularity is not inert. It is not on our "plane" and confronts us, so to speak, fron an "ultradimensional" position. We shall call these moments of confrontation by the singularity "epicalic" (from the Greek *epikaleo*, "call upon" or "summon"). As epicalic, the moments of summons require naming. Postmodern thought or theory, according to Jean-François Lyotard, "activates differences and save(s) the honor of the name."[15] It was that type of gesture which summoned Levinas to infinitize the other and Derrida to infinitize the interval (*espacement*) in the deconstruction of the text as the "making safe" of "the name" in negative theology. It is no happenstance that Derrida's odyssey takes him from the hypertextual readings of *Glas* to negative theology to meditations on the return of the religious. Negative theology is to deconstruction as a "wounded writing" is to the writing subject in Derrida's grammatology. It is what Derrida calls a *post-scriptum*, a writing that is post-writing, a writing that does not merely name but honors and "saves" the name. Negative theology is language's own soteriology. What would be its eschatology?

Negative theology, Derrida contends, is not about God, but is a kind of *beyonding*, or transcendence of both language and theology. "The beyond as beyond God is not a place, but a movement of transcendence that surpasses God himself, being, essence, the proper or the self-same, the *Selbst* or *Self* of God, the divinity of God." It "surpasses positive theology as well as what Heidegger proposes to call *theiology*, that is, discourse on the divinity (*theion*) of the divine." Such a "movement radically dissociates being and knowing, and existence and knowledge. It is, as it were, a fracture of the *cogito* (Augustinian or Cartesian)."[16] There is a hint here of Levinas's illeity. But Derrida, even if he saves the name, cannot name it, perhaps in deference to his own Jewish, *not* Greco-Hebraic, deference to the *tout autrement* of the inscription that is the Tetragrammaton. Postmodern religious theory per se leaves us standing before the holy of holies, unable to enter.

Religious theory after postmodernism rips aside the veil of the temple of the apophatic. Our option is not—to paraphrase Wittgenstein

—to keep silence in the presence of that which we cannot speak because of its unpresentability. It is to let the *signs themselves and singular signifying events speak* to us as a symphony of *e-vocative, in-vocative,* and *pro-vocative* figurations of discourse that constitute religious theory after postmodernism. We have a foretaste of this rhetoric of infinite singular significations when we consider the incredibly powerful tropism and multi-instrumental metonomy of Deleuze's "philosophy." Deleuze's philosophy is not simply postmodern because it is post-representational, but because it is a cascading and rhythmic *rhetorology* where difference reaches its own catachresis and morphs into meaning at the next level. On that score it outdistances everything that is postmodern. It lends the thrust to break the being barrier. It allows us to say we are now "after" the postmodern moment.

That is something perhaps Nietzsche, who inspired Deleuze, had in mind when he proclaimed that the thought of eternal recurrence, as the dwarf who shadows Nietzsche's Zarathustra whispers, was the "gateway" for the advent of *Übermensch,* for coming to the juncture when thinking itself would break the barrier of the human-all-too-human and have us embark us on a "higher history." Nietzsche's discovery was not the power of difference as negation, as it was for the Hegelian tradition and its poststructuralist progeny, but the power of *difference as affirmation.* We call this affirmative differencing of difference the semiotic revolution when religious studies is transformed into religious theory, a venture of theorizing that compels us to distance ourselves from Hegel. Such a theory we designate in our own idiosyncratic *façon de parler* as *incarnational.*

Incarnational theory has nothing to do with the Hegelian dialectic. Nor is it some sort of avant-garde Christology, a trapdoor method of theologizing, camouflaged as theorizing. Incarnational theory means that *theos* cannot be made intelligible apart from each singularity that pops up in the infinite semiotic register. The "religious" is both a black hole for any "science" that generalizes according to an inferential schema and a "white hole" out of which is constantly ejected all future signifying eventualities. In order to give a more sophisticated rendering of this model, however, we must turn now to some of the major theorists, precursory and present, from which it develops.

Part II

SOURCES

5

BATAILLE AND ALTIZER

THE SACRIFICIAL BACKGROUND OF POSTMODERN
RELIGIOUS THEORY

■

What was holiest and mightiest of all that the world has yet
owned has bled to death under our knives.
—Friedrich Nietzsche, *The Gay Science*

FOR DECADES the "postmodern" has been defined as indefinable, but
that lack of definition is more a sophistical dodge than a commitment. Let us define it as the lightning storm of the twentieth century
that at last became lyrical.

That century is now past, but its atmospheric conditions remain
with us. Nietzsche himself prophesied an era of wars and upheavals,
climactic shifts in the terrain of values and thought. Postmodernism
has given song to those shifts. Like the angel appearing to the apostles
in prison, it freed philosophy and culture from what Fredric Jameson
has called the "prison house of language." Or it tortured the shape of
the prison itself beyond recognition. The era of postmodernism, conceived by Nietzsche long before its actual historical parturition, found
its signature in the economy of signs and the fragmentation of discourse, first fully exploited in the style of the aphorism. It is no coincidence that the two "levelers" of the philosophical modern terrain—
Nietzsche and Wittgenstein—wrote in fragments and aphorisms.

But we cannot truly comprehend our present circumstances without considering the sublimity of the storm, the harnessing of the

power of the aphorism to disclose, not difference, but ecstasy and excess. All postmodern "strategies" of theorizing, therefore, begin in a strange sense with the writings of Georges Bataille. Bataille should not be read as a "philosopher" by any stretch of the mind. Nor is he simply some curiosity within belles lettres, an avatar of the obscene who happened to draw attention, like ancient Theravada Buddhist techniques of meditation, to the reality of body fluids. Bataille's calculated ribaldry and brutality are no different from Derrida's marginal glosses. They are intended to focus on the alterity generated by all writing. In that sense such theorizing turns out to be, as Žižek has emphasized, merely the final florescence of the modernist project. If the ultimate aim of modernism was pure self-referentiality and the thorough transparency of the creative process itself, then postmodernism fills out the transition. Language no longer speaks from its own bellows. The text talks to itself. It sheds all pretension beyond its own visibility and materiality, gaping with full clarity at its own lesions and anomalies.

The Logical as Lyrical

Yet that is not all theory has ever been about. Nor is it exactly what Bataille was about. We must read Bataille's journal of the lightning storm, the strange epic of a scrivener, the prank of poetic self-mortification that he named *Le Coupable,* or simply *Guilty* in English. The work commences with the Nazi assault on Poland. "The date I start (September 5, 1939) is no coincidence. I'm starting because of what's happening, though I don't want to go into it. I'm writing it down because of being unable *not* to."[1] The scribbling is more than some spirit-infested "automatic writing." All that is happening, Bataille writes, "takes place in a fiery penumbra," an utterly tangential condition hovering above the landscape of awesome and impending devastation. "I won't speak of war, but of mystical experience."[2] It is "blameless, shameless." For days into the war, and as his nomadism and flight from the encroaching chaos take on an ethereal familiarity, Bataille meditates upon those themes that have haunted his imagination since he abandoned Catholicism for the adventures of the avant-garde: the grand inspiration of sacrifice and whoredom. These themes struggle toward the very lyricality that will later become the "language" of the postmodern. "Instead of avoiding laceration I'd deepen it."[3] Laceration and ecstasy—the excess of differentiation—are conjugate with each other. The drive of rhetoric all along has emanated from the delight of nihilation, against what Derrida would later term the "logocentrism" of Greco-Christian universalism, the redoubts of ontotheology. Libertinism is simply the ugly stepsister to a metaphysical particularism, Deleuze's univocity or "logic of sense." It all concerns the abdication of language. "A few Christians have broken from the language world and come to the ecstatic one. In their case, an aptitude has to be supposed which made mystical experience inevitable *in spite of Christianity's essential reliance on speech.*"[4]

The death of God is a celebration of incompleteness. Death is not really a finality; it is the imperfection of life, the sovereignty of the unfinished. It does not take mathematics but rather rhetoric to illustrate Gödel's theorem that the demonstrable is paradoxically incomplete. The very idea of meaning as a "deconstructive" moment first occurs in Bataille's jottings over two decades before Derrida. "Constant human errors would express the incomplete character of reality—and so of truth. Knowledge proportionate to its object—if that object is incomplete in its very being—would develop in every way. This knowledge would be, as totality, a huge architecture in *deconstruction and construction,* both at the same time, uncoordinated or barely so, but never through and through so they overlap."[5] Although the postmodernist theory signification begins with Derrida's "grammatology," it is Bataille's writing that makes possible the "deconstructionist" project in its own right. Bataille, who died just as Derrida began to write and publish, sought the holiness of excess that transfigures writing as something *more than* writing. *Guilty* is the writing of excess, the excess of war, the Second World War. The Second World War did not, unlike the first, purport to end all wars, but abolished the illusion that war can be ended.

When Nietzsche wrote that the denial of God's death has been aided and abetted by a misplaced confidence in "grammar," he was giving voice to a prolepsis concerning the twentieth century. Twentieth-century thought is commonly demarcated by what has been called the "linguistic turn," which might be better characterized as a dogmatism of representational coherence, of the regimen of sentences, of *linguisticism.* Nietzsche's prolepsis is much more profound than we ever realized. In *The Will to Power* Nietzsche had made his well-known distinction between "active" and "passive" nihilism. Active nihilism is the job of the Zarathustran prophet. It is the assault on cultural and moral platitudes which remain tenacious but unexamined—the work of philosophy in its classic operation, the critique of belief and value Socrates first undertook. Active nihilism, which Nietzsche could only push forward by abandoning the "argument" and perfecting the aphorism, runs the risk of transforming reasoning into rhetoric, mainly because it applies the philosophical "hammer" to grammar.

But, as those who have repeatedly corrected the popular misreading of Nietzsche understand, philosophizing with a hammer does not amount to the shattering of perceptible idols. Hammering amounts to a *semiotic intelligence gathering,* to a discernment of the *substance-lessness* of substance, of the emptiness of the construct, of the unreason of the rationality that is circumscribed within the "limits of reason alone." Active nihilism reveals the passive, or unacknowledged, nihilism that is part of the architecture of pure reason. The architecture discloses the *nihil* that insinuates itself into every *ens,* a realization which Heidegger dubbed the "end of philosophy" and which applies to theology as well. The active "nihilism" of postmodernism is, as Bataille first descried, the "deconstruction" that belongs to the mobile and morphing architecture of signification. The death of God and the baring of the *nihil* inside civilization require a "writing" that amounts to what Nietzsche described as the "hardness" of creation. Bataille is neither an artist nor a philosopher, but a writer/creator.

The Flowing Signature

Writing is for Bataille, as desire becomes for Lacan, a flowing "signature" that both disperses the metanarrative of Western theogrammatology and reconstructs for an instant at least its uncharted reserve of signifying possibilities. Like all signatures, it is unique, a rhythm and a kind of "fractal geometry" of projections and eruptions, of labyrinthine breakages and errant flows along the lines that Deleuze characterizes as the "conceptual persona." *Logos* becomes *rhetor,* the flux of intimations and signs. Bataille writes as much about the reddening sunrise or a woman's sensuality as he does about the role of philosophy. Postmodernism is the "alternative universe" of the pure writer, but it is a universe into which we diehard "grammarians" are slowly fading, inexorably but blissfully and triumphantly. It is our retreat from the advancing armies of scientific, cognitive, and discursive precision.

Postmodernism is the great escape from the prison house of language. More precisely, it is the confession of the false transcendence that "modernism" has bestowed with its metaphysics of the sovereign subject. The idol of the sovereign subject is nothing more than a historical monument signaling the "mirror stage" of an increasingly conscious strategy of collective desire. Bataille maps out this originary strategy in his discussion of the prehistoric cave art of Lascaux, in the engineering of art and sacrifice. The birth of art coincides with the overflow of "life" beyond its forms and boundaries. That was of course Nietzsche's point. The difference between Nietzsche and Bataille is that the former understands the moment of overflow, or superfluity, as a transition beyond the human, the "all too human," as the advent of the mysterious symbolic asymptote, the trope of tropes, that Nietzsche names *Übermensch*, or "overman." The overflow is a prolepsis; it is futuristic. For Bataille, it is aboriginal. The human has not yet comprehended its own intrinsic eschatology.

> What remains uncertain is at what moment did transgression, given free rein in an outburst of festivity, first obtain the decisive role it had in human behavior ever since? Such a principle does not contradict the specific interpretations every work separately inspires. A work of art, a sacrifice contains something of an irrepressible festive exuberance that overflows the world of work, and clashes with, if not the letter, the spirit of the prohibitions indispensable to safeguarding the world . . . a work of art in which this desire cannot be sensed, in which it is faint or barely present, is a mediocre work. Similarly, there is a specific motive behind every sacrifice: an abundant harvest, expiation, or any other logical objective . . . every sacrifice has its cause in the quest for a sacred instant that, for an instant, puts to rout the profane time in which prohibitions guarantee the possibility of life.[6]

In his *Theory of Religion* Bataille explains this "sacred instant" as a return to the innocent inseparability of consciousness from its immediate world, where human agency differentiates itself from the production of things as use-objects and the technical regimen associated with what Heidegger terms the "calculative." "The sacrificer's prior separation from the world of things is necessary for the return of intimacy, of immanence . . . between the subject and the object."[7]

The common practice of sacrifice among "primitive" humanity betokens this urge toward self-transcendence. It is a point Nietzsche himself made obliquely. The "idea" of God is something extraordinarily different than the will to power that invents gods and plays God. Theology is to art as taxidermy is to the creative event. Art is the surging of life into its ocular alterity. The "representations" in the flickering torches of the cave chamber at Lascaux have little to do with the craft of imitation. They are the ceremonial production of the "animal-human" that drives toward its most "lifelike" figuration. But this lifelikeness is paradoxically nonfigurative, at least not in its intent. The anonymous Lascaux painters aim to inhabit the vitality they limn with ochre. Their art is "deconstructive" in the measure that it becomes an exhibition of excess.

Bataille's "sacred instant" is achieved only through a sensual transgression of workaday routines that must somehow be put aside and, if only for a while, left behind. Bataille notes that the act of *mimesis* in the primitive aesthetic of the kind discovered at Lascaux is quite different from the stylized and formalized "naturalism" that served as the spark of the early modern art. In the spirit of Nietzsche, Bataille remarks that the first works of art "were something new: out of nothing, they created the world they figure."[8] "Man" begins, rather than ends, as overman. Only later does humanity settle into a regime of emulating and replicating the past which we call "tradition." Civilization thus is more a fall than an advance. Humanism is not exaltation; it is decadence. The civilizing process amounts to an ordering of the sacrificial impulse, which slowly turns "sacramental" and religious. The ecstasy of the aesthetic transgression vanishes into the normalization of sacred forms, rites, and symbols.

The familiar furniture of the sacred becomes Durkheim's "collective representations" out of which language and thought spring. Just as Nietzsche understood, Greek philosophy is the progeny of Dionysus. The Dionysian is prior to the "Apollonian." Philosophy is the Dionysian consciousness expanding beyond the mere furor of the instincts. "What then is it that brings philosophical thinking so quickly to its goal? Is it different from the thinking that calculates and measures only by virtue of the greater rapidity with which it transcends all space? No, its feet are propelled by an alien, illogical power—the power of creative imagination."[9] The dawning of culture is synchronous with the "birth of tragedy," which is intimately entwined with the frenzy of the blood sacrifice. And it is the tragic destiny of thought that it must seek its origins in the moment of transgression, in the nocturnal excesses of the sacrificial rite. Like Pentheus sidling up to the Bacchae in their ecstatic celebration, thought always runs the risk of coming too close to the chaos it is compelled to contemplate. The question is not what Athens has to do with Jerusalem so much as what Königsberg has to do with Lascaux. For Bataille, the two are much closer than we realize.

Bataille and the Genesis of Postmodernism

Bataille, rather than Nietzsche, epitomizes the birth of postmodern theory. Bataille's prose is one that contains the most exacting reflection. In a sense it supersedes philosophy. The very concept of a "postmodern philosophy" amounts to a strange sort of catachresis. The postmodern is also postphilosophical, as Bataille's writings illustrate. Bataille's "general economy" in which the calculus of exchange gives way to a grandiose, "solar" potlatch—a festival of sacrificial exuberance—prefiguring the turn of philosophy to writing, where all discursive restraints are now lifted and where the "gift" of being—Heidegger's *es gibt*—is now iterated as the word untethered. Bataille's writing goes beyond writing to the *pure mobility of the sign*. Writing itself belongs to a general culture, which in the postmodern venue consists in a pastiche of all artistic practices and gestures.

Bataille does not invent the theory of the sign by any means. But he transforms thought into signification through the evocation of all extremes of eroticism, obscenity, cruelty, and violence. Thought can only accomplish its task when it ponders the unspeakable, Žižek's intractable real, the "obscene supplement." But Bataille's perversions, real or conjectured, are in themselves tropes for something far more rarefied and consequential. They are the effort to make our notions fluid, even if it requires a preoccupation with orgies and somatic excretions. This fluidity is the "gift" of language and ontology taken to excess. It is transgression with a global and epochal strategy, a latter-day Lascaux. What we might call the "post-ontology" of postmodernism has its signature in the esthetics that emerged at the time of the First World War. Just as classical art and classical philosophy go together with their supreme valuation of proportionality (*ratio*), representation, and form, so the conclusion of classicism coincides with the Nietzschean "transvaluation," the transit from pure being to pure becoming.

The sign is the apotheosis of "creative destruction," the sacrifice. As Bataille writes of art in his day,

> The image of sacrifice is imposed on our reflection so necessarily that, having passed the time when art was mere diversion or when religion alone responded to the desire to enter into the depth of things, we perceive that modern painting has ceased to offer us endearing or merely pretty images, that it is anxious to make the world "transpire" on canvas. Apollinaire once claimed that cubism was a great religious art, and his dream has not been lost. Modern painting prolongs the repeated obsession with the sacrificial image in which the destruction of objects responds, in a manner already half-conscious, to the enduring functions of religions.[10]

Postmodernism is a "religious" act.

Postmodernism is Bataille's gift. The theory of the "gift," which becomes so prominent in French postmodernism from Derrida to Marion, does not originate with Heidegger. It is seeded with Bataille. Bataille read closely Marcel Mauss's analysis of the potlatch, of the sacrifice as *donum gratiae*, of the exuberance of excessive giving which has no "economy" in the strict sense but which calls into question all discourses and signifying economies with their logical and syntactical architectures that must now be "deconstructed" in the track of the German guns. Bataille's metaphor of the "solar phallus" signifies all plenary force in the sense Hegel uses it in his *Phenomenology*. It is both the overture to, and the climax of, the symphony of spirit. Hegel's spirit must drive itself into night. Nietzsche's Zarathustra must "go under." What Bataille seems to have given us is something exceedingly strange, Nietzsche's "strangest of guests." Postmodernism is the "stranger" (*l'étranger*) whose "strangeness" means that it is ungrounded and without a home (*unheimlich*).

We can imagine Bataille's flight from the Nazi occupation forces, a solitary, animal-like restlessness and wantonness confronting the cold, collectivist rationality—and wantonness—of the Third Reich. The stranger bears a gift, the gift of a "infrahuman" freedom that perishes in its own nocturnal excess and yet crafts the primal stutterings of a new philosophical and theological rhetoric. The infrahuman confronts the inhumane. From this "gift" of *disiecta membra* of the old Christian millennium a new one is reassembled and reborn.

Mors Dei as Sacrificial Exchange

If Bataille first enunciated this new rhetoric of the sign, which would serve as the marrow of the postmodern theory of religion, Thomas J. J. Altizer formulated its "theological" framework. What Bataille discovered in the pure "Dionysian" undercurrents of culture, Altizer found in his own curious version of "counterenlightenment" during the age of excess known as the 1960s which combined Hegel with William Blake to engineer a popular rehabilitation of Nietzsche's slogan "God is dead" that still resonates today. Altizer is not simply the "prophet" of "postmodern theology," as he has been called, but the forerunner of postmodern theory. Like Bataille, he relied on the same root metaphor of the sacrificial offering. But the "sacrifice" is not of the human but of the divine itself, the core concept of the grand "theological" enterprise that dominated religious studies up until the era when Altizer emerged. As the éminence grise who inspired many among the first generation of postmodern religious thinkers, particularly

Mark C. Taylor, Altizer loiters at the threshold between the "secular theologians" of the Vietnam era and the Derridean revolution of the 1970s and 1980s. His writings—visionary, declamatory, and breathlessly oracular—have no parallel in the writers he has influenced.

The postmodernist turn indeed has its origins in death of God theology, about which Altizer almost single-mindedly created a frenzy in 1965. Postmodern thought, at least in America, has leveraged in spades both the cultural sentiment of a dead God and the disturbing metaphoricity of the expression itself, which has been institutionalized in Nietzsche's haunting parable of the madman. The "undecidability" of what is connoted in such an expression has been the stimulus for an endless recrudescence of the parable's invocation by both theologians and philosophers, usually in a gesture toward impressing upon us the particular crisis of the age with which we are confronted.

As the dominant force in the death of God movement, Altizer gave impetus to this set of trends. Over a generation later it is perhaps time to call a moratorium on the overuse and misuse of the metaphor and to decipher further what has been meant by the "death of God" on the theological level. The death of God, as Altizer himself has insisted, signifies the culmination of the apocalyptic yearnings of the West. Apocalypticism is the eschatology of the modern, insofar as it is imaginative apprehension of "total presence," the *parousia* of what has not yet been realized in the thought of Calvary.

What do we mean by such a *parousia*? The death of God, according to Altizer, is something far more momentous than the erasure of the West's premier *theologoumenon*. For Nietzsche, who first proclaimed *mors Dei*, it is a crime of Deicide, a "murder" committed by "all of us" as both plotters and perpetrators. It is a crime that we want to deny, not merely our complicity in it, but the very fatality of it. Who are the "us"? That is a question "death of God theology" has never addressed. It has nothing to do with the two-millennium-old canard that a *gens*, a people, or as the anti-Semitic vitriol runs, the "Jews," have killed God. Deicide is at once an act of "mass slaughter," but it is not a terroristic spectacle. We discover the secret "grave" of the victim only after the empire of the conspirators has crumbled. So long as we heed the proviso that it is the many—Heidegger's *das Man*—who have perpetrated the slaughter, the "we" does not seem at all problematic; we have, as the Christian confessional goes, all in some manner of speaking cried "Crucify him."

One can imagine the historical episode, the curious mise-en-scène, when the even stranger prophecy of the dying and rising "Son of Man" becomes instantiated in the passion narrative. Stranger yet remains Pilate's quandary concerning the justice of exchanging Jesus for Barrabas. The regulative metonymy in what René Girard calls the "surrogate victim" of the blood sacrifice is at a stroke dissolved. The crucified Messiah no longer "signifies" by the thaumaturgy of symbolic exchange those who are destined to be redeemed from the violence of that historical site and figuration. The savage act of torture and execution can no longer redistribute the elements of cultural economy that invariably align the "sacred" with death, the "sacrificial" or "sacred-making" with crime. Pilate's protestation of the man's innocence bespeaks this terrible realization. *Ecce homo*, "behold the man." It is a homicide that conceals the apophatic expanse of Deity!

The "foundational" event of Christian thought is inseparable from this very aporia. Orthodox tradition has called it the "mystery" of the Incarnation. But the mystery reaches far deeper than the logical antinomy that befuddled the early Church Councils. How does the death of a man, the Son of Man, manifest the eternal nature of God? The first-generation Christian community resolved the issue by the testament to the Risen One. God died, but he rose again. Yet it was God's death that fascinated the Conciliar movement and compelled resistance to such heresies as Docetism, patripassionism, Montanism, and even Arianism.

The affirmation that God had died, and not merely taken on the "appearance" of mortality, penetrated to the marrow of both pagan and Hebraic thinking. And it served as the setting for a convulsion in Western thought that would be felt as late as the dialectical philosophies of the nineteenth century—the transformation of the classical theory of representation into the idea of "sacred history," of ontology into narratology, of metaphysics into soteriology, of the doctrine of essence into the romance of existence. Nietzsche's "murderers of God" are all of us, precisely because by embracing dialectical thought we have acceded to the abolition of the boundary between the two signifying planes of thinking itself: presentation and representation, immediacy and mediacy, intimation and articulation, *ousia* (in the Heideggerian sense of that which simultaneously shows and hides itself) and *parousia*, temporality and eschatology.

Eschatology and White Mythology

The question of eschatology is impossible to consider within the *metaphysicism* of Indo-European grammar and language, what Derrida terms our "white mythology." The signifying dyad of metaphysics which enables the novelty of dialectics is that of permanence and change, stasis and kinesis, time and eternity. The linguistic sign is double-bound and schizoid; it emerges out of the incision of the text. The sign of the "eschaton," however, is plenipotentiary; it gathers and fuses all forms of signifying action into itself; it draws them all into itself at the same time it shatters them and breaks them down into what they "are" before the judgment throne. Eschatology means the effacement of all double sentences, the unmasking of every duplicitous system of signification. It is "allness" and "nothingness" in an identical instant.

The very prospect of an "eschatology" sequestered within our very white mythology was actually discerned by Kant in his third critique, the *Critique of the Power of Judgment*. In the third critique Kant sought to push beyond his efforts to delineate the conditions of possible knowledge (a metaphysics of cognition) in the first critique as well as the conditions of ethical decision making (a "metaphysics of morals") in the second critique. If these two critiques aim to explore how general concepts or representations effectively provide an "architecture" of different faculties that make intelligible the concrete singularity of both sense experience and individual volition, the third critique is essentially, as Lyotard puts it, an undertaking that reconciles them in explicating the "paradox of a judgment that appears, problematically, to be doomed to particularity and contingency."[11] The critique of judgment concerns the possibility of any "theoretical" insight into the singularity of aesthetic experience, involving both the beautiful and the sublime.

In aesthetic experience no conceptual generalization is possible. The aesthetic object simply is what it is. It is not a "quiddity," but what Deleuze calls a "haeccity"—a singularity constituted by an unrepeatable act of signification. What pressures thought into making a determinate judgment of an object's intelligibility without resort to any sort of predicative logic is the indeterminate but overwhelming character of what the mind encounters itself, especially when contemplating the power of nature. This encounter Kant calls the experience of the "sublime." The power of nature summons forth not only the power of the imagination (*Einbildungskraft*) but the force of certain judgment (*Urteilskraft*). The force is generated from the "resistance" of the finite subject to the overpowering presence of the infinite.

God as a theological concept is completely "unrepresentable" in this experience, which "is not a feeling of the sublimity of our own nature but rather submission, rejection, and a feeling of complete powerlessness that is the appropriate disposition of the mind to the appearance of such an object."[12] The experience of sublimity amounts to what Clayton Crockett, following Žižek, dubs a "logic of exceptionality." A logic of exceptionality is nondialectical. A logic of exceptionality, unlike a logic of predication, is not concerned with either the general or the specific inference. It concentrates on an exclusive "thingness," not the thing as *Ding an sich* as in Kant's case, but in the thing of Lacan's psychoanalytics. Kant's "thing" is a limit-notion, the horizon of representation itself. It is this "horizontality" of the thing that Heidegger seizes upon in his program of fundamental ontology to configure it as, however, a reserve of real and inexhaustible presence rather than a heuristic construct (with Kant), a formal *incognito*. In Lacan the thing is an intrusion of the unrepresentable as *singular signifying moment*. It is comparable to Heidegger's "thingness of the thing." It is an irreducible moment of difference in the undifferentiated field of desire, the expanse of the Real as it wrestles with the emerging Symbolic order. The thing is "indicated" by the eruption of a dissymmetry in these two orders. It is a product of semiotic rather than linguistic processes. "The Thing burns a hole in the Real, and it is the nothing organized in the work of art or creation of a signifier that enables 'authentic' signification to occur. The Thing is not God, but it can encapsulate the desire for God."[13]

The desire for God as in the encounter with the Kantian sublime "object" culminates in an irrepeatable event of recognition—what Kant would call *apperception*—the profound sense of a *singular signifying event*. This singularity defies representation; it is pure presence, though not in either the Heideggerian or the Derridean connotation of the word. It is comparable to the *tout autre*, the "wholly other," what phenomenologically has been named the "holy," the "sacred," or the "religious"; but it is even more than that. Otherness always implies a relation, an infinite dialectical relation.

Yet the singular signifying event of which we speak knows neither self-identity nor absolute alterity. It is, to repeat, nondialectical and, as Derrida would say, "undeconstructible." It overwhelms; it is impossible to resist while at the same time it obliges resistance. It is closer to what both Nietzsche and Freud named *das Unheimliche*, the "uncanny." In Deleuze the singular is always associated with "force" and with "sense," the two terms in the post-Platonic philosophical lexicon that imply signification without sameness, semiosis without representation. But in the case of the sublime, which has a different kind of force—the force of the *revelatory*—the singular signifying event inaugurates the impossibility of transforming force into representation, of "making sense" out of what is there in its overwhelming and overpowering manifestation with some kind of theological follow-up or intervention.

Even for Deleuze, who eschewed all talk of God and the religious, the singularity of signification has its own "payoff." It is the virtual becoming real, which is Deleuze's take on Nietzsche's assault on epistemology in the cause of affirmation, the "will to truth," and "creating new values." Only when God as "transcendental signifier," as the representation of all representation, has died can the overman, who creates new values, "live." The death of God is the death of representation, but it does not yet call into play the power of the singular signifying event. The singular signifying event is something Nietzsche perhaps had in mind, but could not articulate, with his "abysmal thought" of eternal recurrence, a thought that Deleuze appropriates as the thought of pure difference that is infinitely "repeated" *as difference*. But difference is only "singular" in the abstract. The singular signifying event remains singular in its concrete anticipation, the moment "to come" when all that remains veiled will be revealed. As historians of religion have long reminded us, a founding myth requires a final expectation, a "protology" as well as an eschatology. The eschatological is a term for the singular signifying event that, following Derrida, remains messianic, that is *avenir*, "to come." Eschatology can never, as Hegel deeply *misunderstood*, turn out to be a dialectical synthesis, even a synthesis that results from a "death of God" and the "Golgotha of Absolute Spirit." The *eschaton* is always singular.

It is to Altizer's credit to have used dialectics to turn eschatology on its very head. Hegel's "Golgotha of Absolute Spirit" can only be described as a genuine philosophical apocalypse, but it is still philosophical in traditional reading. For Altizer, it is the great speculative moment of silence in heaven, but it is not the end. It is only the precondition for the movement from divine transcendence to divine immanence, to the event of "total presence" that is at the same time God's self-presence as complete divine self-reference, secular theology that has become secular eschatology, the *eschaton* that is once and for all *saeculum*. "Despite the Nicene formula, the Word cannot be fully God and fully man, if, on the one hand, it continues to exist in an eternal form and, on the other, it is unable to move into the present and the full reality of history."[14]

In this peculiar volte-face, this transposition of millennial revelation, in this strangest of "scenes" where mythic construct of "the end of time" signifies time itself as end, the dialectical drama of history, which Hegel envisioned as culminating in the abolition of limited consciousness, can no longer come to fruition. The death of God

intimates something far more epochal than any triumphal "humanism," as theologians a generation ago suggested.[15] The orthodox formula for "incarnation"—that curious, doxological compromise of the
Church Fathers between the Hebraic reverence for the unspeakably
"beyond" and the pagan valorization of the senses—is also upended in
the Altizerian world of metadoctrine, transforming itself into a rhapsody of pure immanence, a Dionysian *sparagmos* of theological limbs
and entrails where hitherto there had been some kind of coherence in
the ecclesiological idea of the *corpus Christi*.

We must begin to understand the death of God, as perhaps even
Altizer himself has not understood it, as an "end times" of *dismem-
berment and sacrifice*. So much of the so-called death of God theology
derives from the glory, as well as the bathos, of Hegel's phenomenology. The Hegelian stamp is evident as well in Altizer, not to mention
the influence of Eliade and Nietzsche's notion of "eternal recurrence."
But the thought of Altizer carries us beyond the now obsolete "modernist" controversy between theism and pantheism into the more
complex, and fateful, biblical problem of Jesus's death as divine sacrifice. The work of René Girard, of course, has alerted us to the intimate
correlation between the semiotics of the sacred and ritual sacrifice.
What Altizer seems to suggest, perhaps without a recognition of the
dramatic implications of his own thought, is that the Nietzschean
metaphor of the "murder of God" points to the profound analogy of
the death of God as sacrificial slaying. What could such a metaphor
mean in terms of the secular theology Altizer's work has spawned?

The relationship between Christology and the cult of sacrifice is
evident in the book of Hebrews—a segment of scripture that is usually
ignored, or overlooked, by modern theological authors. Hebrews is a
strange document; it is attributed to Paul, but was most likely composed by the Levite Barnabas. It is a treatise on soteriology that deconstructs by a miscellany of metonymical transpositions the rhetoric of
the already defunct sacrificial system of the Jewish temple priesthood.
More than any other "work" in the New Testament, Hebrews follows
through with the theo-logic of "God's death," but it does so in a way
that is bereft of the cant of theological modernism.

Hebrews begins with the assertion that God's "speech" in these
"last days" is no longer direct, but "by his Son." The Son is the "radiance of God's glory and the exact representation of his being [*character tes hypostaseos*], sustaining all things by his powerful word"
(Heb. 1:1–3). On the face of it, there is nothing remarkable about this
statement, insofar as it prefigures the kind of orthodoxy that for two
millennia would be the ideological staple of Western Christendom.

But the subsequent unfolding of its soteriological implications in Hebrews is indeed remarkable. Although Hebrews affirms the Pauline as well as Johannine proposition that Jesus through his death "shared in [our humanity],"[16] it transports it to a more radical site of interpretation: the "humanity of Jesus" is revealed in his concurrent role as hierophant, or sacrificial priest, and sacrificial victim. The Son that is the *hypostasis*, the full but particularized signification of God's Being, sacrifices himself in order to leap the chasm between Being and representation itself.

Christ's self-sacrifice, elsewhere in the New Testament characterized as God's self-emptying, or *kenosis*, is something far more telling than the Chalcedonian formula of God becoming "man." It points to what in Hegelian terms is the abrogation, the *Aufhebung*, of God's eternal self-diremption, the negation of the divine self-negation, which in turn fulfills the concept of the Son as *hypostasis*. The evangelical shibboleth of "blood redemption" entails an astounding form of *theosemiotics*—namely, that the unity of divine essence and simulacrum, of presence and re-presentation, is not achieved by any kind of transcendent synthesis of the religious imagination. Rather, it manifests itself in the movement when God's own "blood" is shed, when the sacrifice from below to above is transferred into the literal "dying of the Lamb" on the Cross of Cavalry. Incarnation only becomes explicable at the site of pure divine carnality, the inescapability of flesh and blood which Bataille celebrated. Any "death of God theology" must take into account the butchery as well as the "obscenity" of the sacrificial instance, the resolution of holy as profane, the "carnivalesque" character of Christian experience in its utter primality.

The Semiotics of Blood Sacrifice

The connection between Dionysian symbolism and Christological speculation, therefore, is not accidental. Hegel's phenomenology of "Spirit" mirrors a more primitive phenomenology of religion that is pretheological, pre-Chalcedonian, prespeculative. Again, it can be found in Hebrews. "This is the blood of the covenant, which God has commanded you to keep."[17] If the death of God is grounded in such a blood covenant, the suggestion is staggering. Anthropological theories of blood sacrifice rest on the premise that the "life" of the victim is in the blood, and that the spilling of blood conjoins the sacrifice with the ontological source from which all emanates.

Ancient theology, of course, was confounded by the paradoxical quality of this relationship. The gradual elimination of the practice of human sacrifice in the archaic world underscored the perception that the shedding of human blood in the sacrificial ceremony was not an act of consecration but an incidence of "barbarism" that mistakes the sanguinary for the liturgical. The movement from human to animal sacrifice, particularly as manifest in the evolution of Hebrew ritual, however, resulted only in a heightening of the paradox and the incapability of the archaic complex of religious signification and representation to encompass it.

The difficulty of making intelligible the notion within ethical monotheism of an all-loving, thoroughly holy, and mysteriously merciful God whose worship must still be based on ritual slaughter must have seem to ancient devotees to have been weighted quite precariously. The theology of Hebrews, which some scholars believe was composed after the destruction of the temple in Jerusalem as a means of explaining to early Jewish Christians how the act of "making sacred" could be accomplished without sacrifice, attests to a tentative resolution of this quandary. It is not the transfiguration of the dead victim into a form of divine life that matters. It is the dying of God himself on the "altar," the redemption of all things through the eschatological shedding of blood, "God's blood."

But the semiotics of blood sacrifice, which remains ultimately an anthropological question, must not obscure the basic and most original problem of God's death as the "end" of representation itself. The end of representation, the overcoming of the inherent ontological dualism of the West, is what the death of God is truly all about. The key to this intricate hermeneutic of divine semblance can be found in the opening verse of Hebrews, which we have already referenced. The realization of the nature of the Son as the "exact representation" of God through death on the Cross betokens a type of radical theology that the formalism of Greco-Roman thought could never articulate. The orthodox conception that God "sacrificed" his Son to redeem fallen humanity transfers into the ontological insight that the infinite divine presence, and its reproduction in the sacrificial victim, is overcome once and for all in the moment of crucifixion. The victim as representation, or surrogate, is abolished—not momentarily as in the sacrificial system—but decisively and irrevocably. Presence and representation are no longer terms of difference, a difference that makes an ultimate difference. Heaven and earth, word and flesh, are equalized in a signifying singular event.

The "blood covenant" between God and humanity in Christ's death becomes a root metaphor for the erasure of the boundary between God and the *imago Dei*. The boundary, metaphysically expressed as "sin,"

is washed away in the blood. There is but a temporal, not a logical, gap
between God's presence (*ousia*) in Christ and *parousia*. For *parousia*
itself can be deciphered as the full, post-representational expression
of what the troped notion of "God's son" truly entails. It is not, as
philosophical idealism understood, the *Aufhebung* of finitude into a
"speculative infinity," of the concretization of "Absolute Spirit."

Such a vision is already labored in the main writings of Altizer. We
must therefore pose the question whether the death of God in all truth
signifies the sacrifice of God, which would imply a singularity that
neither theology nor philosophy, which shrink from blood, can abide.
The analogy of sacrifice, of course, was prominent in Nietzsche. The
cry of the madman that the divine murder is bleeding "under our
knives," a translation to a "higher history than all history hitherto,"
has all the resonances of ritual sacrifice.

But a theory of sacrifice as applied to any theological dialectics
must first take into account Bataille's economics of expenditure and
excess. As Bataille observes, a theory of religion cannot in any way
be derived from a doctrine of utility. Indeed, the opposite is true. The
experience of the sacred arises out of what Nietzsche described as
the joy of self-expenditure, the "overflowing" of power, an economy
that like a swollen watercourse overruns its banks. Only economies
of consumption and excess are capable of sacrifice. The element con-
sumed in the sacrifice—the victim, the ensign of excess—is Bataille's
"accursed share," and it is in this accounting "accursed" that the production of the sacred becomes possible.

The centrality of the sacrificial motif in the Christian doctrine of
atonement underscores the importance of Bataille's hermeneutics of
excess. We can begin to understand the Nietzschean parable of the
murder of God and the classical dogmatic formula of God's sacrifice
of himself as a kind of *obversity* within all forms of religious discursivity. The "death of God" can therefore be comprehended as a con-
trolling catachresis, as the distension of the dialectics of sacrifice to
the point where the "paradox of incarnation" is no longer a linguistic
stumbling block. But the structure of the catachresis, wherein the expenditure of what is "all too human" logically communicates at the
same time the idea of divine self-exteriorization, cannot be resolved
by any Hegelian juggernaut of the negative. The catachresis remains
an impenetrable membrane through which yet sift hints of divine singularity and, therefore, truly *divine presence*.

Here we surpass all forms of "secular" as well as "negative" theologies—the metonymy of the divine *ousia* expressed in the *mysterium
tremendum* of sacrifice, both anthropologically and theologically.

In Hebrews, and then overtly in Altizer, we cross over the semiotic threshold into the postmodern. If we systematically reread Altizer's writings, we discern the way in which he uncovers a startling relationship between variant epochs, divergent semiologies. As Altizer says, "The real ending of speech is the dawning of resurrection, and the final ending of speech is the dawning of a totally present actuality. That actuality is immediately at hand when it is heard, and it is heard when it is enacted. And it is enacted in the dawning of the actuality of silence, an actuality ending all disembodied and unspoken presence."[18]

After Altizer, nothing can remain hidden. The bones of the dead God are there for all to see. They are the dry and glistening remains of everything that has been said about God and as the grammar of God. After all, as Nietzsche pointed out, even with the death of God we still have grammar—in this case a theological grammar. Yet there is no longer any representation of God that we can reconstruct or revivify within theological discourse. That is why postmodernism has always involved the "end of theology" and why a "postmodern theology"—especially what has now come to be known as *deconstructive theology*—is an unmanageable, if not an indecipherable, expression. But the impossibility of theology does not preclude by any means a new possibility for theory. If Altizer's and Taylor's a/theology have brought us as well to the necessity of denying any truthfulness to "unspoken presence," that forecloses only the hidden *logos*, not the singular sublimity of *semeia*. The Johannine moment of *logos* become *sarx*, word as flesh, has been the unthought "death of God" from the very outset.

Incarnation is such a singular sublimity. The sublime cannot be illumined; it is pure difference, a cataclysmic disintermediation. The singular signifying event constitutes the plentitude of semiosis, not a bare clarification of what previously had been merely glimpsed in an "ordinary" light. Nietzsche in vain pursued this unmediated sense of a singularity that fulfilled the aim of an eschatological redemption. For him, the thought of eternal recurrence was "abysmal" because it was one kind of metaphysics—the metaphysics of cyclical renewal—made strange, *made singular.*

There is no science of the negative—even the negative that could be called "total presence"—when it comes to the religious. There is only the singular that derives from the sacrificial metaphor while fascinating and drawing us into a signifying moment that is endlessly available to interpretation, and interminably deconstructible if we try to take it as *Vorstellung,* as a representation. The semiotics of singularity as our postmodern move of religious theory has a stunningly different provenance from the Hegelian dialectic, although both are rooted in the "event" of incarnation. For semiotics, it is the meaning of the empty tomb, the figure at first that goes unrecognized on the road to Emmaus, that singular signifying event that means ultimately that "every knee shall bow" in the *parousia* before the name of Christ Jesus. But it is at the same time the meaning of *satori* in the Zen koan, where focusing on the sense of nonsense yields the singularity of truth in the revelation of the no-mind.

We do not mean the ceremonial or the mythico-symbolic when we talk about the religious. We have in mind those forms of catachresis, the stretching to the limits of language through the deconstruction of its textual memes and components, that transport us beyond the *negative to the singular,* or what we call the *religious.* The theory of the singular is the theory of "exception" to language, even theological or familiar religious language. It is naming *sauf le nom.*

6

LEVINAS AND THE FINAL
À-DIEU TO THEOLOGY

.

That which was from the beginning, which we have heard,
which we have seen with our eyes, which we have looked upon
and touched with our hands.

—1 John 1:1 (NIV)

IT IS THE "proper name 'Sinai,'" which Derrida says is "as enigmatic
as the name 'face,'" which is "untranslatable."[1] The death of Levinas
called forth this peculiar "spirit" for Derrida. But it is a spirit that
does not allow us to simply say "farewell" to the celebrated postmodern Moses who brought down from the mount of modernism the
tablets of a new ethic, the (post-Kantian) "law" of responsibility to
l'autre. This spirit, specter, or "ghost" (Geist) is, at the same time,
a "guest" (Gast). The specter of infinite alterity oscillates with its
seeming "opposite pole," its parallax position, which in the argument
against ontotheology must be considered.

In the *Will to Power* Nietzsche spoke of nihilism as "the strangest
of guests." But the spectrality of the Infinite trace, the "saving" of the
holiest name—which should not be confused with linguistic trace at
the moment of deconstruction—is even stranger; it is indeed strangest
among all "strangers." If in Nietzsche's words nihilism "stands at the
door" of the twentieth century, and by Heidegger's reckoning skulks
at the borders of Western philosophy, then the strangest thing is the
way in which the trace can be recollected as a double inscription, as

the gratuitous and gloomy ghost of a dead Deity, or as the *parousia* of the unpresentable present that history has named "Sinai."

Specters of Levinas

The aporia of postmodern religious thinking is itself a kind of aporia, a displacement of the fundamental zone of undecidability for the "Western," not simply Greek, philosophical tradition. Derrida himself sought to frame his own project within this zone of undecidability, in the "hypocrisy" that is our philosophical "history."[2] *The real "undecidable" in postmodern religious thinking, however, has never been between Athens and Jerusalem; it has been between Derrida and Levinas.* The Derridean trace marked through temporality of the text is the true conjugate of the Levinasian trace of interpersonal responsibility that is deposited by all relational investments in the Other, which is not ontological in the Greek sense, but *heterological.* This heterological trace arises not from the "grammar" of reading, writing, interpretation, and exposition, but from the very *grammar of address* that constitutes the intersubjective relationship. It is genuinely the *duplex Hebraicum,* the two "faces" of Western thought. It is Torah, Law, Word, Scripture—the *signature of a singularity* behind the philosophical production of signs.

Thus Derrida's famous question ("Are we Greeks? Are we Jews?") that early on in his career called Levinas into question actually in its own manner *calls Derrida himself into question,* a question which he was never able to resolve and perhaps "unconsciously" motivated his own turn toward the "ethical" in the early 1990s. If one examines carefully the spate of Derrida's writings following publication of *Specters of Marx* (1993), one is struck by the finesse with which he almost completely renounces, without ever saying so directly, the very baseline "semiological" position of deconstruction enunciated in 1964: "Ethico-metaphysical transcendence . . . presupposes ontological transcendence."[3] In fact, ethico-metaphysical transcendence—for instance, Derrida's *avenir,* the "to come"—both determines and conditions the semiotic value of the textual trace, for it places the text itself in relationship to the claim of alterity, including the Infinite Other that conditions all intersubjective and ethical claims within the Jew-Greek, "hypocritical" history of the West. Caputo's influential, *quasi-theological* reading of Derrida, which has had such tremendous impact in recent years, would have been impossible without Derrida's own terribly subtle but "hypocritical" move in the early

1990s. Thus the term "deconstruction" as Derrida originally meant it, as a radical Husserlian and post-Heideggerian revision of the history of ontology, really does not apply to what has been going on in the "theological" realm in the last twenty years in the aftermath of publication of Caputo's *Prayers and Tears*.

Yet the Levinasian—as opposed to the "deconstructive"—legacy, if it is no longer relevant for theology, has tremendous ramifications for religious theory. Ontological transcendence, the transcendence of the "negative theology" characteristic of Derrida's midcareer, still belongs to the "Greek" side of the equation. However, on the Hebraic side it is not the contingency and temporality of the sign itself but the "command" from Sinai that "justifies" all signification. Kant's own aporia of the two main critiques of "pure reason" embodies Derrida's two centuries later.

The problem of metaphysics for Kant, which is at the same time Heidegger's and in an extended sense Derrida's as well, is not the unique dilemma of postmodern religious thinking. But in problematizing the metaphysical in the manner that both Heidegger and Derrida are most famous for, they have raised a more compelling problem, the problem of signification inherent in the address of the other, the "inscription" that requires a "society" in Levinas's usage, a type of semiosis that utterly transcends the self-presence of consciousness. Nietzsche's aporia was simply *God or "overman."* But what if *Übermensch* itself was a tracing, an unrepresentable ghost/guest of the unity of self-presencing, the phenomenologist's "consciousness," which Kant dubbed the "transcendental unity of apperception," the Hegelian *an und für sich*?

Nietzsche's guest is Descartes's ghost, the infinity that both logically and existentially overwhelms the positivity of the finite. But it is even more the specter that cannot be exorcized by any deconstructive reading. Without knowing it, in his attempt to subdue Athens, Derrida threw his incense finally onto the altar of the temple in which is enshrined the Law of writing, that interminable *metaphorization* of the text that is the legacy of philosophy. In the temple endless sacrifices—sacrifices of representation or acts of "deconstruction"—are conducted.

Sinai is not a temple; it is the *fons et origo* of all signifying moments that take us back to the revelation of the infinite in the finite. As the author of Hebrews informs us, when "Sinai" is reconstituted as the Cross, it is the end of all sacrifices. The stylization of the mountain from the standpoint of philosophical writing, as Derrida understands, is the pyramid.[4] The pyramid situates the altar, the site of sacrifice; it sublates the letter to produce difference. But the pyramid of sacrifice is not identical to the mount of Sinai. The mountain is where one discerns the Infinite Face. The mountain reveals the infinite "altarity" of the letter itself.

Derrida understood with Hegel that Spirit is sublation—*Aufhebung*. *Aufhebung* is the jarring of the literal, the pattern of differentiating enfolding within itself all of writing. Derrida's "*a*" of difference thus comprises a subtle moment of totalization. But the *a* of différance is not the kind of *à* that we encounter in the "later" Derrida when he seems to make a half-circle turn toward Levinas himself. This turn is particularly obvious in Derrida's valedictory testament to the great modern Jewish philosopher entitled *Àdieu to Emmanuel Levinas* upon the latter's death in 1995. In this publication Derrida, in fact, seems to contravene his own assertion of the primacy of the "ontological" thirty years earlier. "Each time I read or reread Emmanuel Levinas," Derrida gushes, "I am overwhelmed with gratitude and admiration, overwhelmed by this necessity, which is not a constraint but a very gentle force that obligates and that obligates us not to bend or curve otherwise the space of thought in its respect for the other." We are called "to yield to the other infinite precedence of the completely other."[5]

In the sixties Derrida had maintained the primacy of language itself in the face-to-face encounter, for without grammar—or an ontology embedded in grammar, a "grammatology"—there can be neither recognition nor enunciation of one's responsibility to the other. In the nineties the orientation is quite different. The "a" of ontological difference, or différance, is a negation, an absence or "being away" (*Abwesen*). The *à* of *À-dieu* (literally "to God") is the *à* of "being toward." Any "deconstructive theology" confirms the "a" of *a-theology*, the "a" of the *law* of the text that leads to death, as Paul would say. Yet the *à* of *Àdieu* marks the very curvature of the ontological toward the Levinasian ethical, the address of Sinai.

When Derrida relatively early on speaks of "spirit," he speaks of what is dead, absent, what has "passed on" into the trace that is beyond the present, the *geistliche* guest in the house of philosophy that forever haunts us. Derrida declares at the opening of *On Spirit:* "I shall speak of ghost [*revenant*], of flame, and of ashes."[6] The flame is Hegel. The ashes are the event of deconstruction of the text of speculative philosophy. Not a spirit in ashes, but *a* spirit of ashes.

In *Of Spirit*, composed on the eve of Derrida's own *Kehre* toward the infinite other, he imagines that he has thought through Heidegger as follows:

Do you find that what we have in our memory, the abyss of our memory, is not enough?), the thinking of this *Frühe* to come, while advancing towards the possibility of what you think you recognize, in going towards what is quite other than what you think you recognize. It is indeed not a new content. But access to thought, the thinking access to the *possibility* of metaphysics or pneumato-spiritualist religions opens up something quite other than what the possibility makes possible.

Here we have here echoes of Nietzsche's well-known polemics. Such a "new content" keeps alive, if only as catachresis, the allusion of presence in the Derridean trace. The "trace of the trace" that is at the same time the "spirit which keeps watch in returning [*en revenant*, as a ghost] will always do the rest. Through flame or ash, but as the entirely other, inevitably."[7]

In this Derridean excerpt we detect a "reverence" for a *revenant* as "reference" that is endless repetition, the endless differencing of difference, Nietzsche's "eternal recurrence of the same" now deconstructed as the "origin-heterogeneous," the trace. It would appear that the entire Derridean project had succumbed to a kind of Nietzschean exhaustion at the rim of the abyss. Derrida did not overcome Nietzsche, but impaled himself on Nietzsche's own "most abysmal" thought, the thought of the eternal recurrence of the same, the mark of/as the same. The same that eternally recurs is the presence of the present that presents itself as pure presence, that keeps erasing itself as *ecriture*, but remains "eternally" *la meme.*

Descartes's Ghost, or the "Otherwise"

Derrida's *Geist* is Descartes's ghost as well. In his 1962 essay "Transcendence et hauteur" Levinas writes about "the rhythm of Cartesian thinking," which "only rejoins the world by passing through the idea of the Infinite." If, Levinas says, "Descartes begins with the *Cogito*, he says a little later that in fact it is the idea of God that is primary, that is, the idea of the infinite. The idea of God was prior to the *Cogito*, and the *Cogito* would never have been possible if there had not already been the idea of God. . . . it is in the direct act and not in the reflective act that philosophical critique begins."[8]

Levinas makes a critical observation that Derrida, or Heidegger for that matter, wound up passing by. Levinas has observed that the "question of Being" is "over and above" ontology. Levinas talks not about differencing, but of the "trace" in the sense that Plotinus long ago meant it, as a "signature" upon Being of that which is beyond Being, as an Opening within being that reveals that Being itself is "beyond itself." "This *hither side* of identity is not reducible to the *for itself,* where a being recognizes itself in its difference beyond its immediate identity."[9] The "hither side of identity" is Levinas's "otherwise than being." It is the radical troping of even the most allusive ontological determinations toward what Levinas terms a "height." The troping of the language of predication on which even Heidegger's "fundamental ontology" depends drives the "science" of Being in the direction of what Levinas calls "prophetic signification."

The site of Sinai, for Levinas, both grounds and confounds the history of Western philosophy. While in no manner does Western philosophy, according to Levinas, "lose its right to the last word . . . it is not the place of the first meaning of beings, the place where meaning begins."[10] Sinai recurs in philosophy, particularly in the dead zone of ultra-Cartesian subjectivity.[11] This *siting* is the difference in both philosophy and theology that takes the "end" of both philosophy and theology, of which Heidegger spoke, to the top of the mountain, to the height. Sinai speaks for the site from which it is possible to speak ontologically at all.

The "phenomenon" of religion for Derrida, however, is "phallic"; it is projective from its invisible origin. It follows "the law of iterability" inherent in textuality, "or of duplication that can *detach* it from its pure and proper presence." Is such a presence, Derrida asks, "also its *phantasma,* in Greek, its ghost, its spectre, its double or its fetish?"[12] The ghost Derrida embraces is the "spirit" of the text, the infinitely iterable text. The "ghost" of writing is the theological body of Christ, the strange apparition that appears on the endless road to Emmaeus that we know as history. Theology, which forever writes, is incapable of saying *à-Dieu,* as was Derrida himself.[13]

How then does one truly say *à-Dieu*? Levinas himself observes: "As the relationship to the absolutely other—to the nonlimited by the same—to the Infinite—would transcendence not be equivalent to an originary question?"[14] The *à-Dieu* is without doubt the "originary question." The *à-Dieu* is a saying "good-bye" to the "deconstructive" concept of Spirit become letter, of the word made text. But the *à-Dieu* is also a saying "to" the infinite that is the "absolute other," which spectrally haunts all subjective philosophies. The *à-Dieu* is always "outside" the Cartesian circle. In contrast with spectral haunting, it demands embodied presence.

Emmaeus: The "Otherwise" as the Singular Event

It is the sign, as Levinas reminds us, as "being's other," *autrement qu'être*, "otherwise than being." The sense of *autrement*, or "otherwise," frames Levinas's "alternative" to the ontotheological strategy of regaling the "transcendent" in language. "If transcendence has meaning," Levinas says, "it can only signify the fact that the *event of being*, the *esse*, the *essence*, passes over to what is other than being."[15] It corresponds in a sense to Heidegger's "way back" to the garden of Being, to which Heidegger often alludes. But it is also the "way toward," a "going forward" into the temporalization of time that shows us what Being, or human existence as *Dasein*, genuinely *is*. We would compare it to Abraham's trek up the mountain to "the hither side."[16]

Levinas's "hither side" naturally resembles the "unsaid" of Heidegger, but with a critical distinction. "If being and manifestation go together in the said, it is natural that if the saying on the hither side of the said can show itself, it be said already in terms of being."[17] To speak *on the hither side of the said* is to speak at the heights of Sinai. It is to say *à-Dieu*. The alterity of ontology is not so much "the way of faith," though faith is crucial. It is the way toward what the scriptures, as well as both Hegel and Heidegger, term *parousia*.

Jesus's disciples on the road to Emmaeus encountered a "ghost," who happened to be their risen Savior. The *Geist* become their "guest" later at dinner. From the temporal standpoint though this singularity is encountered as spectrality. This spectrality is what has haunted not only the early Derrida but Žižek as well. It is what compelled Derrida to turn from the trace to the specter, to *khōra*, and finally to the "return" (*revenir*) of the religious. Only in the sense of the specter (*revenant*) as the "returning" of what cannot be sited, or *placed*, in the history of the full play of text and discourse can we "give place" to the meaning of the Sign that signifies the very law of meaning that renders the text significant and intelligible, the Sign that is Sinai.

For Žižek, of course, it is the other way around. Such a Sign is a reversal, a reciprocal transposition of the "g" and the "n," *nicht Gott*, Sign as dead Singularity, the corpse at Calvary. In Žižek *parousia* "comes" with the rolling of the stone to close the tomb that harbors the corpse. In Derrida there remains an "uncanny" sense of something unfinished, a Saturday that feels *unheimlich*. Nietzsche's guest pays his last respects. But with Levinas, who has been named not so much a Jew-Greek as a Jew-Christian, the singularity is an "essential" one. In other words, it is what confirms, sustains, promises;

"it gives" (es gibt) what Derrida in his latter "religious" years spoke of as the gift. The gift is what is given from "on high," the singularity of Emmaeus.

The question of the à-Dieu, therefore, pushes us in multiple directions when it comes to religious theory. The event horizon of the sign-singularity can be encoded in not just two, but three parallax dimensions. What lies "over" the horizon can just as well be Žižek's "monstrous" Reality; it could be Derrida's indeterminate, messianic expectancy, which could just as well turn out to be the "theoretical" equivalent of a "waiting for Godot"; or it could be the High Sign itself, the resurrected God. It constitutes, we might say, from the Derridean standpoint, the final differànce. The final differànce is the one Levinas has enunciated in such a way that renders the distinction between theology and philosophy less consequential than we are wont to acknowledge and underscores how the "end of theology" is at the same time an eschatology of each and every sign, consolidating and abrogating at once the metaphysical regulation of equality between signum and res, running back to Augustine.

We find a slightly less cryptic construal of this eschatological differencing stated by Levinas toward the end of Otherwise than Being. The challenge by the infinite, the calling of Presence, Levinas's "one-for-the-other," is "the very signifyingness of signification," Levinas asserts. It is a challenge to philosophy to discover the Sinaic site of "saying." "Philosophy has at its highest, exceptional, hours stated the beyond of being and the one distinct from being, but mainly remained at home in saying being, that is, inwardness to being, the being at home with oneself, of which European history itself has been the conquest and jealous defense."[18] Western thought, therefore, bears "the trace of events carrying another signification." And this signification is one of utter alterity, the final difference of thought that is the ending of the thought of alterity itself.

Such a signification is something even more momentous than the "absolute deterritorialization" that occurs in eschatological thought, so far as Deleuze is concerned. It is the singularity of singularities. It is far more than the transcendent gaining a foothold in the domain of immanence and leaving its semiotic signature in religion, culture, and the arts. Through the philosophy of territoriality that Deleuze has roughed out, theory/thought articulates its siegeworks for the assault on standard "culturalist" methodologies, eventuating in a far more comprehensive, sign-based model of the human sciences that we may christen religious theory.

But if the human sciences are capable after their anticipated rein-vention by Deleuzian semiotics of mapping culture and signification in an entirely new register, they are still not fully equipped to grapple with the inbreaking of the Levinasian *autrement* that defies the de-mands of immanence. The conventional presumption of the work-ings of a transcendent operator within the plane of immanence—the classic theological framing of the issue that cashes out as the famil-iar distinction between "natural" and "revealed" theology, or even as "ontotheology"—cannot solve the problem for either philosophy or religious thought. Can religious theory comprehend not just the plane of immanence, but also the *orthogonal* manifestation of what is wholly "otherwise"? The orthogonal is not merely the vertical, which pertains to transcendence. Orthogonality refers to what comes in "at right angles"—*extradimensionally*—to the plane of immanence. It does not subsist within the plane (i.e., the "transcendental") or apart from the plane ("transcendence").

The implication of Levinas's notion of the infinite, which follow-ing Jewish convention relies on the argot of transcendence ("on high," "Most High"), is however something quite unique. The *autrement* sig-nifies what is both inseparable and separable from the plane. Levinas's infinite resides in the infinity of the "face," where the "otherwise" traces its signature. Levinas, therefore, completely recasts the context in which philosophy and theology alike have adduced the connota-tions of the term "subjectivity."

Modern philosophy, which has evolved from the Cartesian moment of self-referential singularity, has its beginning, its *prius*, in the sub-ject. In Žižek this self-referentiality returns to itself as the barred subject, unlocking an eschatology of pure self-recognition and self-responsibility, the Lacanian correlate to Sartre's "dreadful freedom." But Levinasian subjectivity replaces Lacan's—and Žižek's—*objet petit a*, the surrogate object of desire, with the both "near" and "distant" other, to whom in our subjectivity we are infinitely responsible. *Le sujet est un hôte.* The subject is both "stranger" (*étranger*) and "guest" (*hôte*), to whom we must be "hospitable" (*hospitalier*). Levinas raises this simple precept of ancient Hebraic regard for the foreigner as so-journer to a philosophical principle that *transcends transcendence*, to the idea of the *face-singularity* as the orthogonal expression of what empowers and defines every subject-singularity within the plane of immanence, which is no longer the Hegelian *an-und-für sich* but the Levinasian *an-und-für-einander* ("in and for another"). It is on this account that Derrida's à-dieu to Levinas becomes at the same time his own swan song, a kind of à-dieu to deconstruction itself.

The Levinasian specter, which Derrida finally domesticates, appears in *The Politics of Friendship*, first published in French in 1994. The question of the "political," which deconstruction first raised in *Specters of Marx*, now becomes the question of the ethico-religious. Without mentioning Levinas, Derrida cites Augustine's "turning" to God in the latter's *Confessions* as the cipher of any "model of fraternal friendship." Here we see in Derrida himself the intimation of a *postdeconstructionist theory of infinitization*, a role formerly performed by the *textual* trace. Here we also find something very close to the Levinasian trace of the Infinite within the face. "The *infinitization* qua conversion *in God*, if this can be said of this model of fraternal friendship . . . is not only the friendship of the friend, but the enmity of the enemy. . . . The friend should be loved in God; the enemy must be loved not—to be sure—in God, but *because of* God."[19] Later, Derrida concludes that "there is thought for man only to the extent that it is *thought of the other*." Furthermore, "all thought does not necessarily translate into the logic of the cogito."[20] The Cartesian circle has now come *full circle*, in the Levinasian circuit between subject and Infinite Other, even in Derrida.

Can religious theory, therefore, bid à-dieu to Derridean deconstruction in such a manner that it remains theory and digresses neither as negative theology nor as raw apophanticism that generates its own weird intertextuality, its own semblance of theoretical discovery that is philosophy's one true "empty set"? Would the suggestion that theory can comprehend the orthogonal in tandem with the vertical *and* horizontal make any sort of sense at all? Here we need recourse to a theory that takes us beyond both Derrida and Deleuze—*beyond postmodernism itself*. Derrida's musings on the return of religion and his desert trek from textuality to existential faithfulness amid the relentless annexation of the world by the technological imperative of which Heidegger prophesied raised the prospect that a theory of the religious in a global sense is not only possible but absolutely necessary.

Deleuze's indigenized transcendence under the aegis of the philosophical "concept"—and by implication the metonymy of the nomad as well as the war machine—creates an occasion for the overlay of the historical and the semiolinguistic onto what was traditionally referred to as the "theological" task. The consequence is a theory—or even a "science" in the somewhat elliptical sense we sketched earlier—that genuinely surveys the perimeter of the religious but is not a concealed theology, not even a covert *postmodern* theology. However, theory itself stumbles over an alterity that is neither the transcendent epiphany nor the *apophasis* that lays bare the intrusion of the negative

sign into the intertextual as well as the *contextual*. This alterity
Derrida—once again—addresses as the problem of faith, which is also
Levinas's. But it is faith not as a stance or position, but as a response
to the *mysterium tremendum*. Theory stumbles as Abraham climbs
Mount Moriah.

Secret Responsibility

In *The Gift of Death* Derrida explores the fateful story of Abraham and
Isaac that occurs in Genesis, the narrative of the dutiful response on
the part of the progenitor of the elect to Yahweh to sacrifice his son. In
unraveling the tale Derrida probes the limits not just of any modernist, or Enlightenment philosophy, of rational agency—which forever
lurks in the background of Kierkegaard's "teleological suspension of
the ethical" for the sake of the "religious"—but also of all postmodernist strategies of multiplicity and difference along with their exotic
dance of reservedness and transgression, of sameness and otherness.

Derrida discusses this limit in terms of the "secret of responsibility." The secret of responsibility derives from the strange "gift" con-
ferred on the West, the gift of transcendent monotheism. The secret
cannot be circumscribed within the methodology of any history of religions, or any metahistory of the religious in general. The secret both
compels and disrupts. It is truly "uncanny" in the fashion Nietzsche
meant it. It bids *à-dieu*. "The *à-dieu*, for God or before G and before anything else or any relation to the other, in every other Àdieu.
Every relation to the other would be, before and after anything else,
an Àdieu."[21] The gift of transcendence is at the same time the gift of
death, as the remembrance of Moriah underscores. Early Christianity associated Calvary with Moriah, except that this time the hand
that stayed the slaying of the son of the father of the elect has now
slain his only begotten son. A "transcendent" immanence is what the
"death of God" is all about. But it is a death required in order to attain
Deleuze's "pure immanence," the immanence that allows the stream
of pure figurations unfolding within the horizon of all spatiotemporal
tensors and coordinates.

Still, the death of God does not smooth out the mystery of the
response to what Christian theology casually dubs the "incarnation."
The incarnation may be a kind of Deleuzian concept in which the
fundamental antinomies of Hebraism versus heathenism are forever
played out, and *splayed forth*, within the arena of world history,
even if the paradox can ultimately be reconciled in thought, as in the

Hegelian absolute, or remain a perennial "absurdity" to challenge one to existential resolve and to faith (Kierkegaard). Yet it is more than a concept. As an instant of "absolute" deterritorialization it affirms neither earth nor sky. It is neither transcendent nor transcendental, neither an orthogonal connection between what is immanent and transcendent nor a pure trace of the infinite. As Derrida suggests, it is a concept-sign of a divine "gift," the gift of infinite love. The "gift of infinite love comes from someone and is addressed to someone; responsibility demands irreplaceable singularity."[22]

Infinite love, according to Derrida, entails "religious" responsibility, because it is the sine qua non according to which responsibility is possible. Responsibility is possible "on the condition that the Good no longer be a transcendent objective, a relation between objective things, but the relation to the other, a response to the other."[23] But the "other" to which one responds in a "responsible" fashion is not posited, as the other was for German idealism and in large measure for much of postmodern philosophy, in terms of nonsubjectivity or nonselfsameness. One responds to the voice before Moriah, to the *mysterium tremendum*, "a frightful mystery, a secret to make you tremble."[24] The gift of infinite love is the secret, "the dissymmetry that exists between the divine regard that sees me,"[25] yet who has given us assurance of his love through incarnation. But the incarnation takes place for "secret" reasons. Yahweh did not give reasons to Abraham for his command to slay Isaac, nor did God give reasons, or a rationale, for sending his son to the cross. There is no teleology, as opposed to ethical deliberation, in God's decisions. There is only his "ultimate plan" for creation, his *eschatology*.

The Problem of the Vocative

Levinas and Derrida, who are both Jews and in varying proportions "Jew-Greeks," call attention to the conundrum that a thoroughly Gallic and European thinker like Deleuze cannot countenance or express—the essential problem of the transcendent, *paraenetic voice that summons and commands*, as contrasted with the question of Greek and "globo-Latin" ontology, the question of Being and the unity—or "univocity"—of all attributes, modes, and predications, that comes to be worked out as the pure immanentism of Spinoza, the "subjecticity" of a Descartes, or even the "pure immanence" of a Deleuze. Can there be such a thing as the *philosophical vocative* (a "grammar" of address as compared with the logic of predication) that is impervious to both ontology and phenomenology, that is *un-Greek*, or at maximum authentically "Jew-Greek," without becoming overtly pietistic or "theological"?

After Heidegger we know that the vocative presents its own unique perplexity. Even the later Heidegger was compelled to address the problem of the vocative by switching from the metaphors of "world" and "horizon" to "voice" and "call"—the "poetic" phrasings of so much of his work after the Second World War. Heidegger could only accommodate the ontological to the vocative by making philosophy oracular and using a putatively nontheological discourse that has always sounded irremediably theological. The Levinasian "solution" was to translate the mystery of the vocative into the enigma of the "face." The face bears the "trace" of the most Holy and unnamable and summons us to "ethical" responsibility. But, as Jewish as he was, even Levinas had no way of coping "phenomenologically" with the transcendent voice. The face makes us responsible because it is the "other" that transports us toward the "otherwise," the pure ulteriority, the absolute deterritorialization, that evokes the *mysterium tremendum*. Yet conceptually the face is silent, and Levinas remained a philosopher. As Derrida observes, "There are no final secrets for philosophy."[26]

It is not exactly accidental that Derrida "comes to faith" through Kierkegaard, insofar as the former's reading of *Fear and Trembling* as the insoluble aporia of the relationship between gift and command—salvation and ethical responsibility—is quite congruent with his lifelong project of dispossessing the immediacy of texts—commonly called "deconstruction"—and demonstrating where their apparent continuity generates a more full-orbed sense of the abyss intercalated between their surface textures. *Fear and Trembling* and the *Gift of Death* are both troubling meditations on a sacred text that confounds the "civilized." There is a profounder understanding of "faith" in Derrida's *The Gift of Death* than in *Faith and Knowledge*. The reason is that Derrida is wrestling neither with the ethical nor with the mystical, but with the vocative. After wrestling all night with the angel of the vocative, Derrida in his essay "Khōra" is close to having a new name.

"But since Levinas also wants to distinguish between the infinite alterity of God and the 'same' infinite alterity of every human, or of the other in general, then he cannot simply be said to be saying something different from Kierkegaard," Derrida writes. "Levinas is no longer able to distinguish between the infinite alterity of God and that of every human. His ethics is already a religious one."[27] Derrida proposes "linking alterity to singularity" as the secret that "hides and reveals itself" in language.

The secret, however, turns out not to be "religious," as it is for Levinas, but "political," the first principle of democracy, the nonexchangeability even in a capitalist order of every singular personality. This singularity is Derrida's "infinite alterity," and it is founded on the "gift" of infinite love that does not have to be paid back. The concept of singularity, as Derrida understands it, takes root with the pagan experience of ecstasy, an idea that is tacit in Nietzsche's *Birth of Tragedy*, where his later thoughts of "overman," "overcoming," and the transvaluation of the divine command as self-command and becoming a "creator" begin to percolate. Derrida poses a tempting and extremely valid question that has been advanced by scholars in different guises for generations: to what extent is "Christian" salvation a reenactment with a different outcome on the celestial plane of Abraham's response to God's vocative at Moriah and to what extent is it a strange sort of Greek thaumaturgy?

As a Jew, Derrida would hope for the former. But he also realizes that a politics of singularity must in the final analysis be based on a faith contingent on concealment from the outside of our private spiritual interiority. That realization frames the distinction between simple, anarchical "individualism" and an "ethics" of responsibility. An ethics of responsibility stems from the formation of moral conscience that, as even Kant the child of the Enlightenment intuited, cannot exist without a God to whom the self is accountable. For Derrida, the question of the *tout autre* is the issue of "to whom" (rather than to "what" in teleological or eudaimonistic morality) we are accountable. "Then we might say: God is the name of the possibility I have of keeping a secret that is visible from the interior but not from the exterior."[28]

But such a move—even if his earlier critique of Levinas goes to the heart of what the latter conceived as alterity—compromises both Kierkegaard and the question of the *mysterium* and demonstrates that Derrida, even as he moved into the last decade of his life, was at heart a secular thinker. Derrida makes many of the same gestures Kant actually was forced to make in his post-critical period, particularly in the *Opus Postumum,* surrendering the entire architectonic of "pure practical reason" to a proto-Feuerbachian acknowledgment that the word God is really a name for moral conscience.[29] The inscription of pure interiority as a philosophical codex that deciphers the *mysterium tremendum* fails to analyze the semiological power of the vocative, the Infinite through the Other that *calls us to responsibility* (which Derrida in *The Gift of Death* conveniently ignores).

At the very end of his book Derrida seems to fall back (although one never figures out exactly where Derrida is going with his exposition of crucial texts) on Nietzsche's interpretation of Christian interiority as a "self-destruction of justice by means of grace." The gift of death in the divine self-sacrifice is the forgiveness of all indebtedness, which in turn abolishes all circuits of exchange, or recompense (i.e., "justice"). The gift of death is inescapably inward, as Kierkegaard emphasized. It is this lack of visibility, its inaccessibility to every gaze except one's own, that makes it problematic and makes it ethically meaningful and *aesthetically inconsequential.* Responsibility lacks a gaze and in its most extreme manifestation appears absurd, which is why faith as the extension of responsibility beyond what is prudent and calculable walks not "by sight."

How does religious theory apprehend the "cryptic" in Derrida's sense? As we have already argued, there is more in Levinas than Derrida will admit, just as there was always far more in Heidegger than the early Derrida would concede with his critique of "logocentrism." The signification of the voice—the power of the *vocative* as a discursively transgressive semiosis, as its own special vehicle for a non-predicative presencing—provides the occasion for a radical and still unreflective alterity in the domain of thought that is more appropriate to Hebraism than to Hellenism. Derrida takes what is implicit in Levinas, perhaps because it did not need to be explicated at all for a rabbinic thinker, and makes it the key to his exegesis of the "secret." The cryptic character of the face is also the secret to an alterity that can only become evident *after postmodernism.* The "secret" of postmodernism itself is the erasure, the space, the *khōra*, the lesion in the carefully stitched web of both formal and natural language that discloses the negative not as a logical sign, operator, but as the impossibility of semantic closure. What remains *sur erature* also remains semiotically indefinite, the alterity of endless difference.

The postmodern secret is less a secret than the premise of inescapable fallibility, or incompleteness. Quentin Meillassoux has attacked the gradual *secretization* of this secret in all modern philosophy since Kant with his attempts to set forth a new kind of realism—mistakenly christened by its admirers a "speculative realism"—that opposes to this secretization, or dogmatic finitization, of thought what he calls "ancestrality," or being that "is" apart from its givenness.[30] But Levinas's secret, the secret of the face, is something that neither the modern philosophy of finitude—what Meillassoux terms "correlationism"—nor "speculative realism" can account for, since both "speculative realism" and correlationism are joined at the hip with the ontology of predication. The secret of the face is, by extension, the secret of the voice; it is a vectoring of signification that does not belong to any logic, onto-logic, or even a *semantics.* Nor does it follow the contemporary misreading of Kant that he is an advocate of "divine command theory," the view that moral values have their source of valuation in the nature of God, and that the incommensurability of this divine nature with finite experience makes them appear as injunctions of a personal Deity.

The secret of the face *commends* rather than commands. The sense of ethical obligation is a responsiveness to this commendation. The commendation, in turn, can only be deciphered as a *pure semiotics* of the trace of the holy in the face of the other.[31] Because the face fields the voice, it has both an exteriority and an interiority. Indeed, God has a "face" in the Jewish sense because he is capable of double vectoring. The Hebrew word for "face" (French *visage*) from which Levinas derives his philosophical concept is *panim,* which exhibits a fruitful kind of connotative duplicity. The word means both the physical look, or expression, and personal inwardness, an undisclosable privacy. The voice emanates from the physiognomy, but its intentionality is kept within the sphere of interiority.

But can there be a "theory" of the voice? And is a theory of the voice contained within the *theory of religion*? If one starts from the modern theological position, particularly neo-orthodoxy and its subsequent permutations, the vocative as the basis of faith is an *existential peremptory* that cancels out the "religious," which can be considered strictly indicative or statutory. But this distinction has no real application if by theory we mean—as we have meant it all along—an inquiry into the modes, aggregates, and intricacies of textual or quasi-textual signification that are commonly termed "religious." The signification of the religious does not depend on the reduction of the ethical to the ontological, as in divine command theory, nor on its degradation into the transitory negative "spacing" of language and textuality, as in any deconstructive theology or a-theology. The signification of the religious belongs to the orthogonal relationship between the addressed, and addressing, "subject" of all intersubjective pairings and the boundless signifying praxis and generativity of such relationships. Derrida's divine "gift" does not derive from the Heideggerian *es gibt*—"it gives" or "there is"—of ontology, but from what Deleuze would call a certain "donation of sense" arising out of

the orthogonal "cutting across" of the plane of pure subjective immanence in the event of divine confrontation and address. What "gives"
is the singularity of address.

The Levinasian "Otherwise"

For Levinas, the Being of beings which Heidegger views as the transcendence of Western predicative logic remains inseparable from the
being of Cartesian self-referentiality. But any possible exit from the
subjectivist morass does not lie in the deconstruction of substantivist
formalities. The deconstruction of both subjectivism and substantiv-
ism is an endless loop that can never ultimately be abrogated. *The end
of philosophy and theology is not a more "fundamental" ontology,
but radical alterity.* And alterity can only be pronounced when one
comes up, according to Levinas, against the presence of the infinite,
which annihilates presence in the ontological sense. It is the moment
Levinas calls *autrement,* the "otherwise" that is other than Being.

This horizon of the "otherwise" can be traced in Descartes himself, Levinas proposes. Cartesianism deconstructs itself insofar as
with Descartes the *I that thinks* "maintains a relationship with the
infinite."[32] Therefore, if we are to rethink modernism, as we have
already proposed, we will indeed have also to rethink postmodernism itself by rethinking the ontology of the Cartesian *subjectum.*
How? The problem was already thought—insufficiently—by both
Descartes and Husserl. At the end of the third meditation Descartes
pondered over the "production" of the notion of an infinite Deity.
The puzzlement over the idea derives from the paradoxical character of what nineteenth-century theology would have termed "God
consciousness."

As Levinas affirms, "The idea of infinity is exceptional in that its
ideatum surpasses the idea. In it the distance between idea and ideatum is not equivalent to the distance that separates a mental act from
its object in its representations."[33] Furthermore, the idea of infinity
"has been put into us. It is not a reminiscence." It is out of this previously unreflective Cartesian aporia that Levinas offers a philosophical justification for the first time in Western thought of a "personal"
God. But Levinas reverses the chain of inference normally implicated
in any "personalistic" theism. The *subjectum* is a consequence of
the radical experience of alterity. "God is the other." Furthermore,
the site for this pure moment of generative signification that the encounter with otherness provides can be found in the very Cartesian
rumination on self-presence.

Such a "total" alterity is the precondition for the freedom of the ego. The reciprocity between the infinity of God as *totaliter aliter* and what Kant would later term the "constitutive" role of the *cogito* forces us to rethink the very essence of thinking itself. The "I think" must think of necessity not only a world but an infinity that reveals itself in the world through a unique mode of signification—the infinite qua "finite" personality, the "face."

Theology and the Impenetrability of the Face

The face is "signifying" presentation independent of representation, beyond the nexus of logical and syntactical properties that makes "theological" talk in the traditional sense possible. Theology belongs to the grammar of the third person. But the face demands the dialogical, eluding all possibility of predication. It is "otherwise" than what can be formulated in ontological language. Its relationship to the sentence remains mysterious, because it does not consist in a determination. It can only be addressed, its "grammar" thoroughly confused by the *orthogonality of the second person.* The face cannot be comprehended; it requires instead an *invocation.*

The unrealized genius of Levinas lies in this breakthrough, which he himself never fully expounded. It is the dialogical, not deconstruction, that drives us beyond ontotheology. Deconstruction in the final summation belongs still within the history of ontotheology, because it is captivated by the rondo of presence and representation, of the eidetic and the mimetic, which it renames presence and "absence," or text and its dissemination. Theological thinking can never go to the place within discourse where the other as Infinite Other intrudes and intersects. This denial of access has nothing to do with the "ineffability" of otherness qua otherness. It has to do with the *strange semiology* of the second person. The semiotic shift between first and third is thoroughly "natural," so far as the grammar of attribution is concerned.

The Derridean *supplément,* which connotes a kind of "parapresence" within the space of representation, becomes *suppliant.* This relationship of "suppliance" appears as a null factor, an "erasure," but also as a revectoring of the force of signification within predication. Just as a cube appears as a square, a square as a line, and a line as a point, if we strip away progressively the dimensions of geometry, so the infinite appears as the other, the other as a "not I," and the "not I" as a mere *negative sign,* if we move from the mode of address to the formality of logic. God is *Nichts,* not because *nothing of God can be spoken*, but because God is the One not *of* but *to* whom we speak. God is signified "strangely" as the *à* of *à-dieu*.

The Levinasian *autre* along with its semiotic *autrement* entails a "transcendence" that is entirely different from the differentialism of the sign. The differend of the sign emerges from the play of syntactical collations that constitute propositional discourse. The difference of *engaged alterity* stems from the disruption of syntax with the act of address. Kierkegaard's "infinite qualitative difference," which implies the absolute alterity of the God-human or eternity-time disjunction, has something of this tenor.

The difference between the other of Hegel and that of Levinas is the difference between the declarative and the prophetic. The prophetic discloses an "exteriority" which "does not become simply the content of interiority." It is the *vox auditu*. It is sustained by the "paradoxical" relationship between signification and communication, between saying and conversation, between the self-mediation of the "speculative sentence" and "the explosion of the 'more in the less' that Descartes called the idea of the Infinite."[34]

We must ask ourselves what would be the meaning, plainly and simply, of a theology that is "otherwise than" theology? What is otherwise than theology—what is not simply the "end of theology"— would be a "paratheology" in its own right. Is it the nomenclature we would give to the investigation of the religious? Would a "hetero-theology" be the expression we use for the consideration of theology from the standpoint of the "heights" of radical alterity?

The "Archimedean point" for modern philosophy that Descartes supposedly uncovered in the certainty of the *cogito* thus disappears from our gaze. The uncertainty and instability of postmodernity do not arise from a critique of Cartesianism—standard postmodernism is more Cartesian than it fancies itself—but from a researching of the very standpoint from which both modernism and postmodernism proceed. The dialectical division in Descartes, and later on in the critical philosophy and in phenomenology, between the *je suis* and the *il y a*, which at the same time frames the agenda for modernist thought culminating in Heidegger, is put out of commission by the very catastrophe of thinking the "idea of God," which the third meditation precipitates. It is not the *cogito*, but the infinite, which forces the dialectical separation.[35]

Theology and philosophy, therefore, as historically constituted, have always been nonnegotiable, not so much as a result of the opposition between "reason "and "revelation" as because of the *two-foldness* of speech. Philosophy says "it is." Theology, as we find for instance in the *Confessions* of Saint Augustine, originally spoke the words "thou art." The *thou art* of the *Confessions* is drawn from the *duplicity of the voice.* "Let me know you, for you are the God who knows me; *let me recognize you as you have recognized me.*"[36]

The same aporia manifests itself in Calvin's famous *duplex cognitio Dei*—the "double knowledge of God"—a method of argumentation that derives from Augustine. Knowledge of God as infinite power and presence necessitates a self-knowledge that reveals one's own radical finitude and incommensurability with the divine. Thus the more the supplicant comes to know a truly holy God, the more the "wretchedness" (in Calvin's terms) of the human creature becomes apparent, and vice versa. If God cannot be thought, still it is possible to have a "relationship" to him, and that relationship is one of vocative address and responsiveness. The signifying link is intersubjective, not conceptual. It is what has been known for ages as faith. Faith must always be instantiated in the vocative mode.

The Grammar of Address

There is an essential "theoretical" issue when one considers the grammar of address—when one simply says *you*. But the problem does not need to be mystified in order to be confronted. The grammar of address is the grammar of *fidelity*, of "trothfulness" (whence the word "truthful"), which in turn boils down to the parlance of first- and second-person discursivity, of promise making and promise keeping, of such performatives as willing, obeying, desiring, and answering. The theory of address is the theory, regarded pragmatically and productively, of the *re-ligio*, the theory of the bonding of the finite agent to a transfinite velleity, to "others" in service and communion and to a *tout autre* in meditation, reverence, and worship.

Levinas anticipates this performative strategy in the section entitled "Beyond the Face" in *Totality and Infinity.* "My being is produced in producing itself before the others in discourse; it is what it reveals of itself to the others, but while participating in, attending, its revelation. I am *in truth* by being produced in history under the judgment it bears upon me, but under the judgment that it bears upon me in my presence—that is, while letting me speak."[37] This condition of *in-truthfulness* while in the vast historical, evolving latticeworks of intersubjective communication at the social and political levels and of dialogical discussion in more intimate settings establishes what is uniquely religious. "In my religious being I am *in truth*."[38]

For Levinas, the truthfulness of religious being is grounded in the struggle against violence, tyranny, alienation, and every constraint upon recognizing the "epiphany of the Other." This struggle arises from the unquenchable desire to meet one who desires us, who desires us even more than we desire, and demands a response of speaking intimately and proclaiming *thou art*. Signification as a linguistic project confirms human subjectivity and the very possibility of performance and response. Without *responsibility* there can be neither an act of signification nor a "semiotic" approach to the theory of meaning and significance.

Levinas thus loops us back to a reappraisal of Derrida's religious "secret." Religion is the secret of language and signification only because it is the secret of desire, the secret that discloses language not as an arabesque of predications but as a multidimensional process of intersubjective venturings as well as interpersonal trust-binding and mutual promissory obligations. The face, as readers of Levinas well know, consists in the space where infinite alterity intersects the realm of existents. This intersection spins the logic of predication on its axis and repositions subjects and objects, or things and their properties, as the meeting on the interpersonal plane of reciprocal addressees. *The interlocutory supersedes the semantic as well as the syntactical.*

Levinas's critique of Western philosophy as "ontological imperialism" is founded on a protest against the steel-fisted sovereignty of the inferential relation, forever taking precedence in philosophy over the vocative relation. But just as in language there are different types of relationships, so it is also the case with ethics as "first philosophy." Even Lacanian psychoanalysis implies this reading. The analyst teaches the analysand to break out of his or her "Cartesian" monologue and bring to a halt the endless metaphysical allocation of the familiar semantic segments of one's own constructed discourse. "Analysis can have as its goal only the advent of true speech and the subject's realization of his history in its relation to a future."[39] In this regard Lacan agrees with Levinas that "'we' is not the plural of 'I.'"[40]

Both Lacan and Levinas understand linguistics as merely the initial set of circumstances for a *transversal semiotics* that registers as a theory of signification by shattering the representational clarity of the *cogito* and sketching a nexus of speech-moments that depend on the reciprocal alterity of interlocutors. For Lacan this clarity is disrupted through the methodology of transference employed by the analyst. For Levinas it is the presence, transformed into the thought, of an infinite God. *We-ness* is a roaring chasm which the logic of propositional truth cannot span. *We-ness* is the site for a summons from the *tout autre* and elicits responsibility to the other. Both speech and responsibility arise out of the intermeshing and clashing of differing natural loves and desires that at last are synchronized with each other.

The insight that *signification becomes vocation* in the presence of the other—in the epicalic transversal—depends on an equal recognition that the concept of "alterity" in postmodernism is landlocked by the linear predicative positioning of all sign-complexes and correlations inherent in our legacy of ontotheology, in our "white mythology." Postmodernism has reveled for decades now in its "conquest," its *Überwindung*, of metaphysical communication. But it has failed to break the spell of ontology as a whole and move into the era.

Why is postmodernism incapable of breaking through? Why does it slowly sink in the quicksand of a "flat earth" ontology, even when that ontology is subtly reversed in the religious realm as a negative ontology or an "apophatic theology." Even Nietzsche's call to be faithful to the earth *cannot break the "being barrier" that has haunted Western philosophy since the pre-Socratics.* Even Levinas himself, who has offered us a glimpse of the epicalic transversal in the *autrement*, does not break through. The difficult notion of illeity—the vanishing tangent that bespeaks infinity in the recognition of the other as "third person"—provides us only with an opening that is inaccessible because of our lack of a multidimensional imagination.

Deleuze and the Breaking of the Predication Barrier

The thinker who has come the closest to breaking this barrier, of course, is Deleuze. With his postulate of "pure immanence" Deleuze presses ontology toward its absolute limits. "We must think of philosophy as a force," Deleuze writes in his extended musings late in life concerning Nietzsche and the overman en route to thinking what it might mean to be a "Dionysian philosopher."[41] Just as Nietzsche worked out a new way of thinking aphoristically and polemically, Deleuze envisions a "new image of thought," a theory of thought, or a thinking through of thought, for the future that is *postmodern* to the extent that it is postpredicative and postanalytical.

Like Nietzsche, Deleuze sees what we tend to call the "postmodern condition" as infected with the nihilism of a decadent thought, particularly in its obsession with the negative spaces of the textual and the grammatical. Like Nietzsche, Deleuze seeks the fullness of affirmation in a new epoch of thinking that reconfirms the principle of univocity, which was originally in the fourteenth century the sledge to break through the battlements of neo-Platonism, Aristotelianism, a nd Scholasticism. Now it is the battering ram against the remnants of postmodern nihilism. Univocity is a metonym for the *affirmational* force that is philosophy. Univocity abolishes philosophy's categorical distinction between the One and the Many, or even between Same and Other, between identity and difference, between existent and alterity.

Univocity is the name for the coliseum in which multiplicity puts on a semiotic circus where the games never cease. "What is affirmed is the One of multiplicity, the Being of becoming."[42] Just as Deleuze drew his inspiration from Scotus and Nietzsche in setting forth the rule of univocity, he also relied heavily on Spinoza. In his voluminous work *Expressionism in Philosophy* Deleuze explores the "underlying theory" of univocity that dominates Spinoza's work. The theory of univocity, we shall see, is the quintessential theory of the postmodern, inasmuch as it provides a classical philosophical precedent for "imaging" the differential diffusion, or "dissemination" (Derrida's terminology), of ontological properties and of the instances of logical predication throughout the galaxy of signification.

In Spinoza the theory of univocity deconstitutes all metaphysical architectures by denying that language about God can ever be of an "equivocal" or "analogical" nature. God is "expressed" through his attributes. "The attributes are, according to Spinoza, univocal forms of being which do not change their nature in changing their 'subject.'" They are also "infinite forms of being, unlimited, ultimate, irreducible formal reasons." Furthermore, "attributes are words expressing unlimited qualities; these qualities are as it were involved in the limits of the finite."[43]

Spinoza's philosophy of immanence, according to Deleuze, is a reaction against the Cartesian theory of "eminence," which assigns different degrees of reality to things in proportion to their transcendent quality. Descartes's positing of God's eminent reality, as we know from the *Meditations*, is the second "Archimedean point" by which he establishes the existence of God, which in turn reestablishes the certainty of the *cogito*. But an eminent God is also a transcendent God of which being or reality can only be predicated in a nonequivocal, or misleading, sense.

What does Being "say," therefore, when it comes to theory? Deleuze's writings are both an effort to express "life" in Nietzsche's phrasing *and* to generate an immanent semiotics that takes us beyond ontology and onto a "plane" of discourse that gives unfettered expression to the multiple and the temporal. *The theory of univocity is the key to this immanent semiotics.* In *The Logic of Sense* Deleuze makes this project quite apparent. "Philosophy merges with ontology, but ontology merges with the univocity of Being (analogy has always been a theological vision, not a philosophical one, adapted to the forms of God, the world, and the self)."[44]

The Vocative Transgression: Toward an Orthogonal Semiotics

But the "voice" of Being—even if we are to follow either Heidegger's oracular pronouncements or Deleuze's stripping down of all philosophy into an *ultra-postmodernism* fusing ontology with a neo-Peircian perfection of sign theory—is not the same as the vocative transgression of both the onto-theological and the onto-philosophical. Only a *semiotics of the vocative* with an appropriate theoretical framing can in the last analysis make intelligible what comes into play after postmodernism. In a semiotics of the vocative it is not Being that gives "voice," *but the voice that makes "Being" present.* It is our white mythology alone that is responsible for this *tromp de langue* that we know as ontology and privileges it over any other mode of signification.

But how do we make sense out of the voice, particularly the theological signification that is familiar to us as the "divine" voice? Does the sensation of voice have its own "logic" in Deleuze's manner of speaking? Could a mapping of the vocative from the standpoint of religious theory be akin to a radically new "image" of thought—or even the "sound" of thought—that Deleuze adumbrates? Can there be a radical or essential "phonology" that has nothing to do with the simple immediacy of reference in speech (Ferdinand de Saussure's *parole*) that the early Derrida criticized as a source of confusion and *mis-representation* in the history of Western thought and the philosophy of language, a phonology that has less to do with the spoken word per se and much more to do with the trajectories of signification that intersect all two-way conversations as well as those of multiple interlocutors? Do all these trajectories add up to a new "logic of sense" that is more than dialectical, or even simply dialogical (although it is the moment of dialogue that is the paradigmatic instance from which all these trajectories emanate)? Can we make any sense out of such a phonology without a conjugate grammatology, a new theory of textual signification to complement the theory of the vocative sign?

If the *theos* in all religion—and not just the God of the monotheistic religions—is capable of speaking, which popular traditions as well as the magisterial ones take in large measure for granted, then why have we not broached the problem of how the provenance and character of that voice are a compelling task for theory, and not simply a side issue? It is, after all, the "voice" that bears the *revelatory* power of that religion. We are accustomed to asking what, if anything, is actually revealed, but dare we wonder how such a "revelation" is communicated and takes hold?

Levinas offers us some guidance not so much in his philosophical as in his "religious" writings. In his essay entitled "Revelation in the Jewish Tradition," Levinas poses the question of the "content" of what is revealed by compassing the span of exegesis of that content from Sinai down through the formation of the Talmud. He asks: how is the Mosaic revelation, which "is alleged to be unusual, extraordinary, linking the world in which we live to what would no longer be of this world," indeed "thinkable"?[45] What would be the model, or theory? Levinas argues that there is a "structure" to the revealed, a structure that embraces both the primal event and the long Jewish tradition of exegesis and commentary. It is important, Levinas notes, that revelation is profiled in the Jewish context as "commandment" (*mitzvah*).

Levinas therefore echoes Derrida's proposal concerning the uniqueness of revealed language, not as an exchange of signs, but as an infinite gift. Yet he does not associate it with "death," as does Derrida, the death that is an ingredient in the sacrificial motif and the *nihil* that seems obvious to the observer without faith who cannot grasp why God requires mutilation, or murder. For Levinas, and for Jews (though not for Saint Paul), the commandment does not bring death, but gives life.

The commandment, however, gives life because it is not capable of "plain meaning." It involves a polysemy, a fathomless surplus of significations, still to be worked through and hammered into form. Revelatory words in the Hebraic language "co-exist rather than being co-ordinated or subordinated with and to one another, contrary to what is predominant in the languages that are said to be developed or functional." They are not logically covalent, but semiotically dense and *intensive* in their own right. They are Deleuzian singularities that thunder "from the mountain." Truth does not arise anonymously or idiosyncratically in history, the revelation that comes to the "inspired" or prophetic recipient and is then accepted, or later "understood." The Word reveals, *but the Spirit interprets.*

But how does this "revealing" make its initial impact as vocative or command? Revelation is not quintessentially an act of cognition; it is correlative with the "turning" of the whole person to God in an act of submission. According to Levinas, "Jewish revelation is based on prescription," on command. The "content" of this revelation is not some kind of philosophical datum that is preserved in its logical aseity but a shifting correlation between text and reader, and ultimately between Voice and voice, the vocative and the responsive. It is the vocative nature of Jewish revelation that makes the oral tradition of the rabbis so critical. The vocative that Abraham first hears at Ur becomes both the Great Commandment and Jesus's Great Commission, but it is still our "calling" as religious personalities, as respondents to the Other who calls. The vocative is not metaphysically intelligible, despite two thousand years of Christian ontotheology. *When one says "thou art," one says something entirely different from "it is."* The Torah is irremediably "given" and given in a way that Being is not given (Heidegger's *es gibt*).

But what is "given" through the voice? The question of the givenness of the voice is haunted by ontological presuppositions that distort the radical depth of the question itself. A semiotics of voice must indeed be orthogonal to any deconstructionist semiotics that exposes the numberless lesions and spaces in the raddle of grammatical operations. An orthogonal semiotics would add a vectorial dimension to the play of signs, where direction is just as crucial as intensity. It would challenge the *formalization and logicization* of the canons of theory.

Buddhism as Negative Science

But ironically the importance of the vocative, not so much as the "call" but as something akin to Levinas's face-to-face, can also be found in the philosophy of the East. If there is any limit to testing any "theory" of the religious, it is Buddhism. Buddhism has generally been construed as a pure non-religion in the technical sense, or the expressive culture of the negative, a living "a-theology." If religious theory in some sense constitutes a "science of the negative," then the Buddhist way of both thinking and being would come close to such a science. It would be theory and practice joined in marriage with each other. In fact, since the widespread adoption of deconstructionist language and method in American religious thought, the insight that the "negative theology" of Derrida is intimately related to Buddhist philosophy, particularly Madhyamika, has been widely acknowledged.[46] Deconstructionism as the theory of the de-centered and de-negated text brings to light the same hidden "Khōric" character of all representationalist discourse in the same way that Nagarjuna brought against *nyaya*, or Buddhist logic, the argument that all forms are constituted as emptiness (*sunyata*).

But the negative space of the text, the negation of the propositional posit contained in the Hegelian dialectic, and the negation of self-same subjectivity that the face-to-face precipitates are not the *deep negative* that Buddhism ultimately discloses and that can never be assimilated to any kind of negative "theology." As we have seen, a negative theology remains above all a theology. The deep negative in Buddhism has been analyzed structurally as well as philosophically by Keiji Nishitani in his well-known book *Religion and Nothingness,* which explores the general problem of the "religious" and the manner in which it can be conceptually adduced from the doctrine of emptiness. Paradoxically, the "a-theistic" rigor of Buddhist meditation and philosophical analysis, according to Nishitani, arises from the same source as the intuition of the "personal" God in Hebraic thought which becomes the staple of Western theism. Nishitani's approach is very subtle, if not at times convoluted, and depends heavily on the "Dasein analytic" of Heidegger's *Being and Time.* But it makes apparent what is at stake in a theory of religion that comprehends the negative in this distinctly "personal" sense which, according to Nishitani, is grounded in the "the relationship between God and man."

For Nishitani, to be religious is to be "personally in the world." But is not Buddhism an "impersonal" avenue of salvation entailing the intuition of the "not-self" (*anatta*) as well as the impermanence of all forms and entities, including the phenomenon of individual consciousness? Self is not equivalent to person, however, Nishitani argues. The personal is disclosed in the vision of nihility beyond the human essence. Personhood is "an appearance with nothing at all behind it to make an appearance. Person is constituted at one with absolute nothingness as that in which absolute nothingness becomes manifest. It is actualized as a 'Form of non-Form.'"[47] In a curious fashion Nishitani deploys the Buddhist rhetoric of "nothingness" in the same register in which Levinas's Hebraism characterizes the infinity behind the face. "In this sense we can understand person as persona—the 'face' that the actor puts on to indicate the role he is to play on stage—but only as the *persona* of absolute nothingness."[48] Being is opposed to nothingness not at an ontological level so much as on an "existential" plane of relationality. Ontology is the grim adversary of religion, inasmuch as it substantializes—or we would say *propositionalizes*—the meontic source of the faith relationship that is expressed neither as dialectics nor as negative theology. Nishitani dubs this *me-ontic* source a "nothingness that is living," that engenders the faith personality and a thoroughly responsive personhood.

Nishitani further describes this meontic source of the living faith relation, or the religious personality, much as Kierkegaard understands the relationship between despair and the religious moment in *The Sickness unto Death*. The nihility behind all postures at selfhood is the "sickness" that can only be cured by the "leap" undertaken by the knight of faith. Nothingness—or *sunyata*—is the "home-ground" of religion, according to Nishitani; it is the fecundating abyss from which springs the religious gesture that is counted as "absurd" in Christianity (Kierkegaard) and paradoxical or "non-sensical" in Buddhism. For in the moment of faith, the existential relationship between finitude and its negation which constitutes "personality" is at the same time the axis of relationship that sustains everything that is. "All things that are in the world are linked together, one way or the other. Not a single thing comes into being without some relationship to every other thing." For "to say *that a thing is not itself* means that, while continuing to be itself, it is in the home-ground of everything else. . . . *That a thing is itself* means that all other things, while continuing to be themselves, are in the home-ground of that thing; that precisely when a thing is on its own home-ground, everything else is there too."[49]

Here Nishitani sounds a little like Heidegger with his conception of Being as *physis,* or the emergence of all that is from a matrix of concealment. It also has the ring of Deleuze's semiotics of the univocal. But Nishitani stresses the full "relationality" of that which emerges from concealment. The Buddhist *sunyata* is a "field of force" whereby "the force of the world makes itself manifest in the force of each and everything in the world."[50] It is an "immanent" force in Deleuze's sense, but its immanence is designated not by the force of difference but by the force of relationality. It produces singularities only to the extent that these singularities manifest as an infinite plenitude of relations that are irreducible to any patterns of logical, or grammatical, consistency—"universals" in the Aristotelian vein—as well as to the kind of null set that Badiou calls the "event." Religiosity is the production of these pure singularities, or positivities, that are eminently *non-deconstructable.* A theory of religion, which is thereby freed of any so-called Western bias, would lay the groundwork for how we can speak, if only "poetically," of these peculiar positivities, which appear "negative" only from the metaphysical, or predicative, standpoint. The "deep negative" found in both "monotheistic" and the "atheistic" expressions of religiosity therefore can be equally envisioned as the generative force behind these positivities. It is what is commonly called "divinity." Divinity exists because the self exists in a negative relationship to itself, as Kierkegaard discerned, and this negative relationship is the "personal" relation that is termed "faith" in Judeo-Christianity and "enlightenment" or "liberation" in the broader Eastern purview.

Toward a "Grammatology" of Address

The problem of "metaphysics" is not, as Derrida understood, "phonologocentrism." The problem of metaphysics is the incapacity of the "logical" per se to signify in the most supple and comprehensive sense. Neither texts nor the spoken word can do that. The figurating *figura* is what "grounds" signification, which is far less a logical ground than Nishitani's "figurative" notion of the "home-ground." But this figurative "home-ground" is not found simply in Buddhism's own "antidialectic." It occurs throughout the entire "paralogical" spectrum, the "negative territory" that is *the deterritorialized and antitheological space of signification known as the "religious."*

For want of better nomenclature, we may follow Deleuze and dub this activation of the generative figura *expressive signification.* The "religious" is the expressive signification in countless attributes and modes of the figurative, or virtual, webwork of relationalities that serves as the "home-ground" of all that is perceptible or knowable. The religious can be distinguished from the aesthetic primarily in the measure that it expresses at a figurative level the unity of these relationalities as opposed to certain distinct segments or connections. Art enables us to "see" something special and unique insofar as it offers a close-up encounter with a particular swatch of territory among these infinite relationalities. Art in this sense is always *local.* Religion, however, is always global, inasmuch as it draws the web together into a potent, but immediate, signifying complexity. Religious theory articulates this complexity through whatever discursive tools are available.

The semiotic baseline for a theory of religion, as we have seen, can be found in Deleuze's theme of expressivity. "The originality of the concept of expression shows itself here: essence, insofar as it has existence, has no existence outside the attribute to which it is expressed."[51] The notion of the "essence," of course, harks all the way back to Plato and is integrally associated with the metaphysics of universals and the propositional calculus that predicates, or gives specificity to, the abstract form or idea—the Greek *eidos.* So much of what we know as postmodernism, which begins with the late Heidegger, is the semantic critique of the *eidos.* But Deleuze gives this critique a distinguishing twist by framing it in terms of the medieval question of the "voice" in which something can be said of Being itself. Deleuzean univocity, which is by and large tantamount to his theory of expressivity, betrays a radical shift in both philosophy as a whole and the philosophical doctrine of language. Language is no longer about propositions, predications, and inferences; it is about signification. Even the most "abstract" concept is fundamentally a sign, because in its generality it expresses a virtual infinity.

Spinoza's principle of *Deus sive natura*—"God, otherwise expressivity"—is the same as Deleuze's principle of univocity. *God is the sign of signs* to the extent that all power (i.e., the home-grounding) of signification is condensed into that ultimate semiotic modality. The God of metaphysics is not the same as the "God" that is the "deep negative" of those signifying chains we understand as religiosity. While it may be inappropriate to use God univocally as a "concept" in different religious contexts (e.g., Buddhism and Advaita), semiotically there is a profound convergence among all strata of language that go by the name of religion. Religious theory is a global theory to the degree that this convergence can be charted within an infinite set of variations and permutations of discourse. It is, as we have indicated, not a linear but an orthogonal semiotics.

The sign of signs cannot be decoded; it can only be *addressed*. Otherwise, it must be revered in absolute amazement and silence. In order to designate what we mean by such a form of address we must fall back on Derrida's original term "grammatology." By his own admission Derrida linked the idea of a grammatology—a "science" of writing—with the destiny of Western thought, because the linguistic turn in philosophy that dominates the twentieth century had produced an "inflation" whereby the new "historico-metaphysical epoch must finally determine as language the totality of its problematic horizon." The infinite or transcendental signified, alternately named God or Being, as every introductory account of Derrida's central project of deconstruction and de-ontologizing emphasizes, can no longer guarantee the freedom of writing. Writing liberates the philosophy of language from the absolutism of the *logos* as the anchoring and overarching platform of propositional certainty. All significations are now errant and "nomadized," as Deleuze might say, "particularly the signification of *truth*."[52]

The signifier, according to Derrida, "has no constitutive meaning." No "logical center" undergirds it. Language is the rambling and unwinding of de-centered chains of signifiers, but interspersed within these chains appear gaps or *dis-closures*. A Derridean faith becomes the movement not of the "absurd," as Kierkegaard would say, but of endless *impossible possibilities*, which foreshadow a time that is not of time per se, a messianicity without a messiah, a religion without religion. What calls and convokes these impossible possibilities belongs neither to *logos* nor to writing, which is always writing about what has been written. It is the demand of *what calls us, and to which we respond*. What calls us cannot be signified, as Kant fully understood with his notion of a genuine "categorical" imperative. It can only be "obeyed" in the sense of "harkened to" (*gehorcht*). This harkening or obeying, if we follow closely Derrida's own account of messianicity through his reading of both Kant and Heidegger, is "lending an ear" (*Zuhören*) to what lies ahead (*Zukommen*) in the form of a divine promise (*Zusagen*). The *zu* in German corresponds to the *a* in French of both *avenir* and *Àdieu*. It is the fiduciary prefix that binds us not to grammar and inference, but to address. Such a *grammatology*, which heretofore focused only on the linear structure of exposition and meaning (*Il n'y a pas de hors-texte*), now shows us how this *Zusagen* both intersects and radicalizes the entirety of linguistic significations in the present moment. The *Zusagen* "arrives" from the future (*Zukunft*). Its grammatology is thus future perfect and adds a "vertical" dimension, a rectilinear indeterminacy to what we know of language. Grammatologically speaking, it is the formality of the Levinasian "face-off" of the other, what is spoken in the spectral space when *ich* says *Du*, which even linguistically cannot be finitized.

A grammatology of address is not just discernible in the monotheistic traditions of the West. The grammatology of address, the vocative, the *epicalic*, is an ingredient in all religions. In the epicalic we discover the relationship that we know as *religio*, the deep bonding of the conscious agent to the infinite ground of responsibility and signifiability, where the singular and univocal "voice" of the god makes himself, herself, itself manifest. The faith issue of whether one shall worship different gods or one God only is immaterial here. Religious theory, unlike theology, is concerned only with the forms of signifying praxis that make apparent the divine; it does not pose the ontological question of which form of address discloses the infinite homeground, the true sign of signs. One cannot determine the durability or authenticity of an instance of *religio* from the standpoint of the generic "study" of religion any more than it is possible to figure out which couples one observes in a café will be happily married for years to come.

At the same time, while the significance of the bond between two parties who appear to be a couple in a public venue constitutes an interior datum hidden from a casual observer, the relational quality of the sign that (home-)grounds the immanent signifying connections in a particular religious "system" cannot be gauged as part of that system. It bears down at right angles to the system itself. The sign of signs that appears in the religious contextuality of sign-events signifies the infinite, if not the absolute, deterritorialization of all representations, or forms of "sacred" or "spiritual" expression. This mode of deterritorialization is one way of understanding what is implied in conventional religious vocabulary when God, or the void, is characterized as infinite, illimitable, or ineffable.

Just as religion, because of its illimitability, serves to deterritorialize other modes of limited knowledge, so the unity of signification inherent in all religion is sufficient to deterritorialize the very concept of conceptuality. It certainly deterritorializes and de-privileges the linguistic, which explains why the theory of religion can never be reducible to the theological. The "territory" of religion within the vast terrain of the semiotic is a nomadic realm, a "smooth space" for sojourners and outlaws to inhabit temporarily in their search for greener, richer intellectual pastures. Religion is not an artifice of the state, as the eighteenth-century *philosophes* held, although the politics of the state are eminently capable of domesticating, routinizing, and mystifying the religious impulse. Religion consistently impinges upon and destablizes state territory. It is always outside the walls or across the rivers.

Sometimes the specter of religion is far darker and more menacing than our conceptual schematics can bear. Heretofore religious theory has been comfortable with assessing "static"—i.e., "of the state"—forms of religion, which are ineluctably scribal, archival, ceremonial, and in large measure sedentary. But a change in the world's religious climate these days has made it necessary to draw out the more challenging and contentious significations of the religious that have beset the academic community. In the common idiom this challenge has been posed as making sense of the sudden rise of "fundamentalism." But the word fundamentalism is egregiously misleading. It refers to the rise of intense, uncompromising dedication to what are basically uncompromising religious ideologies, usually based on selected and literal readings of sacred texts, with a universalistic but thoroughly *political* set of objectives. The task instead is to grasp how the momentum of religious signification has been loosed from its orbit around the Western metaphysical sun and has confronted us with a kind of global religiosity that can no longer be construed in terms of its particular histories, its cultures, its legacies.

Globalization amounts to what Deleuze calls "absolute deterritorialization" of all religions as we have known and studied them. This absolute deterritorialization desperately cries out for theoretization, one that recognizes the globally distributive, or what Deleuze terms the "nomadic," character of these dynamic forms and processes. Hence, if we have called on Levinas to help us understand the genuine, infinite force of signification behind the movement of signifiers, we must look at Deleuze much more closely in order to get some fix on how this force distributes the limitless signifying singularities in a limitlessly deterritorializing world.

7

DELEUZE AND NOMADOLOGY

∎

The masters according to Nietzsche are *the untimely.* . . .
Nietzsche says that under the huge earth-shattering events are
tiny silent events.
                              —Gilles Deleuze, *Desert Islands*

A SHADOW is skulking through the borderlands of religious thought. It is Deleuze's "nomad." The nomad is more than a sign of impermanence, or what Deleuze understands as the permanently "deterritorialized." The nomad signifies the errant and global movement of thought that at last bursts the bonds of Judeo-Hellenism, mathematical formalism, or even the rhetoric of poststructuralism. According to Deleuze and Guattari's "Treatise on Nomadology," the fundamental challenge of philosophy is not overcoming metaphysics, subverting ontotheology, or deconstructing the language of presence. It is to find "a way to extricate thought from the State model."[1] The project of emancipating thinking from the "state model" is an unmistakable allusion to the problem of Hegel that lowers over all poststructuralism and Continental philosophy in the twentieth century and beyond. For Heidegger and Derrida, the problem of Hegel is the finality of presence, the inability of philosophy to think the negative, not simply in a dialectical sense, but as a trace that either veils or irremediably vanishes.

In his groundbreaking book on Nietzsche, which on publication in the early 1960s tilted French philosophy in the direction we now call "postmodernism," Deleuze sets himself "against the dialectic" and "against Hegelianism." Virtually all postmodernist watercourses emanate from Nietzsche in some manner of speaking. In a larger sense they all derive from different strategic critiques of Hegelian idealism. One line of critique runs from Nietzsche through Heidegger and Derrida, and it is this trajectory that generally bears the stamp of the postmodern "image of thought," as Deleuze puts it. But Deleuze's own image of thought has a quite different genealogy.

Deleuze bypasses Heidegger (as well as Derrida, who was for a while his colleague and contemporary), inasmuch as he takes for granted the "overcoming" of metaphysics and ontotheology, and elaborates in manifold symphonic registers the Nietzschean semiotics of the *singular site and the singular event* as opposed to the universal principle or concept. All phenomenology is ultimately "semeiology." Deleuze lays out this project at the opening of *Nietzsche and Philosophy:* "A phenomenon is not an appearance or even an apparition but a sign, a symptom which finds its meaning in an existing force. The whole of philosophy is a symptomatology, and semeiology. The sciences are a symptamatological and semieological system."[2]

The Singularity of the Sign

Deleuze's "new image of thought" is to think "culture" where Hegel thinks the Idea and Heidegger thinks the riddle of ontology. Whereas the philosopher of the concept is a philosopher of the state, the philosopher of culture, like Nietzsche himself, thinks the world's "disguises." In other words, such a philosopher thinks only in terms of *signs.* Why does the thinker need culture? It is because "thought never thinks alone and by itself; moreover, it is never simply disturbed by forces which remain external to it. Thinking depends on forces which take hold of thought."[3] A symptomatology, or semiotics, does not disclose but "interprets" phenomena, "treating them as symptoms whose sense must be sought in the forces that produce them."[4] It is this "quality" of generative forces, or their differential relations, that Nietzsche had in mind, according to Deleuze, when he minted the perplexing phrase "will to power," which has nothing to with either volition or domination, but serves as a trope for the creative production of meaning, for the pure affirmation of the singular. "Willing is not an act like any other. Willing is the critical and genetic instance of all our actions, feelings and thoughts."

The "method" of the semiotic is that of "relating a concept to the will to power in order to make it a symptom of the will without which it could not even be thought."[5] In other words, semiotics "values" the exception, or what is excluded from the realization of the concept, or the general predicate, in the negative logic of the dialectic. This exception is neither "rational" nor "irrational," a terminology that is prejudiced by the hegemony in Western thought of subject-predicate rationalization through the proper syntactical operations of discursive *logos*. Socrates, who far more than the stereotyped figure of Jesus is really the arch villain for Nietzsche, "invented" the dialectic by seeking the "truth" of statements rather than their "sense" and "value,"[6] that is, their singular signification as an expression of their force. Whereas Hegel in his *Phenomenology* treats force as pre-predicative and *pre-dialectical,* Nietzsche regards it as both the origin and theme of a "philosophy of the future."

A philosophy of the future is against the general and against the state, which has appropriated for itself Rousseau's monstrous and malformed mandate of the *volonté générale,* or "general will." The philosopher of the state, lionized by Hegel, seeks to contain the violence of history and culture in the dialectical notion. The philosopher of the state ignores the "signs of the times" in order to reconcile the "reactive" negativity of historical turbulence with the eternality of thought as reflection, as a propositional calculus turned back upon itself in what Hegel terms the "speculative sentence." The cultural philosopher, on the other hand, is a warrior flailing and slashing through the violence of the historical. Thinking, says Deleuze, "is always a second power of thought, not the natural exercise of a faculty." Thought is Zarathustra's dancing star. It cannot attain power "if forces do not do violence to it. Violence must be done to it *as* thought." For culture "expresses the violence of the forces which seize thought in order to make it something affirmative."

Culture "is a violence undergone by thought, a process of formation of thought through the action of selective forces, a training which brings the whole unconscious of the thinker into play."[7] Following Nietzsche, Deleuze argues that philosophy, which is always a philosophy of culture, must become an "active force." Active forces are nongrammatical and postsyntactical. Language "expresses" them, but cannot contain them. They are not logic's scalpel, but the anvil against which logic is hammered, forged, bent, and frequently shattered. They do not depend on the play of "active" and "reactive" forces that in the biological world constitute struggle and selection and in the rhetorical universe the process of argument, induction, and the dialectic. Active forces are the joyous affirmation (minus the *ressentiment* of those who always "tarry with the negative") of an immediate and value-intensive singularity. They are, in the language of Zarathustra, the "overrich" and "overflowing" presence of the sign.

The Greeks, Deleuze suggests, understood philosophy as this kind of "training," as *paideia*, as a formative process of "enriching" thought with multiple textures of signification or *de-signs*. In certain respects we may call Deleuze's entire philosophical corpus, and much of post-modernist thought, a *semiological paideia*. Deleuze's commanding metonym of the "nomad" both concretizes and singularizes the field of cultural forces that Hegel sought to domesticate and comprehend in the dialectical movement of thought. There is a profound distinction between the "historyless" nomad on horseback who compels the rise and fall of the state and the march of "God" through history, which Hegel identifies with the historical dialectic. The nomad is not merely "other"; he is a perennial and unnameable provocation to the philosopher as sage, as an icon of the state.

As speculative thought proceeds, according to Hegel, the "alien alienates itself," the negated is negated, and presence becomes fullness of presence (*parousia*). But for Deleuze the problem of Hegel, and even the poststructuralism that follows upon him, should not be located in any reading, or alternative reading, of the dialectical method. Much of poststructuralism, as cultural and intellectual historians of the late twentieth century have long noted, has its genesis, both in France and in the English-speaking nations, in Kojève's famous interpretation of Hegel, which was also compatible with the "humanistic" Marxism that sparked the student revolts of the 1960s. However, as the dramatic events of May 1968 in France showed the nascent generation of thinkers who would later be labeled "postmodernists," the problem of thought does not lie in the nature of dialectics, and it certainly does not arise from any terminal condition in the West of "ontotheology."

Against the State

Deleuze writes toward the end of *Nietzsche and Philosophy* that "there is no possible compromise between Hegel and Nietzsche."[8] That is, there can be no compromise between the philosophy of the state and the philosophy of the semiotic expression, between the dialectic and the affirmation of the singular. The problem *is* the state. So much of Hegelianism—even the "left-wing" Hegelianism of Marx and Engels—is really a crypto-sacralization of state power. Theology is *subliminal* state religion, a theocracy. The cipher for decoding Hegel can be found at the end of the *Phenomenology of Spirit* in the section entitled "Absolute Knowing."

Here Hegel discusses the "moments of which the reconciliation of Spirit with its own consciousness proper is composed." This reconciliation is where Absolute Spirit becomes "certain of itself" through a binding "all into itself." Furthermore, "the Spirit that, in its existence, is certain of itself, has for the element of existence nothing else but this knowledge of itself, when it declares what it does it does out of a conviction of duty, this utterance is the *validating* of its *action*."[9] The "conviction of duty [*Pflicht*]" represents a "Prussianizing" of the Cartesian *res cogitans*, on which all modern philosophy is founded. It "binds" the elements of thought through a phenomenological integration of self-consciousness (Kant's transcendental "unity of apperception," Hegel's absolute knowing) as an "ethical" synthesis of will, intellect, and obligation in the concrete fact of citizenship and service to the state.

This realization, as far as Hegel is concerned, is implicit in all Greek thought, particularly Aristotle, where *nous* is actualized ultimately within the *polis*. For Deleuze, therefore, Western philosophy has an embedded, esoteric component. It is at root a *gnosis* of the state. The development of Western thought is a succession of iterations of this *gnosis*, gradually coming to the realization that is finally articulated in Nietzsche—Hegel's "gallery of images" in both the transcendental and immanent spheres, the representations of absolute knowledge, are empty signs, or mere simulacra. The truth is the state.

In the "Treatise" Deleuze writes:

> Thought contents are sometimes criticized for being too conformist. But the primary question is that of form itself. Thought as such is already in conformity with a model that it borrows from the State apparatus, and which defines for its goals and paths, conduits, channels, organs, an entire *organon*. There is thus an image of thought covering all of thought; it is the special object of "noology" and is like the State-form developed in thought. This image has two heads, corresponding to the two poles of sovereignty: the *imperium* of true thinking operating by magical capture, seizure or binding, constituting the efficacy of a foundation (*mythos*); a republic of free spirits proceeding by pact or contract, constituting a legislative and juridical organization, carrying the sanction of a ground (*logos*).[10]

State and republic, divine despot and "legislator," Romulus and Numa, "binder and organizer"—these different dyads, infinitely substitutable for each other, signify the nondialectical, *conjugate variables* of human history, which is history of the state. Their "opposition is only relative; they function as a pair, in alternation, as though they expressed a division of the One or constituted in themselves a sovereign unity."[11]

Deleuze draws these analytical pairings from the structural anthropology of George Dumézil. The linguist and anthropologist Benjamin Whorff during the era between the world wars discovered that all Western thought, anchored in predicative logic, derives from the distinctive grammar and inferential procedures of the Indo-European family of languages. And Derrida himself describes Western philosophy with its "logocentric" metaphysics as "white mythology." But, as we have suggested, Derrida's effort to dispel white mythology with a "Judaizing" or Talmudic style of anti-logism that refuses to "capture" the transcendence of the transcendental signified by substituting for the denotative sign the endless deconstructibility of the text only problematizes the problem of "metaphysics" even further. Do we not have in Derrida's epigones, if not in Derrida himself, a textual ontologism, a "surfacey" or "*horizon*-tal" metaphysics of algebraic signs, positive and negative literary space, "postscript" and *khōra*, all of which hungers in its soul for a restoration of all things magisterial and theological? The passion is driven by our hardwired habits of uttering Indo-Aryan, magico-priestly, mumbo-jumbo theology with a faint ontological accent.[12]

The imperial paired signs of the Indo-European state are not, according to Deleuze, the be-all and end-all of either thought or political economy. Indeed, there is another strange factor that enters into thought—the lightning strike of a nomadic raid when the a-historical ingresses, suddenly appearing and flooding the horizon of the state and its world-delineating paradigm of reciprocal representations.

Nietzsche himself is the first intrusion of the nomad into Western philosophical space. He is to Plato and the dialectic what Genghis Khan was to both Islamic civilization and Christendom. As warrior-nomad, Nietzsche, like the Mongol nomads themselves, relies on both swiftness and surprise as well as a ubiquity of presence and movement. His wandering, aphoristic style indeed comes "like lightning." His ranging, like a nomad, over the whole of Western philosophy and culture—past as well as contemporary—strikes fear into the defenders of the citadels of whatever theoretical orthodoxy may reign, now as well as in the nineteenth century. In contrast, the state by its very constitution is immobile, hence intrinsically vulnerable to these sorts of forays by outsiders or "outlaws." Nietzsche is such an outlaw. Our "state" philosophies are always at risk of falling to his lightning-like assaults on our seemingly indefensible ramparts.

Nietzsche's well-known characterization of philosophical language as a "mobile army of metaphors" is quite apt in this sense. The "state" of any propositional philosophy of language remains defenseless against such an army. The idea, or the speculative proposition, can only bar itself for so long against the siege of thought wrought by surges of cultural and historical singularity. Nietzsche, Deleuze argues,

> reproaches the dialecticians for going no further than an abstract con-
> ception of universal and particular; they were prisoners of symptoms
> and did not reach the forces of the will which give to these sense and
> value. They moved within the limits of the question "What is . . . ?,"
> the contradictory question *par excellence.* Nietzsche creates his own
> method: dramatic, typological and differential. He turns philosophy
> into an art, the art of interpreting and evaluating. In every sense he
> asks the question "Which one?"[13]

The question of *which,* as contrasted with *what,* is the *question of the sign.* The strategy of the sign, which is wholly Nietzschean, stands radically apart from the strategy of deconstructing texts, even philo-sophical texts. The sign, as Saussure pointed out, is eminent insofar as it "differentiates." It differentiates through repetition and iteration, although the "what" that is repeated cannot be distinguished as a concept independent of this process of re-iteration. For Deleuze, the "what is" derives from the interpolation of "which" specific cases or singular events bring the concept to bear on the situation. The ensem-ble of these interpretative gestures plays itself out as what Deleuze calls a "transcendental empiricism." A transcendental empiricism is always a strategy of referring the instant of signification to an unspo-ken "sense" of what is meant by the deployment of language within a discrete situation. Any event of language can be a sign, and every "hermeneutics" a semiotics, because the singularity of the event is produced by the differential engines of thought that function as an ac-tive force within the configuration of forces experienced as one's life, as culture, and ultimately as history.

The power of every semiotic reading depends on the contextual-ization of meaning and signification *as singularity.* Derrida himself has called Deleuze the great "thinker" of singularity, of a peculiar "sited" philosophy that originates from the event, *the singular event.* "More than anything else, Deleuze the thinker is the thinker of the event and always of this event in particular."[14] The deconstruction of texts, including the operative texts of Western theology and phi-losophy, brings the moment of erasure where the subject-predicate relationship inherent in the propositional structure of logic and ontol-ogy is untangled through a re-reading, or a critical intervention of the interpreter.

Deconstruction strips bare the negative spaces of the text, giving the lie to the monolithic—or *monological*—character of the linguistic. Derridean deconstruction is neither a sporting with words and concepts nor a curious and highly idiosyncratic method of philosophical midrash. It is a dispersal of the presumptive integrity of the text as object into its multiple enumerations that result from exegesis and understanding. In deconstruction, for the first time in the tradition of philosophy, there can be no system of fundamental concepts, principles, or "great "ideas." There can only be the active use, or misuse, of such a "tradition," which in itself is transmuted into the tradition. Derridean deconstruction, however, makes a further tacit contribution to the unraveling of the philosophical legacy, of which it is only vague cognizant. By privileging the text as opposed to the idea, the work of Derrida edges toward affirming the pure singularity of the semantic unit or semantmeme, a *strange ontology* of the sign, which Deleuze designates as the univocity of the event.

Univocity and Singularity

Deleuze's concept of *univocity* bears little relation to the origin of the term in medieval thought. In *Difference and Repetition* Deleuze states rather straightforwardly what he has in mind when he dredges up a well-worn Scholastic expression to frame anew the essential question of signification. The "sense" of any statement requires an intuition of tacit proportionality—a *ratio* on which all theological "rationality" is founded—between the immanent meaning of words and their correlation with a transcendent object of worship and desire. *Au fond* this sense of proportionality demands an inference of sameness or identity, an implicit *homology* that crouches behind the analogy. It was this discovery that led Scotus to reject the doctrine of analogy and to reassert the principle of univocity. The self-sameness of an entity is a feature neither of its abstracted essence nor of its materiality but of its *haecceity*, its "thisness," which is always intuitively grasped and cannot be prescinded from sense awareness. Everything that "is" in this respect is not in itself divisible except at the conceptual level. Conceptual differentiation cannot be construed as equivalent to ontological differentiation. Indeed ontology does not allow of such differentiation at all, even when one is making distinctions between sense objects and so-called transcendentals such as God. God's haecceity is comparable to that of an individual leaf. Therefore, Being is the only "common notion" in Scotus's parlance that truly applies to God and his myriad creatures. Being is never differentiated; it is apprehended in *the act of difference.*

Scotus "deconstructed" Aristotelianism, as well as Thomism, by propounding what we may regard as the first true instance in the history of philosophy of a semiotic theory of representation, locating "difference" neither in the separation of form and matter, nor in the gulf between the finite and infinite, but in the singularity of intuition. The Greek distinction between the sensible and the intelligible—the historical crossroads of empiricism and idealism—fades out in Scotism as it does in Deleuze.

Difference and Event

Difference arises not with any kind of disjunctive algorithm, with every attempt to show up and shore up the relationship between the thing and its possible multiplicity of representations, but with iteration and repetition, whereby the concept "emerges" not as an abstraction but as a string of filiated singularities. It is the repetition of every singular whatsoever in its haecceity that produces the "concepts" of philosophy, a general point Deleuze made late in life in his *What Is Philosophy?* Being itself can never be a concept; it is "eternal recurrence" in Nietzsche's parlance. It is *pure event.* The pure event of a nontranscendental "thisness," therefore, cannot be specified in terms of either the textual differential—Derrida's différance—or the *khōra* of postmodern negative theologizing, let alone the *envoi* of the postcard, the global communiqué. It is the moment of "expression," according to Deleuze. But it is also the *moment of semiosis.*

The emergence of semiotics as *signifying singularity* has been charted by Jean-Luc Nancy in his relentless "deconstruction" of Heidegger's work translated under the title *Being Singular Plural.* Nancy takes up Heidegger's entire project of posing the question of Being and "reverses" it. While Heidegger summons the thinker to think the Being of beings as origin, as what both discloses and conceals itself through the phenomenality of entities in their gathering together and coming-to-presence, Nancy calls for a realization of the singularity of the existent in its "being plural" and commingling with a multiplicity of existents at the very point where origin itself vanishes. "Being consists in nothing other than the existence of all existences [*tous les existants*]."[15] Being is finitude becoming present. In the Heideggerian perspective—especially the later Heidegger—language remains the disclosure, the unconcealing, the coming-to-presence of Being, an event shepherded by the poet, to whom the philosopher must pay deference.

Yet Nancy in many respects brackets the entire corpus of Heidegger after the *Kehre* while veering back to the "analytic of *Dasein*" found in *Being and Time,* and addresses the issue of language as a condition of the experience of worldliness, "thrownness," givenness, and finitude. But, in contrast with now passé "existential" readings of the problem, Nancy takes up anew the "linguistic turn" that some historians of philosophy would argue presages the postmodern turn and returns to Saussure's problem of the signifying nexus of language. The nexus does not emanate from the multiple strands of discourse that are evolving and the differentiation of terms that Saussure identified. Nor does it come from the "spacing" and "erasure" of the elements of meaning in the ongoing deconstruction of the text, as is the case with the early Derrida. Both linguistics and "ontology" take root in the instantaneous expression of significance, which is the act of *signification.* At the ontological level this instant of expression (or what Nancy calls the "shock" of the event, *le coup*) is the opening of the possibility of meaning unto its infinite semantic and syntactical permutations. According to Nancy, "Language is the exposing of plural singularity. In it, the all of being is exposed as its meaning, which is to say, as the originary sharing according to which a being relates to a being, the circulation of a meaning of the world that has no beginning or end."[16] "Being" has no meaning apart from this circulation. The "shock" functions in Nancy's argument very much in the same way the "trace" does for Derrida, just as "circulation" substitutes for the "text." The importance of Nancy's philosophy lies not in its Heideggerizing of classical atomism and materialism—in essence, an endeavor along with Badiou in the great tradition of the republic to re-secularize French postmodern philosophy—but in its capacity to articulate the semiotic agenda not so elliptically in terms of Heideggerian fundamental ontology.

Nancy ponders the question of the sign in ways that neither Peirce nor Deleuze does. Peirce conceived the sign largely as a component of inference, whereas for Deleuze the sign vanishes as a "significant entity" into the *general* signification of the "signifying chain."[17] Nancy's sign is the guarantee of multiplicity in the genesis of lexical or semantic space. The sign singularizes the expression of the concept insofar as it engineers, if we may introduce such a metaphor, a *coup* of the particular against the universal. "This is why there is no ultimate language, but instead languages, words, voices, an originarily singular sharing of voices without which there would be no voice."[18] The univocity of being is one and the same as the plurivocity of the sign. "This does not signify that Being 'is only a word,' but rather that Being is all that is and all that goes into making a word: being-with in every regard. For a word is what is only among all words, and a spoken word is what it is only in the 'with' of all speaking. Language is essentially in the 'with.'"[19]

If Deleuze was the "philosopher of the event," Nancy is its metaphysician. "There is, then, something to be thought—the event—the very nature of which—event-ness—can only be a matter of surprise, can only take thinking by surprise. We need to think about how thought can and must be surprised—and how it may be exactly this that makes it think." For "philosophy [itself] is surprised thought."[20] Furthermore, "the surprise is *not* anything."[21] It is not a portion of the iteration of signs upon signs any more than Being on the plane of fundamental ontology belongs to the order of beings. The surprise is the dynamic and quite un-Platonic Derridean version of the *khōra*, a "black hole"—what in physics is itself termed a *singularity*—at the outlying reaches of the universe of signification that suddenly explodes, then lights and rekindles the discourse of philosophy. Philosophy—and for that matter theology—belongs to the discursive order of history, and broadly speaking of the "humanities." But the surprise is not something historical, even though what are later identified as events of history, such as the Vietnam-era upheavals in America and the student revolution of May 1968 in France, were a "surprising" turn of events that gradually reshaped philosophy and culture. The event, within the Deleuzian framework, is a radical "thisness," a revelation of the singular, a sign—like the fig tree in the gospel narrative is a sign of the coming of the Son of Man. It is Deleuze's rendering of haecceity.

In *A Thousand Plateaus* Deleuze casts the notion of haecceity as "a mode of individuation very different from that of a person, subject, thing, or substance." Haecceities consist "entirely of relations of movement." Very often these haecceities, which may be eccentricities in the signifying schemas of culture, are artistic or literary. They are "surprises" of an intuitive nature, or moments of aesthetic discomfort and wonder. An Oriental haiku poem, according to Deleuze, is a perfect example. In the lines of signification suddenly converge and disappear—as light rays in a black hole—into the haeccity. The haeccity is the vortex of the lines of flight of the narration.

A more contemporary illustration would be "Lorca's 'five in the evening,' when love falls and fascism rises. That awful five in the evening!"[22] The haecceity "means" something only because it generates a chirring spawn of pleasure, fear, confusion, anticipation, desire, and excitement. *Everything* can be said about what happened, or what was heard or seen or read. In our day what is now referred to as "9/11" is a haecceity whose shock is still reverberating. Nancy's—or Badiou's—univocity of the multiple arises. The haecceity "has neither beginning nor end, origin nor destination; it is always in the middle. It is not made of points, only of lines. It is a rhizome. And it is not the same language, at least not the same usage of language." Haecceities have their "own particular semiotic to serve as expression." It is a "semiotic that has freed itself from both formal signifiances and personal subjectifications."[23] Deleuze's semiotic is located in the velocity of signification. In contrast with structural linguistics, Deleuze's semiotic map does not consist in a system of correlations, differences, and equivalences that can be read out of, or read back onto, an ensemble of inscriptions and syntax modules. Deleuze's semiotics requires no *code* to decode the signifying nexus. The haecceity as the matrix of the semiotic stream of production is not an instance of individuation in the grammatical sense. It is composed of "*indefinite article + proper name + infinitive verb.*" The verb "in the infinitive is in no way indeterminate with respect to time; it expresses the floating, nonpulsed time proper to Aeon, in other words, the time of the pure event or of becoming, which articulates relative speeds and slowness independently of the chronometric or chronological values that time assumes in the other modes."[24] For "the proper name is not the subject of a tense but the agent of an infinitive."[25]

Semiosis, therefore, is characterized by an *infinitive-ly* increasing exfoliation of the haecceity. This form of semiosis is sudden, violent, and shocking. Like the nomadic war machine that breaks in on a slumbering sedentary village at the edge of the steppes, semiosis consists in a kind of *Blitzkrieg,* a "lightning war." As David Hale notes in his masterful study of Deleuze's nomadology, "There is only the shock of an intrusion."[26] Deleuze derives much of his thinking about the haecceity from Leibniz's conception of the monad. But unlike the monad, which has a "biography" determined from its inception, the haecceity has no genesis. If the monad is "windowless," the haecceity is "subjectless." "There are no longer any forms or developments of forms; nor are there subjects or the formation of subjects. There is no structure."[27] Deleuze cites the example of Beethoven, who created an amazing polyphony of orchestral music from a handful of simple note patterns. The absence of form, or representation, allows for a semiosis that, like music, is based on temporal rather than structural transformation, a "material proliferation that goes hand in hand with a dissolution of form."²⁸ It is these temporal transformations, or "indications of speed," that generate the "infinitive" of dynamic relations. "It is as though an immense plane of consistency of variable speed were forever sweeping up forms and functions, forms and subjects, extracting from them particles and affects."²⁹

The haecceity is the "becoming of the secret." Semioticians are courtiers of the haecceity as well as "knights of the secret." Deleuze elaborates this theme with an arch reference to Nietzsche's famous, and misunderstood, quotation that "truth is a woman." Or, more aptly stated, truth is "becoming-woman." Women, at least in the male mythology, are known for their secret passions. "It is curious how a woman can be secretive while at the same time hiding nothing, by virtue of transparency, innocence, and speed."³⁰ What is a "secret" that can never be concealed? Signification is this secret, a "complex assemblage" of secrecy that amounts to a "block of co-existence" between lines that indicate a constantly shuffling dance of vectors, and vectorial functions. It is what Nietzsche was driving toward in his sorties against Plato. Deleuze takes up Plato's assault but with literary as opposed to rhetorical artillery. Nietzsche's valorization of "pure becoming" is transmuted through Deleuze's brushstrokes into the "becoming" of the hyphen ("becoming-woman," "becoming-animal," etc.) that marks the alchemy of, or transition between, what manifests as "secrets" at varying intensities and speeds.

Later in his career Deleuze cast these signatures of becoming—the haecceity made mobile—as "concepts." A Deleuzian concept is not a standard philosophical concept—even an Hegelian one—as the phrase has been deployed within the tradition. The concept is the haecceity as it gains velocity. "The concept speaks the event, not the essence or the thing." Concepts are wriggling, jiggling, and comingling strings of expression, complex events that evanesce within and throughout the arc of the virtual. They are schemes of variation that more closely approximate artistic creation than propositional reasoning. Propositions require a linkage between the general and the particular. Concepts are in themselves *accelerated particularities*. A concept "refers back to a chaos rendered consistent, become Thought, mental chaosmos." For "what would *thinking* be if it did not constantly confront chaos. Reason shows us its true face only when it 'thunders in its crater.'"³¹

Territoriality

If we are to be as banal and as unprovocative as possible, we can speak of concepts as "dynamic signs." But Deleuze's very notion of the concept, or haecceity, entails dynamism that in the style of catachresis utterly changes what is meant by "sign." The relevance of the concept/haecceity to a theory of religion, however, cannot simply be located in the brave new world of what might called Deleuze's "quantum semiotics," where signification depends on the energy levels and rhythmic interspersings of phenomena that cannot be formalized, spatialized, or circumscribed. Notwithstanding the *oceanic* character of Deleuze's "general theory" of semiosis, there is also a "special theory" that calls attention to the discrete assemblage of signifying intensities when "something" becomes perceptible within the encompassing "chaosmos." An analogy would be the Buddhist doctrine of the *skandhas* as a counterfoil to the general theory of impermanence, or *anicca*.

Deleuze employs some curious language to work out this special theory of semiosis, but that parlance has become the fastening rod of his lexicon. We refer, of course, to his use of the terms "territorialization" and "deterritorialization." What is Deleuzian territory, semiotically construed? It is important to recognize that Deleuze drew the metaphor of "territory" from his reading of the ethologist Konrad Lorenz on animal aggression and the rituals and rhythms of defending and invading space. "Territoriality" at the same time is neither ground nor location. It is an internal coherence of sign processes—bird song in response to another feathered aggressor or changes of coloring and physical state in insects to ward off an advancing predator are typical examples—that is nevertheless episodic and situation-specific. Deleuze considers these alterations in the behavior or metabolisms of living organisms comparable to musical motifs, which become the identifying "characteristics" or properties of what are misconstrued as entitative in the metaphysical sense. They are "expressive qualities" or "shifting relations" among temporal streams of signification. "We should say . . . that territorial motifs form *rhythmic faces or characters,* and that territorial counterpoints form *melodic landscapes.* There is a rhythmic character when we find that we no longer have the simple situation of a rhythm associated with a character, subject, or impulse. The rhythm itself is now the character in its entirety."[32]

Territorialization is the convergence of these rhythms into a "refrain." It is the moment of the "becoming-expressive of rhythm, the emergence of expressive proper qualities, the formation of matters of expression that develop into motifs and counterpoints."[33] Deleuze elsewhere terms it "intra-assemblage" of the fluctuating heterogeneity. Territory is associated with *consistency.* Deterritorialization on the other hand is both decompression of qualities and a *de-expression,* the moment of vanishing back into the virtual continuum when the rhythm changes or the key is suddenly transposed. Plainly stated, deterritorialization happens, and it happens with its own consistency. Death is the body with its proper name—Michael or Michelle—deterritorialized. It is a different vector for the haecceity. It is the "release" of the refrain into the chaosmos. It is a "note that pursues you, and sound that transfixes you."[34]

Thought itself, according to Deleuze, is the pursuit of these rhythms of territorialization and deterritorialization. The concept is their harmonic, while theory is the vaster musicology. Furthermore, territorialization, as the metaphor suggests, requires a certain level of *indigenization* of thought and theory. Indigenization is not the same as what we today would term "identity politics"—the acculturation and "cultification" of ethnic, racial, gender, or social identity, whether of the infamous Nazi reductionism of *Blut* and *Boden* or the Ibero-Indian mystique of *la raza*. Indigenization amounts to making theory immanent within the territory that is "sited" for thinking, which also means that all thinking is an expression of the site, of the haecceity, of the singularity. Deleuze's sited or indigenized thinking is far more radical than Hegel's "concrete universal." Indigenization is *the theory of what tends toward the singular*, the contrariety of the statistical average, or the "majoritarian" characteristics.

That is why literature takes precedence over abstract reasoning, and "minoritarian" literature is preferable to popular literature. The latter genre is a full expression of the "law" of singularity, the regime of signs. Indigenization also means that the privilege of philosophy and what heretofore was known as higher-order argument and reasoning becomes intertwined with folk narrative, common biography, and the voices of those who have previously been bereft of a voice. Deleuze expands Nietzsche's aphorism that philosophy must become "faithful to the earth" in a much more sophisticated manner. Philosophy must become *immanent* inasmuch as it must capture the territorialization and deterritorialization processes that Hegel only "abstractly" and blindly designated as "reason in history," or Marx in his "socialist-humanist" phase denoted as the elevation of proletarian consciousness to philosophical status. "The philosopher must become nonphilosopher so that nonphilosophy becomes the earth and people of philosophy."[35]

Are we not, however, on the threshold of indigenization when we graph the lineaments of religious theory? If indigenization entails a new kind of semiotic thinking or "survey"—Deleuze's *survoi*, which connotes the comprehension for a fleeting moment of the field of temporal and heterogeneous forces and relations—then the strange sign we call "religious" beckons us to immanentize our thought within that field. Deleuze makes this point in a more oblique fashion, or almost as an aside, in his exposition of the "refrain" in *A Thousand Plateaus*. Art and religion are "territorialized," he says, or they are primary "effects" of territorialization, because they are crucial to the distribution of competitive work functions as sedentary life takes shape in a particular historical milieu. Just as for Hegel art and religion are moments of "picture-thinking" for philosophy long before it becomes self-conscious of itself as dialectical reason, in Deleuze's view they establish the patterns of semiotic consistency as well as the internal coherence of the milieu itself, whereby the lines of flight that "concepts" take can begin to be shown.

Western philosophy has its origins in Greek thought, which in turn can be traced back as a unique coding—in Deleuze's sense a "transcoding"—of the interplay between religious myth, ritual drama, and cosmology. Deleuze terms religion "the other effect" and conjugate condition of territorialization.

> That other effect, which relates not to occupations but to rites and religions, consists in this: the territory groups all the forces of the different milieus together in a single sheaf constituted by the forces of the earth. The attribution of all the diffuse forces to the earth as receptacle or base takes place only at the deepest level of each territory. . . . The forces of air and water, bird and fish, thus become forces of the earth. Moreover, although in extension the territory separates the interior forces of the earth from the exterior forces of chaos, the same does not occur in "intension," in the dimension of depth, where the two types of force clasp and are wed in a battle whose only criterion and stakes is the earth.[36]

This language sounds vaguely like Heidegger and the theme of the *Geviert*, or "fourfold," which has always been something of a dilemma for Anglo-American interpreters seeking to "demythologize" the parlance of his ontological project. Just as in Heidegger, however, the "gathering" of the fourfold remains invaluable heuristic discourse for his initiative to think the origins of philosophy in Greece in a manner the Greeks never thought, for Deleuze the introduction of the trope of territorialization "in the dimension of depth"—that is, in the "religious" dimension—constitutes a critical gesture toward the indigenization of all thought and philosophy. In other words, religious theory is not ancillary to thinking in general. Nor is it derivative of

philosophical conversation that somehow is *applied* to the phenomenology, history, and anthropology of "religions."

Religious theory is a kind of *philosophical* thinking in the strict
Deleuzian sense—not to mention all other iterations of "theoretical"
thinking—because it anchors the entire semiotic project of postmodern thought and beyond in its moment of "territorialization," which
is then deterritorialized by the nomadic war machine (the dimension
of aleatory violence that strikes as an external disrupting force from
"nowhere") and reterritorialized anew as the nomads are gradually
assimilated and "civilized." Religious theory must account, of course,
not just for the moment of territorialization, but for the trajectories
of deterritorialization as well. Religious theory gropes toward and
performs reconnaissance within the dimension of depth, and in the
forces of destruction, dispossession, deracination, and *de-position*
that deterritorialization suggests. It gropes toward a recognizable mel-
ody, an emergent harmony, and a sustainable rhythm (even if these
themes are bold and surprising), toward the kinds of energized "conceptual personae" that Deleuze describes as the semiotic engines of
philosophy itself.[37] Religious theory is the mother lode of philosophy
in a Deleuzian mountain range. But it is also the musicology of the
philosophical mind after postmodernism.

Yet this fullness remains differentiated, disseminated, *deterritorialized.* It is an "absolute deterritorialization," as Deleuze terms it.
In its absolutely deterritorialized diaspora the infinite comes to be
enfleshed, not as an instantiated concept or Hegelian "incarnation,"
but as a Deleuzian event, approximating what Derrida in his later
writings refers to as the "undeconstructible." The undeconstructible,
for Deleuze, is the absolutely deterritorialized, which is also the absolutely indigenized, *singularized.*

We acquire a sense of the fuller significance of this gesture not
only in Deleuze but also in reading the later Derrida. For Derrida,
the terrain of primary signification must be understood in a peculiar
sense, as a "testimonial sacredness," of which Heidegger speaks "under the name of *Zusage* ('accord, acquiescing, trust, or confidence')" as
"that which is most irreducible, indeed most originary in thought."[38]
Derrida construes ontotheology as an "encrypting of faith." Faith
betokens the "place" from which the ontotheological imagination,
which we may call "religion," egresses. "The place is unique; it is
without name."[39] It is a "place without place." It is the One that can
only be "deconstructed" as the infinity of gods, spirits, and place-
names, as revered texts and their distinguished commentaries, as the

production of theological innovations and critical glosses. The One is always "One + n, which 'incalculably engenders all these supplements.'"[40] It is the One that demands, unlike ontic monuments, sacrifice and prayer. It is not the *philosophical* Absolute to be comprehended in the spiral of reflection, but which does not allow itself to be misappropriated, that deciphers the manifold grammars of "world theologies" with the violence of penance, atonement, and immolation. It is found in the "space and time of a spectralizing messianicity beyond all messianism."[41]

Absolute Deterritorialization

Such a space—the place that is "no place" for this faith—is the space of *alternativity* (as opposed to "alterity" per se), a kind of persistent "liminality," mid-rangedness, or *in-transitivity*. Such a terrain religious theory relentlessly explores and charts. The absolute deterritorialization ensconced in absolute indigenization allows us to deterritorialize the signs that can be termed "religious" in their general, conventional, or descriptive connotations. This absolute deterritorialization corresponds to a thought to which a Deleuzian semiotics might direct us. A Deleuzian semiotics—or a Žižekean semiotics for that matter—does not think "out of the box," as the familiar cliché runs, but "inside the skin" of the general representations that inhabit and circulate within our theoretical discourse. Thus the relationship between an indigenous religious thinking and what is commonly called "faith" is constituted in a manner that is far more radical than the way in which the connection between the two terms is largely grasped. We may term indigenous religious thinking *sited*, or "situated," thinking. For Deleuze, to be sited is to have a concrete locus and to unfold within the webwork of tropes and figurative utterances that such a locus implies. This site is the locus of placement, of giving place, of "taking one's place" in the passage from virtual to actual.

Thought advances metonymically, spewing its concrete signifying moments together in an entrained rhapsody. There is no "concept" that remains a general subject for reflection and predicative deduction. The conjunctive and disjunctive relationships between signifier and signified that provide the fulcrum for the propositional calculus in philosophy melt into what Deleuze dubs the "production" of difference. The chain of metonymy is the sequencing of difference. The "differential" does not amount to a deployment of the negative sign in the propositional calculus, but to an intimation of limitless possibilities of inference and discrimination from a language that infinitely concretizes, or "situates," the theoretical insight itself. Indeed, all "ideas" themselves depend on the play of inexorable differentiation and the assimilation of these differences that constitute the syntax of emulation and "representation." "There is the power of the diverse and its production, but there is also the power of the reproduction of the diverse."[42] Metonymy is the genesis of the similar through difference, from which philosophical "universals" finally emerge, but these universals are not general concepts. Rather, they are repetitions that have the force of simulacra. Metonymy, like deconstruction, has no closure. Setting himself against Hegel, Deleuze allows neither for the endless genesis of affirmation and negation, as in dialectical argument, nor for any "negation of the negation" that leads to a new affirmation, or synthesis. Indeed, "the negative is an illusion." It is an illusion "because the form of negation appears with propositions which express the problem on which they depend only by distorting it and obscuring its real structure."[43]

Deleuze cites Saussure's intuition that "in language there are only differences." To adduce an algebraic, or compositional, model of linguistic operations that depends on the balancing of positive and negative is to be on the "lesser side" of language. It betrays "the nature of the play of language—in other words, the sense of that combinatory, or those imperatives or linguistic throws of the dice which, like Artaud's cries, can be understood only by the one who speaks in the transcendent exercise of language."[44] The differential replaces the negative as the register of meaning. Logic gives way to "expression," although there is *no-thing* to be expressed through the combinatory process.

The distinction between possible and actual is replaced by the continuum between "virtual" and real. The virtual is the trajectory of becoming, of a heterogeneity that incrementally comes to pass as part of the string of metonymy, of obscurity becoming ever more distinct, of "differential relations" that amount to the "incarnation of singular points." Deleuze sums up this kind of argument in an aphorism: "The entire world is an egg." For "the double differenciation of species and parts always presupposes spatio-temporal dynamisms."[45] Differentiation is performance, a "dramatization" or theatrics, on the part of a zero-point virtuality. The differentiation expands from a site, not as cogitation or "speculation" on an idea or object, but from a *provocation*. "Something in the world forces us to think. This something is an object not of recognition but of a fundamental *encounter*. What is encountered may be Socrates, a temple or a demon."[46]

Thinking itself is the "deterritorialization" of our initial encounters
—of particular instants of suspicion, clarity, presumption, or self-
assurance—and their reterritorialization as percepts or affects. This
"image" of thinking Deleuze calls "geophilosophy," and it departs
considerably from the paradigm of predicative logic. "Subject and object give a poor approximation of thought," Deleuze writes. "Thinking
is neither a line drawn between subject and object nor a revolving of
one around the other. Rather, thinking takes place in the relationship
of territory and the earth."[47] Here Deleuze elaborates consistently
Nietzsche's demand that thought remain "faithful to the earth,"
where earth signifies—as it does for Heidegger—the context within
which our significations and representations fully emerge. "Earth-
thinking" in the metaphoric sense of the phrase is Gestalt-thinking.
It is ranging nomadically without establishing an identity or location.

The nomadic thinker is the quintessential geophilosopher, who
is not simply "errant" but *extra-territorial* in the way pirates, boat
people, expatriates, and soldiers of fortune are extra-territorial. "Earth
constantly carries out a movement of deterritorialization on the spot,
by which it goes beyond any territory: it is deterritorializing and
deterritorialized. It merges with the movement of those who leave
their territory en masse, with crayfish that set off walking in file at
the bottom of the water, with pilgrims or knights who ride a celestial line of flight."[48] The vertical metaphoricity of "above" and "below" or "within"—or transcendence and immanence—hence evapo-
rates in Deleuzian geothinking, or "geotheory," which is completely
synechdochical. They are part of the deterritorialization and reterritorialization process that propels thought as a whole, which turns
out to be *hyperconceptual.* The philosophical concept, for Deleuze,
is not a concept at all in the analytical sense, but what he names a
"conceptual persona" that constantly reveals its own virtuality, dif-
ferentiality, and rhetoricality.

Movements of thought open onto an "elsewhere." Concepts are in
perpetual flight. They are open-ended figurations that proceed from
their finite and immanent dwelling place toward the infinite *con-
figurability* of anything can be said of anything else, which in turn
entails the univocity of all that is communicable. Throughout his
writings Deleuze does not even purport to develop a theory of religion
as a whole. Yet the importance of the religious as the mother lode
for thought and theory resonates throughout his work, especially his
later writings.

In *What Is Philosophy?*—the capstone work of his collaboration
with Guattari—Deleuze makes some powerful and telling moves in

the direction of religious theory without actually laying it out. He begins by making a distinction between "relative" and "absolute" deterritorialization. Relative deterritorialization takes place within what Deleuze terms the "milieu of immanence." The milieu of immanence is the "plane" of the concept. As "conceptual personae," concepts are not in any sense higher-order or "generic" abstractions, as the history of philosophy has tended to characterize them. Concepts have their own immanent vitality; they cannot be prescinded from the flux of human experience along the lines of Western thought's own genetically engineered Platonism project. Concepts belong to the "plane of immanence" upon which and through which thought expresses itself. The concept "does not have spatiotemporal coordinates, only intensive coordinates. . . . [It] is defined by *the inseparability of a finite number of heterogeneous components traversed by a point of absolute survey at infinite speed.* Concepts are 'absolute surfaces or volumes,' forms whose only object is the inseparability of distinct variations." Thus the "concept is act of thought, it is thought operating at infinite (although greater or lesser) speed."[49] Relative deterritorialization occurs as the concept pushes intensively through its milieu, and there are shifts in the correlation among signifying events that lead to new, overt patterns of thought. These shifts can be synchronic as well as diachronic, insofar as they sort out into what in the theoretical venue are represented as intellectual fields of inquiry, or in the domain of culture as art, science, politics, and so forth.

"Absolute deterritorialization" is a far murkier notion, and Deleuze does not go through all the iterations of such a theme as he does with "relative deterritorialization." "Deterritorialization is *absolute,*" Deleuze writes, when the earth passes into the pure plane of immanence of a Being-thought, of a Nature-thought of infinite diagrammatic movements."[50] If earth is the metonymical signification of "pure immanence," as it is for Nietzsche, then absolute deterritorialization is Deleuze's figurative strategy of positing the "concept" of what has been known from Heidegger onward as fundamental ontology—the overcoming of the representational limits of first philosophy, or metaphysics. But an absolute deterritorialization does not hinge, as it does for Heidegger, on thinking Being within the unity of beings. It is a very concrete, "realized" eschatology of Being that takes us into the intensity and velocity of the world at large, which propositional rationality and predicative semantics can never penetrate. Thought penetrates these spheres only through the deep "expressionism" of religion and art.

Paradoxically, we must begin to think through a Deleuzian theory of religion, anchored in an immanentist semiotics, by addressing the most classical of conundrums in theology and philosophy, the matter of transcendence. Transcendence initiates not only religious thinking but thinking as a whole, according to Deleuze. The transcendent or

> celestial vertical settles on the horizontal plane of thought in accordance with a spiral. Thinking here implies a projection of the transcendent on the plane of immanence. Transcendence may be entirely "empty" in itself, yet it becomes full to the extent that it descends and crosses different hierarchized levels that are projected together on a region of the plane, that is to say, on an aspect corresponding to an infinite movement. In this respect, it is the same when transcendence invades the absolute or monotheism replaces unity: the transcendent God would remain empty, or at least *absconditus*, if it were not projected on a plane of immanence of creation where it traces the stages of its theophany.[51]

The projection of the transcendent onto the plane of immanence is what is meant by *revelation* in the traditional theological idiom, an *epiphany of the sacred* in the discourse of the religious, or the *apophantic* in the grammar of philosophical ontology. Transcendence is made figural in "imperial unity" or "spiritual empire."

"The transcendence that is projected on the plane of immanence paves it or populates it with Figures. It is a wisdom or a religion—it does not much matter which. It is only from this point of view that Chinese hexagrams, Hindu mandalas, Jewish sephiroth, Islamic 'imaginal,' and Christian icons can be considered together: *thinking through figures*."[52] The power of the figure is the key to religious theory. The figure deterritorializes the transcendent along a vertical axis and reterritorializes it as the religious sign or emblem that invades the space of the *imperium*. That movement corresponds precisely to how the Cross of Christ "won over" the ancient Roman Empire until it was reterritorialized as an imperial symbol itself after Constantine's vision in the sky of the *chi rho* before fighting the battle of the Milvian Bridge, or to how the figuration of the serene Buddha captured for a time an evolving Indian civilization during the reign of Ashoka. The religious figure—the beachhead of a deterritorializing movement of transcendence—is the sign of signs that generates the signifying richness of conceptual personae on the plane of immanence.

Religious theory is a transcendental semiotics that explores the multivalency of the "history" of religions and religious experience within an immanent frame of reference. "Theology," or the science of the divine, makes no sense without this sort of immanentist analysis.

A theology of pure transcendence—even a Derridean negative theology that transcends through the porousness of language—is vacuous theory; it is not theory at all. The Derridean epoch has been a blessing for us because it has thoroughly disabused us of our propositional, inferential, and representational thought habits. But it has left us with nothing more than a *nirvana of the sentence*. It cannot transport us into the fullness of a future overshadowed by a semiotics that for the first time in recent history replaces the "study" of religion with the theory of religion.

A theory of the religious as a semiotics of the figurative in Deleuze's sense would also link our methods to the other "human sciences," as the nineteenth century called them. But this kind of *scientia* is more wisdom than hypothesis making. It drives us from "projection in a figure" to "connection in the concept."[53] The interfacing of the vertical signifier with its horizontal (that is, its immanent) nexus of conceptual relations conjoins the theory of religion with the fields of art, history, philosophy, and to a certain extent even psychology and anthropology. But this conjoining—or *enjoining*—has nothing to do with some bold "interdisciplinary" venture across the wide terrain of knowledge. It is tracing the Nile with all its vast cultural and physical geography to its source, then traveling down it to where it debouches. In religion as well as in the explosion of globalized capitalism "even the skies become horizontal," as Deleuze says.[54] Ideas stay with the state. Figures expand and rhizomically multiply, as happens in fractal geometry. All concepts are this infinite expansion of figurative vectors and intensities. "The concept is not object but territory."[55]

Religious theory is our "earth-concept." It is our absolutely deterritorialized "strange" territory, not only because it creates a duplex coding of the transcendent as both vertical and immanent but because it makes our thinking through the transcendent wholly *indigenous*. The theory of religion is both thought's infinity and its infinitesimal movement of indigenization. In religious theory we are space-time travelers in such a territory. We are neither citizens of Derrida's great globolatinized imperium nor resident aliens from the fourth dimension that we call the transcendent. We are nomads wandering in the steppelike "smooth space" of this infinite territory that is constantly being deterritorialized and reterritorialized by the very concepts that incite us to think both the totality, and the *total heterogeneity*, of thought.

We are raiders of the citadels of signification. Yet in mapping, traversing, and wandering throughout this smooth space we must come to terms with that other "conjugate" dimension of the religious which neither a Levinasian infinitization of the immanent relation nor a Deleuzean topology of global, nomadic distributions can manage. We must come to terms with the concurrent process of "subjecti-fication" in the postmodern context, a process we realize does not consist in "becoming" a religious subject, as Kierkegaard would have it, nor in infinitizing "subjective experiences" along an infinite grid of fluid point-events everywhere on a rapidly deterritorializing planet, as New Age enthusiasts would have it. We must realize that absolute deterritorialization requires a subject that is also absolutely deterrito-rialized, a subjectless subjectivity to go along with any "religion with-out religion." This subjectless subjectivity, however, is implied in the radical semiotics of the formation—actually the *failure to form*—of what we regard as religious subjects. For such a perspective we must turn back to Žižek.

8

ŽIŽEK AND THE FAILURE OF
THE SUBJECT

▪

The psychoanalytic problematic concerning identification and its failure is, if anything, more pertinent than ever in today's world.
    —Slavoj Žižek, *Conversations with Žižek*

THE SOMEWHAT recent claim of Žižek to speak to the religious academy as a "theologian," more precisely as a *Christian thinker*, has unsettled traditional practitioners of the profession. Žižek's exchanges with John Milbank, the would-be guardian of orthodox Christianity against secularist postmodernism, in the volume entitled *The Monstrosity of Christ*, and his impromptu monologue about the "death of God" (which was supposed to be a dialogue) on the same platform with Altizer at the American Academy of Religion meeting in November 2009[1] have both entranced the field and left many scratching their heads. Even more puzzling is Žižek's declaration on the book jacket of *The Monstrosity of Christ*: "My claim is that it is Milbank who is effectively guilty of heterodoxy, ultimately of a regression to paganism; in my paganism, I am more Christian than Milbank." Here Žižek, of course, is making a claim similar to that of Altizer, whom he discovered not too long before propounding this position. But what makes Žižek's recent forays into topic areas that European philosophers since Hegel have left largely untouched is the implications of his arguments and statements for the problem of religious theory rather than theology. Like Derrida a generation earlier, Žižek has cultivated his own kind of celebrity presence by relentlessly applying a novel theoretical procedure—the Lacanian analysis of the split subject as applied simultaneously to popular culture, neo-Marxist politics, and the history of modern philosophy—in a repetitious manner that gorges itself routinely on the intellectual fads and fashions of the day by means of an endless juggernaut of published books and articles.

However, what does, and most likely will, endure as Žižek's legacy is his resuscitation of German idealism as the authentic precursor of postmodern philosophy.[2] His omnivorous Lacanianism will most likely fade into the historical background of ideas. Yet as a result we will perhaps realize once and for all that the road routinely followed from Kant through Kierkegaard to Heidegger and beyond makes a fateful, but barely noticed, bend in its brief, initial passage from the critical philosophy to Hegel. The occasion for this fateful turn is the philosophy of Schelling, whom Žižek regards as the true wild card in the career of "ontotheology." Prior to Žižek, Schelling, a contemporary of all the German idealists, was regarded largely as a strange sidebar to the philosophical revolution of the Napoleonic era, or at most the missing link in the patrimony of Hegelianism.

The "Barred" Subject

Nevertheless, it was not Kierkegaard's assertion of the absolute primacy of *Existenz* as the original foil to Western philosophy's inveterate logocentrism, but Schelling's insistence on an *Ungrund*, a "Not-ground," a "God before God" that is responsible both for the creative nature of God and the historic-conceptual process of opposition, strife, and differentiation that makes possible the overcoming of metaphysics and the inauguration of the age of signification. Žižek obviously over-Lacanizes Schelling. There is far more to the odyssey of Schelling's work and its long-term effects than Lacan's radical Freudianism can freight. But in the current sepulchral twilight of the once scintillating poststructuralist project, which fronted for Lacan for a long while just as Marxism fronted for Hegel, Žižek's persistence has forced us to confront not the arbitrariness so much as the lack of intellectual transparency commonly attributed to postmodern thought.

So much of Žižek's exposition of Schelling, if we bracket the Lacanian lense through which he reads most of his sources, derives from the latter's key statement in his *Philosophical Investigations into the Essence of Human Freedom* that "the law of the ground [*Gesetz des Grundes*] is just as original as the law of identity."[3] What Žižek adds to the postmodern "dialectic," which runs the entire gamut from the Hegelian negation of the negation, to Derridean *différance* as the anomaly of the passage from utterance to inscription, to Deleuze's identification of the event as the virtual production of the actual, is the recognition that the Same is neither beginning, nor end, nor a kind of "halfway house" where alterity can take account of itself as somehow positive. Sameness, or *Identität*, has a genealogy, or, as Žižek himself puts it in various ways, every beginning itself has its own beginning. Unlike Deleuze, who in *Difference and Repetition* extrapolates from Nietzsche's "abysmal thought" of eternal recurrence to *identify* identity with the affirmation of difference, Žižek refuses to play the breezy and familiar postmodern—especially Derridean—game of *oui et non*. Yea-saying and nay-saying is the tired, formal Hegelian way of thinking by disjunctions. Rather, following Lacan's core notion of the *objet petit a*, we must realize that Žižek's notion of parallax discontinuities between things is not an epistemology, a theory of how we come to know the real by considering both opposite or varying perspectives, but *a theory of the real itself.* The real "in reality" is *in itself* discrepant, asymmetrical. If modern thought from Descartes to Derrida prioritizes epistemology over ontology (Heidegger's famous principle of "subjecticity"), a *post/postmodern* thought returns to a kind of ontology *in situ*, but only in the sense of an ontology that is essentially "dysfunctional" from the get-go. Hence Lacan's famous "barred S," or $, the crossing out of the algebraic letter to indicate the split subject as the subject matter of psychoanalysis, is in Žižek far more than a symbolic notation. It becomes the depositional sign of his parallax ontology.

The bar denotes the irreconcilability of the divergent trajectories of the self-reflection that is named the subject's *subjectivity*. As Bruce Fink in his careful exposition of Lacan puts it, "the subject is nothing but" a split between the false sense of ego constructed around the attributes of selfhood generated from the attributions of parents and significant others and the dynamic logic of the unconscious, which has "no concern whatsoever for the ego's fine opinion of itself."[4] Both of these discontinuous trajectories Fink calls "avatars," mobile and internally expansive complexes of signifying assemblages that manifest what we understand as the conscious and unconscious personalities. The "metaphysical" assumption of all psychology is that these trajectories somehow are complementary aspects of an implicit unity. In the familiar model of "ego psychology," as opposed to the Lacanian one, the aim of therapy is to integrate the disparity between these two strands of a presumed unitary psyche.

But the Lacanian paradigm supposes that the disjunction is real, not simply apparent. The postulate of unity derives, like the sense of the integral I or self itself, from the operations of language, in much the same way as the child becomes aware of himself, or herself, through the interventions of speakers, who serve to shape and structure the plasticizing capacity of infantile drives and desires at that early point in life known in Lacanian lingo as the "mirror stage." The disjunction marking the split belongs to the expansion of discursive operations that we understand as language. The barred subject therefore amounts at one level to a linguistic operator ("shifter" in the nomenclature of the structural linguist Roman Jakobson, on whom Lacan relied) that somehow renders disjunctive the two different streams of what we would otherwise regard as "consciousness." The barred subject does not manifest simply a paucity, or a gap (a "lack" in the ordinary sense of the word), as it might do when applied to any "deconstructive" type of semiotics. It is not so much a negative as a transpositional operator. As Fink points out, "Lack in Lacan's work has, to a certain extent, an ontological status; it is the first step beyond nothingness."[5] The subject's "lack" constitutes an actual incentive to move beyond the frustration of desire, and the alienation that goes along with it, and to locate itself within the symbolic order. The barred subject, therefore, in a broad manner of speaking indicates the impossibility of congruency between the different orders of language that communicate in different registers within the total matrix of psycho-somatic impulses and operations. Subjectivity does not amount to the recognition of abysmal freedom, as in existentialism or Sartrean phenomenology, but to the parallax relationship between complicated semiotic protocols that perform disparate functions within the economy we call the personality.

Žižek "ontologizes" the subject, however, even further than Lacan does. In *The Ticklish Subject,* his monumental tome on subjectivity in German idealism and philosophy, Žižek characterizes the subject as what

is strictly correlative with the ontological gap between the universal and particular—with ontological undecidability, with the fact that it is not possible to derive Hegemony or Truth directly from the given positive ontological set: the "subject" is the *act,* the *decision* by means of which we pass from the positivity of the given multitude to the Truth-Event and/or Hegemony. This precarious status of the subject relies on the Kantian anti-cosmological insight that reality is "non-All," ontologically not fully constituted, so it needs the supplement of the subject's contingent gesture to obtain a semblance of ontological consistency.[6]

Following this account, we can understand why Žižek prefers to use the terms "subject" and "subjectivization" (as opposed to the familiar "subjectivity"). The subject is neither a mark nor a locatable terrain of meaning (a *significandum*), but a locus of "circulation" among elements in the interplay between desire and language. There is no *object* per se that can be identified "subjectively," merely a shifting object-supplement, the *objet petit a*. Žižek's ontology of the subject, therefore, effectively translates Schelling's mytho-cosmology into the argot of poststructuralist Freudianism and language theory while sustaining the pretence of preserving the German idealist project. Ultimately, however, Žižek's project is "political," as he himself constantly stresses and as the subtitle of *The Ticklish Subject* makes clear. In ontologizing Lacan, Žižek is seeking to de-ontologize politics and ethics altogether while putting to rest once and forever the idea of Sartrean responsibility, the Derridean aporia, or any other overt or covert version of decisionism. The sign of the split subject entails an endorsement of what he describes as "the pragmatic paradox of ordering you to be free," which also "exhorts you to dare."[7] The dare corresponds in a not-too-indirect manner to the divine act of creation in Schelling. Both creation and dare are what Žižek terms a "self-relating negativity," which is not a negativity in the dialectical sense or even a productive one in the sense of the Derridean *khōra*. This self-relating negativity comes close to "the 'impossible' relationship between a drive *qua* real and its object, *objet petit a* (a drive is doomed to circle for ever around its object-cause)."[8]

Hence, the function of the *objet petit a*, for Žižek as opposed to Lacan, is to have stick in our mind the brutal truth that we cannot depend on ontology, or even any kind of anti-ontology, as Derrida is frequently read, to move philosophy à la Marx from interpreting the world to changing it. We must read all philosophy, and by extension all theory, as the impossibility of philosophy, or theory. The point is not to theorize; it is to act. If the motto of the Enlightenment for Kant was *sape audere* ("dare to know"), for Žižek it is *sape agere* ("dare to act").

Failed Subjectivity

At the same time, Žižek's resuscitation of German idealism amounts, in fact, to a *re-Hegeleanizing of the poststructuralist Hegel* for the sake of a new, self-conscious (or perhaps we should say "subjectiv-ized") political actionism that will wean people away from Hegelian-ism in its entirety. It has nothing to do with helping us bring Kant, Schelling, and Hegel up to date, as an "interpreter" would be wont to do. Bringing anyone "up to date," as the specific German word *aktualisieren* suggests, is to "actualize" latent potentials that were already there in the legacy of a thinker, but have remained dormant, like "sleeper cells," within the legacy itself. But no "actualization" of the latent Hegel takes place in Žižek. Like a good therapist, Žižek helps us focus on our obsession with Hegel in such a way that we are eventually cured of the obsession.

Žižek writes that "what philosophical idealism, at its most sub-versive, effectively amounts to is *not* a kind of gradual emanation of material reality from the Absolute, *à la Plotin*, but the Hegelian notion of 'reality' as something which exists only in so far as Idea is not fully actualized, fulfilled.'"[9] Žižek therefore locates the subjectification of the subject not in German idealism, or any other type of idealism per se, but in the *failure* of the subject. The failure of the subject is coordi-nate, both theoretically and historically, with the failure of idealism, that is, the kind of subjective idealism inaugurated with Descartes, which finds its true bearings in Kant's "transcendental" philosophy, and which allegedly reaches its apotheosis in the Hegelian thesis of the Absolute *becoming* Subject through the dialectical movement of self-reflexivity, becoming in its unique concretely universal totality *an und für sich.* Žižek keenly and brilliantly recognizes that postmod-ern philosophy went off track, starting not so much with Derrida as with figures like Foucault, by conflating the subject to a mere type of regime or *praxis.*

This insight explains his otherwise somewhat puzzling hostility to the collaboration between Deleuze and Guattari, not to Deleuze's own philosophical contributions. Under the spell of Guattari, the radical Freudian, Deleuze apparently succumbed, as Žižek at times intimates, to a kind of materialism that may have pandered to the New Left of the 1960s and 1970s with its pseudo-Marxist sexual Dionysianism, but failed to banish the totalizing impulse from West-ern philosophy, as the avant-garde of that period claimed to be doing. Detotalization requires a subject, not the substantial subject, but the split subject. The split subject in turn guarantees the perpetual exor-cism of even the most subtle totalizing specters.

Žižek, in fact, makes this point somewhat ironically in his preface to *The Ticklish Subject* by parodying the oft-recited opening lines of *The Communist Manifesto* to make his point.

A spectre is haunting Western academia, the spectre of the Cartesian subject. All academic powers have entered into a holy alliance to exorcize this spectre: the New Age obscurantist (who wants to supersede the "Cartesian paradigm" toward a new holistic approach) and the postmodern deconstructionist (for whom the Cartesian subject is a discursive fiction, an effect of decentered textual mechanisms); the Habermasian theorist of communication (who insists on a shift from Cartesian monological subjectivity to discursive intersubjectivity) and the Heideggerian proponent of the thought of Being (who stresses the need to "traverse" the horizon of modern subjectivity culminating in current ravaging nihilism); the cognitive scientist (who endeavors to prove empirically that there is no unique scene of the Self, just a pandemonium of competing forces) and the Deep Ecologist (who blames Cartesian mechanist materialism for providing the philosophical foundation for the ruthless exploitation of nature); the critical (post-) Marxist (who insists that the illusory freedom of the bourgeois thinking subject is rooted in class division) and the feminist (who emphasizes the allegedly sexless *cogito* is in fact a male partriarchal formation).[10]

But what Žižek *actually* means by the "Cartesian subject," as our analysis already implies, is something radically different from any kind of orthodox or even a "transcendental" Cartesianism. Žižek is not really advocating a "return to the subject," nor is his *cogito* by any means a retro-incarnation of Descartes's *res cogitans* or Kant's unity of apperception. His gesture of "back to the subject" is but a feint that allows him to insert both Schelling and Lacan into the discourse in a powerful and strategic manner. Subjectivity becomes "the indivisible remainder," the barred S that can never be rubbed out, rolled over, or bracketed in the discourse *de rerum natura*, whether it be metaphysical, ontological, critical-transcendental, idealist, structuralist, or whatever. Heretofore we have always referred to this remainder as "consciousness," but the term is too long heavily laden with mystified implications of autonomous selfhood, an "identity" that leaves completely out of account à la Schelling the realization that such an *Identität* is always *pre-ontological*. It cannot be speculatively determined. What remains is the irremediable incommensurability of the ontological nomenclature we have at our disposal.

We can only understand Žižek's apparent "prioritizing" of the Cartesian subject when it dawns on us that he is reading Descartes in a radically different way, as does Levinas, as we shall see later. What is

truly at stake in Žižek's reading of the *cogito* is the view that it ultimately "brings us to *madness* as a philosophical notion inherent in
the concept of subjectivity." Just as the subjective, or creative, drive
in Schelling's God serves as exit route from his own pre-ontological
madness, so the *cogito* becomes "the founding gesture of 'human-
ization.'"[11] Furthermore, the "gesture of withdrawal" in Descartes's
method of hyperbolic doubt, which constitutes an "absolute negativity" akin to madness that is at the same time "the gesture that opens
up the space for the Light of Logos," succeeds fatefully in constituting subjectivity once and for all as "a kind of substitute-formation,
destined to recompense us for the loss of the immediate symbolic
Real."[12] All etiologies of realism and idealism constitute parallax
viewings of what we see after the loss of the immediate Symbolic
Real. They circulate around this impossible positioning of the subject,
which Žižek compares to a "strange attractor" in mathematics, a set
toward which a dynamic or chaotic system in flux tends in its evolu-
tionary changes. The history of philosophy can be located as a series
of events, or event-formations, which in Žižek's eyes always have the
self in this profound sense as their limit or horizon. That is because
philosophy itself would be impossible without the intervention of
subjectivity. But this place of intervention cannot be located within
the territory of philosophy itself. It belongs beyond its own horizon.

Against Deleuze

Žižek's conviction that in the discovery of an indivisible remainder,
rendering impossible the claim of self-identity through the fact of
a "zero-level" subjectivity, he has somehow delineated for the first
time the horizon of philosophy (as if he had photographed Sasquatch
for the first time) leads him to take on Deleuze as a kind false prophet
of immanence. Žižek's argument against Deleuze, contained for the
most part in his 2004 book *Organs without Bodies: On Deleuze and
Consequences*, makes basically two essential points, which are unfortunately not as effectively pressed as against other rivals such as
Derrida and Badiou. The first point he makes is that Deleuze, the
self-professed anti-Hegelian, is in reality a closet Hegelian. The second point, which he argues more indirectly, is that Deleuze's vaunted
notion of a "transcendental empiricism" anchored in his own assertion that philosophy must assume a "pure immanence" must at the
same time always come back to the indivisible remainder.

If Deleuze seats all empiricism in the production of difference, this
production is unintelligible without the "minimal difference," as

Žižek calls it, of subjectivization from the production process itself. Deleuze's well-known concept of the virtual is carefully enunciated in *What Is Philosophy?* The virtual is the ontological region of the cosmos that somehow conditions the experience of the event. The virtual is what perpetually "haunts" the manifestation of the actual. It is the "pressure" that keeps the ordered system as close as possible to chaos. "The virtual is no longer the chaotic virtual but rather virtuality that has become consistent, that has become an entity formed on a plane of immanence that sections the chaos. That is what we call the Event, or the part that eludes its own actualization in everything that happens."[13] The productivity of the virtual through its ongoing "expressionism," as Deleuze calls it, in the radically temporalized event can be attributed to the kinetic movement of the putatively "timeless" substance of metaphysics. Hence, Deleuze reads Spinoza as a precursor of the theory of dynamic immanence with the latter's notion of "substance" playing the role of the virtual. "Expression is inherent in substance, insofar as substance is absolutely infinite; in its attributes, insofar as they constitute an infinity; in essence, insofar as each essence in an attribute is infinite."[14]

Here we have Deleuze's answer to Hegel, perhaps calling into question Žižek's contention that the former is secretly a Hegelian. It is hard to read this statement of Deleuze's in even the remotest Hegelian manner, as Žižek proposes. Expressionism does not countenance the dialectic. Infinite substance is not something that can be codified by either classical idealism or "materialism." Deleuze quotes approvingly Merleau-Ponty's observation that the "idea of a positive infinity" in seventeenth-century philosophy happens to be "the secret of grand Rationalism."[15] One can detect in this citation Deleuze's long-standing position that the infinite cannot be seen as any kind of "attractor"—either in the sense of *a terminus a quo* (the infinitely small) or *a terminus ad quem* (the infinitely vast)—but as a *potentia infinita*, the "originary origin" of the real, the intelligible, and the actual, that is, the virtual.

Žižek mistakenly interprets Deleuze's discussion of the virtual as a slam against the dialectic. According to Žižek, Deleuze's "proper site of production is *not* the virtual space as such, but, rather, the very passage from it to constituted reality, the collapse of the multitude and its oscillations into one reality . . . the determination and negation of the virtual multitude (this is how Deleuze reads Spinoza's *omnis determinatio est negatio* against Hegel)."[16] It is not clear how Žižek establishes this particular reading of Deleuze. The insinuation is that Deleuze's virtual site of production is just a lot of hocus-pocus for the process of dialectical self-negation. Žižek wants a truly materialist Hegel, and he therefore is compelled to construe Deleuze as a kind of renegade materialist Hegelian as well, which is slightly plausible given the latter's French Marxist incubation period, yet misses the critical themes that distinguish Deleuze from all the other poststructuralists. Further on in *Organs without Bodies* Žižek claims that "another subterranean link between Deleuze and Hegel is that of *immanence*."[17] Hegel is truly, he insists, "the philosopher of unconditioned immanence," according to Žižek.

The dialectic by and large can be considered the "transcendental" movement of self-negating categorial rescissions in the fabric of being, the fluttering of its momentary "folds" (as Deleuze might say) in such a way that everything is eventually ironed out, though with the wrinkles still visible.

Contra Deleuze, "*immanence is not an immediate fact but the result that occurs when transcendence is sacrificed and falls back into immanence*," Žižek maintains.[18] Hence, there cannot really be any such thing as a "transcendental empiricism," because such a somewhat sophistical construction fails to recognize that the very momentum and *ontologic* of the transcendental, as Kant first crafted the concept, cancels out the conditions that would keep it going. The dialectic captures this immanent sense of the real in a way that no "empiricism" could ever manage. The sacrifice of the transcendental representation, even the ultimate representation of God, is a necessity of the gesture toward immanence itself, whether that immanence be posited as a start point or an end point. It is no accident that Hegel in the *Phenomenology*, borrowing from Luther, minted the expression "God is dead" three-quarters of a century before Nietzsche.

Of course, the production of the multiple at the site of the virtual is something much different from its own negation. Deleuze, with the possible exception of the Heidegger of *Identity and Difference*, is the first philosopher to elaborate the *difference* between negation and difference. The production of the multiple, for Deleuze, is its differentiation from the not-yet-actualized potentiality of the generation of infinite assemblages and singularities within the space of the actual. The line that separates virtuality and actuality is traversed not by an act of dialectical disclosure in reversal, a "passage" from the not-here to the here, but a passage from *what could be here* to *what is now here*, something akin to Schelling's infinite potentiation in God before creation, his *Seinskönnen*. Despite Žižek's misplaced polemics against Deleuze, his misreading of the latter's account of the event serves a valuable purpose in framing his own theory of radical subjectivization. According to Žižek, "subjectivity" is the site of "true infinity," not the passage from virtual to actual, or "the infinity of pure becoming."[19] In Deleuze, of course, the "infinity of pure becoming," a motif first introduced by Nietzsche, is the infinity of affirmative—not negative—differentiation, Zarathustra's transformation of every "yes it was" to "thus I willed it." For Nietzsche and Deleuze, willing, or "repetition" *as* willing, differentiates.

What Žižek means by the "true infinity" of subjectivity does not range far afield from this kind of differentiation as willing. But if Žižek did not make a straw man out of Deleuze, his point would be far less forceful, and his misprision would not be as fruitful. What gives Žižek a slight edge over Deleuze in this particular confrontation is his hint that subjectivity as a way of naming the site of infinity draws our attention toward the *ultimate singularity*—misidentified in the philosophical tradition as the self or ego—around which all evanescent events of cognition and signification must circulate. Can this peculiar singularity, whether we dub it an "attractor" or an "event horizon" or something else, be considered religious? Žižek tends to think so, which explains why his thesis of the split subject must ultimately lead to the same problems to which Hegel, Nietzsche, Heidegger, and Altizer keep coming back—the singularity of the crucified, "dead" God.

Žižek and the Question of the "Religious"

Žižek's foray into the question of the religious tactically follows the one-lane access route of Christian thought, and even in this seemingly capacious domain takes the treacherous, narrow jeep trail of what several centuries ago we would not have hesitated to envisage as a brooding "pietism," especially the old Germanic kind with its focus on the Good Friday passion, the divine *via dolorosa*. Although Žižek occasionally compares himself to historic Protestantism, his project is really to show that the entirety of the Reformation imagination must inexorably collapse into a Marxist materialism, especially the odd "libertarian" kind that he with various flourishes avows over and over again. And this new kind of libertarian Marxism comes down to a "perverse core" of so much of the Western political and ethical heritage, which includes both Christianity and Marxism, yet can be assimilated to neither concept as these "traditions" are normally understood. Contrary to some of his critics who are quick to pounce once they think they have figured out exactly what he is saying about the connection between the history of philosophy, politics, and religion, Žižek does not use the religious as a form of leverage to get beyond the religious. It is safe to say that is exactly where he has always wanted to land, though he is perhaps more comfortable with his surroundings, which he at last recognizes, than his critics would be, if they actually understood his stance.

Žižek's seemingly playful notion of a "perverse core"—comparable taxonomically to the Real in Lacanian theory, or to everything that gets shoved aside in the struggle between our desires and the machinery of the Symbolic order—is not a hyperbolic gesture whatsoever. A "perversity" is something that ends up tortured and twisted into unrecognizable shapes through the incommensurability of these two kinds of signifying processes. Perversion is not a type of rhetorical caricature; it is what remains embedded, coiled, and concealed within the very illusions of normativity and the performance, including linguistic performance, of those things "done decently and in good order" (as a Calvinist might say). It is the kind of "truth" a psychoanalyst strives for the patient to uncover through the unwinding of the tightly structured dissemblances peculiar to his own discourse. The quest for philosophical truth is no different, as far as Žižek is concerned. What we call "religion" has its own perverse core, and that perverse core is Christianity. Christianity, in turn, has its own perverse core, which is the crucified God.

In *The Puppet and the Dwarf: The Perverse Core of Christianity,* Žižek hammers together the scaffolding for the more complex kind of analysis he carries out later in *The Monstrosity of Christ.* Any theory of the "religious" cannot be essayed by theorizing from the singular to the universal. It is always the other way around. *One must theorize from the universal to the singular.* Religious theory is not about the grand commonalities of the multifarious religious kinds of religious "data," including beliefs, practices, and idiosyncrasies. It depends on discovering not the "rule" but the *exception to the rule,* which paradoxically yields the rule. "Christ was, before his death, a universal concept ('Jesus the Christ-Messiah'), and, through his death, he emerged as the unique singular, 'Jesus Christ.' Here universality is *aufgehoben* in singularity, not the other way around."[20]

This backward reading of what makes Christianity significant is more than just a "perverse" reading of the history of Western philosophy and theology. It is the cipher for Žižek's insistence that the secret of Christianity is its radical materialism, its progressive own "auto-deconstruction" (my term, which I employ here ironically) to the point where the death of God is, not a temporal, but an eternal event necessitated by the nature of God himself (a strong version of Schelling's cosmological argument). God singularizes himself *in time* in order to sacrifice himself for the sake of his human handiwork made in his "image," a loving act of divine suicide. God dies, so that the "overman" may live, as Nietzsche puts it so well in *Thus Spoke Zarathustra*. That is what Žižek, of course, means by the "perverse core of Christianity." It is perverse because it is like a surprise Hitch-cockian ending (a theme that fascinates Žižek to a fault) to the seemingly coherent narrative of Christian salvation. It is summed up in Lord Chesterton's phrase, which Žižek cites forcefully, as "a matter more dark and awful than it is easy to discuss." The Cross was never an option, as far as God was concerned; it was his own inexorable "coming of age," as the incarcerated Diedrich Bonhoeffer, the only theologian in the history of Christianity who has ever truly carried out Kierkegaard's "teleological suspension of the ethical," strangely intimated while awaiting the gallows. The movement is not from eternity to time and back to eternity. The movement is into time once and for all, a point Altizer made more than a generation ago without the benefit of Lacanian analysis or the history of German idealism—only the kind of "apocalyptic" insight communicated on the eve of the Industrial Revolution by the poet William Blake.

Hence, it is not too difficult to grasp why Žižek has nothing but contempt for all ideologies of religious pluralism, perennialism, neo-Gnosticism, transcendentalism, what he brands "New Age obscuran-tism," and all the other kinds of cheap, happy-go-lucky affirmations of religious relativism masquerading as "postmodernism" that consti-tute the hard-wired ideological core of the "study of religion." Žižek does not even spare the recently modish neo-Derridean notion of a deconstructive theology, a "religion without religion." The task of the theoretician of the "religious" is not to open up broader horizons but to narrow them to the point of exclusivity, even more exclusively than what we might term certain discourse-bound forms of "privileg-ing" texts, points of view, or "traditions." If one looks at the actual history of religions, Žižek contends in *The Puppet and the Dwarf*, we find three distinctive ideal types (to employ Weber's locution): the tribal-communitarian, the universalistic, and the exceptionalistic.

Although Žižek has little familiarity or patience with the history of methodology in the effort to sketch out a religious theory, it is evident he discerns clearly that the *idea* of religion qua religion is normally something that can always be derived from a close study of the differ-ent patterns and interrelations among the first two types. Indeed, the actual history of religious theory, perhaps dating all the way back to the Enlightenment, if not the Greeks, unstintingly swings back and forth between ethnography and a general phenomenology, between the anthropological and the morphological, between historicism and comparativism. The third type is truly something "dark and awful" for religious theorists to contemplate, yet that is where we must go if in the twilight of postmodernism we have no choice but to go. Religion is the "universal exception," not simply with respect to other dimensions of the "Symbolic order," but also regarding what we normally regard as "religious." The dreadful *religiones*, those nonhumanistic "exceptionalities" to our pious universalities, are our genuine data. Hence, Christianity becomes a starting point for Žižek (as for Badiou), not because it is the "only true religion," but because it has nothing to do with what we consider to be "religion" at all. As Paul says, no one "preaches" the Christian religion; "we preach Christ crucified."

One of Žižek's most shocking claims is that "fundamentalists" may know something that we "enlightened" scholars think we know, but don't. It is not that fundamentalists, who think they have the truth, do in fact have it. Fundamentalism is always about the priority of texts or doctrinal formulations, whereas "truth" for Žižek is far more radical than all that. The religious is the Real, the terrible revelation of naked singularity, par excellence. As Žižek claims in his earlier book *The Fragile Absolute*, religious truth—that is, "Christian" truth—in its raw singularity is "monstrous" in its role as a kind of pure "fantasy." "Fantasy is not an idiosyncratic excess that deranges cosmic order, but the violent singular excess that *sustains* every notion of an order."[21] There is no "language" in the sense of *parole* as opposed to *langue* without the "symptom." There is no truth without the incommensurability of the different "orders" of truth. Žižek here pulls in Marx's own complex trope of the "specter," which Derrida of course utilizes to evoke the *revenant*, that which forever "returns," as does the religious, in the disordering or "disjointing" of our current sense of semiotic order for the sake of unlocking the *avenant*, the pure messianic, what is "coming."

For Žižek, the "specter" or *revenant* does not point to the "impossible" impulse toward a future messianic "paradise" of pure indeconstructible justice that is never locatable "historically," but what he calls the "impossible Real" of a present "structure," which is truly the "Event." "The "Event" is the "engendering violent gesture which brings about the legal Order that renders this very gesture retroactively 'illegal,' relegating it to the spectral repressed status of something that can never be fully acknowledged-symbolized-confessed."[22]

Curiously, Žižek here follows Derrida's own analysis in his treatise "Force of Law," where he inaugurates the problem of the religious within the project of deconstruction by rereading idiosyncratically

Walter Benjamin's famous essay from the time of the Weimar Republic entitled "Zur Kritik der Gewalt" ("Critique of Violence"). Derrida draws on Benjamin's famous distinction in his "critique," which is actually a critique of the state, between *rechtsetzende Gewalt* ("law-imposing" violence) *and rechterhaltende Gewalt* ("law-preserving" violence). Derrida inaugurates the religious question in terms of the problem of justice, which requires both a law-founding and a law-sustaining violence that is aboriginally divine, or religious, though seemingly "unjust," in character.

Žižek demystifies this famous observation in Derrida by suggesting that the Derridean question of the religious does not have its genesis in the problem of the political, but in the problem of the Symbolic order. The problem lies in the failure of the subject for the sake of its own subjectification through the *spectralization* of impossible desire in the formation of the *objet petit a.* The religious, which generically or institutionally belongs to the Symbolc order, in a broad sense is equivalent to the commodified *objet petit a.* Thus the "return of the religious" in the era of hypercapitalism can be interpreted as the proliferation of such *objets* in all their spectral, structurally dysfunctional, splendor. The messianic, even the Derridean messianic, is inscribed within this commodified order. The "perverse core" of the religious *revenant* with all its promiscuous progeny is really the dead God, the singular, abysmal *realissimum* around which all such specters in their commodified supplementarity circulate and create a cloud of distracting signifiers through which we cannot penetrate to the Real, the very "truth" of religion.

The Monstrosity of Christ and the Death of God

It is in his recent encounter with Milbank's own version of what Žižek considers such "obscurantism" that he finally lays out the perverse core as theory, rather than suggestion. The "conversation" between Milbank and Žižek entitled The Monstrosity of Christ (actually, it is a reciprocating polemic with Žižek having the final say) is supposedly, as Milbank himself says, a "question of the interpretation of Christianity."[23] But it is not about Christianity at all, not in the sense that Milbank implies. The debate is really about method in its broadest meaning.

Milbank views Žižek with his would-be Hegelian obsessions as the truly "last" of the modernists, where his sophisticated Lacanian refinement of Altizer's "Christian atheism" amounts to nothing more than a "heterodox version of Christian belief" that is uniquely Protestant.

Milbank plays on Žižek's rhetoric of the "post-metaphysical" to make much the same point early in his career when he claimed that radical orthodoxy with its own "strange" reading of the historic doctrines of the Eucharist, as opposed to Žižek's caricaturing of Wittgenstein, Heidegger, and Derridean postmodernism, was the only possible navigable transit route beyond "ontotheology." What he terms "the nub of the issue" between himself and Žižek is putatively a simple dispute over who is truly radically heterodox or radically orthodox.

At one point, however, he paradoxically accuses Žižek of "orthodoxy," albeit not a sufficiently radical one. "Is it more radical and Christian to say," Milbank asks, "in heterodox fashion (with Hegel), that the infinite 'is only the absurdly self-grounding finite,' or is it more radical to say, in a kind of hyperorthodox fashion with Eckhart, that the infinite and the finite both coincide and do not coincide"—in other words, the "orthodox" Chalcedonian "fully God and fully man." Milbank adds: "In the first case we have the tediously mysterious abolition of mystery; in the second case we have the fascinatingly mysterious exposition of mystery in all its simplicity."[24]

Milbank, of course, entirely misses the point of what Žižek is up to. The question of Christianity—and we should add the question of the religious, especially if the object is to theorize—has never been about "mystery." The category of mystery is one of the arch categories of the process of "postmodern" mystification, which Žižek sees as an expansive Enlightenment universalism, following the trajectory of a dying star in its "red giant" stage (or, as Žižek calls Milbank, a "Red Tory" who wants an all-encompassing socialist state largesse specifically under the umbrella of a reactionary Catholic-feudal class structure) collapsing into the form of a "white dwarf," an even more "obscurantist" style of "religion without religion." Milbank confuses simplicity with singularity. Singularity is what both draws both *infinitely* and *abysmally* all the structures—even the most *paradoxical* or even *paralogical* ones—of language and signification in the direction of a *parallax*, or "split," subjectivity that is truly primordial in its postmodern *postmetaphysicality*. The "Christ event," as Rudolf Bultmann originally named it, is the "true event." When "the Christian God," Žižek writes, "'manifests himself to other men as an individual man, exclusive and single,'" we are then "dealing with the singularity of a pure event, with contingency brought to an extreme—only in this mode, excluding all efforts to approach universal perfection, can God incarnate himself." Finally, "this change can be succinctly described as the shift from the upward movement of the becoming-essential of the accident to the downward movement of the becoming-accidental of the essence."[25]

There is a strange logic that demands the metaphor from astrophysics of the so-called black hole, alternately referred to as a "singularity," which becomes the so-called event horizon beyond which we cannot peer, yet we know it influences the appearance of everything visible in both its immediate and more remote neighborhoods. We locate the black hole, where all the laws of nature (and by extension of logic and language) collapse, also by the infinite "gravitational" pull of this singularity, toward which everything tends. The black hole signifies the possibility of infinite destruction and infinite renewal for cosmic processes, all within its event singularity that is the ultimately real and determinative. The event singularity, circumscribed by its horizon of its ever more intense "downward" circulation, is not a mystery. In physics it is eminently predictable, though not observable, by the computations of arcane mathematics. Is not the religious singularity eminently predictable, though not immediately observable, by the complex and esoteric inferences of all poststructuralist theoreticians, including Žižek?

We must remember the sudden death-plunge of Nietzsche's tightrope walker, the one who seeks to transit the abyss but falls into it. That is what Žižek perhaps has in mind with his provocative and "perverse" signification of Christ's "monstrosity," which he characterizes as a tenebrous "truth," wherein "the entire edifice of reality hinges on a contingent singularity through which it alone actualizes itself."[26] That is also what it comes down to in Hegel's absolute self-disclosure of Absolute Spirit, according to Žižek. "In the triad of art, religion, and science (philosophy), religion is crucial as the site of a gap, of an imbalance between form and content."[27] Spirit is the horizon, the Absolute is the event, which, as Hegel says cryptically at the conclusion of *The Phenomenology of Spirit*, must undergo its Golgotha to become actual.

Žižek puts it as starkly as possible. "What dies on the Cross . . . [is] indeed God himself, not just his 'finite container,' a historically contingent name or form of God."[28] Žižek criticizes Caputo's suggestion that events such as the death of God are not happenings per se, but something that "goes on in what happens," the virtual productive that can be conjectured yet never derived from the experience of things within the temporal dimension.

For Žižek, God dies in the exact same "univocal" sense that my friend Doug died in 2005—in the latter's case from cancer, in the former case perhaps from "pity," as Nietzsche wrote ironically. The event, for Deleuze and of course Caputo, is always an "excess" over its determinations. Yet, as far as Žižek is concerned, the excess is in its effects. That is why the death of God, which we can understand as a concretized, determinate event on the Cross (or when we look at a crucifix we perhaps have a kind of kitschy *memento mori* of it), is more shattering than any metaphor can contain. Žižek professes that he much prefers Altizer's "apocalyptic" depiction of God's death over Caputo's putative "deconstructive" account of it as the final disclosure of the impossibility of ontotheology. He asks: what if "the entire history of Christianity, inclusive of (and especially) its Orthodox versions [not to mention its deconstructive ones], is structured as a series of defenses against the traumatic apocalyptic core of incarnation/death/resurrection?[29]

The history of Christian theology—from Paulinism to Christian Platonism to "dialectical theology" and beyond—is, therefore, "structured" against acknowledgment of this perverse and "monstrous" incongruity between God as a sustainable "idea of God," nested within a certain inaccessible revelatory particularity, and the particularity itself. Altizer's essential theme, which he has drummed home for most of his career, is that "apocalypse" is not like Derridean messianism, that is, what *is to come*. Jesus's memorable yet ambiguous, word on the Cross—*telestai*, "it is finished"—means exactly that, as far as Altizer is concerned. *Fini!* Done! But with a bang, rather than a whimper. According to Žižek, the "finished" singularity of this non-iterable actual event establishes not "truth" in either a religious or philosophical sense, but perhaps something akin to a truth-event that is more than truth. But this truth-event, the most real event, the singular event of all singular events, contains something even more significant than all religious formulations can allow.

The concept of the truth-event, of course, does not have its genesis in Žižek, but in Badiou. One can only grasp the meaning of the truth-event, whether it has a "Christian" or a materialist nomenclature, says Badiou, if one realizes that the whole of Western philosophy since the early nineteenth century has been slowly replacing the process of logical determination with what he calls "suturing." It has incrementally surrendered the autonomy of philosophy to separate independent "truth-procedures," such as science and politics, to which it is subsequently joined or "sutured." Philosophy, or theory, can never revive the once grand opera of unfolding concepts à la German idealism, declaring at the highest level of synthetic thinking what something *is* in its concretized generality. Philosophy must move in the direction of making "determinations" that are indeterminate, that is, "eventful" and "singular." Although Badiou does not use the term, we can say that these indeterminate determinations are "semiotic" in the broadest meaning of the term. If the failure of the subject is the source of subjectification for Žižek, what Badiou dubs "disobjectification" is the source, for him, of the philosophical registering of the event. In order to grasp how this kind of perspective plays out with regard to religious theory, we must now turn to Badiou himself.

9

BADIOU AND THE PROSPECTS
FOR THEORY

■

New: that which is unforeseen by the order of creation.
—Alain Badiou

BADIOU WOULD seem to be a genuinely bizarre source of inspiration for "religious theory." While most of our present-day celebrity postmodern thinkers, including even Deleuze, have been amenable to God-talk or religion-speak in some fashion, Badiou has resolutely maintained his youthful stance of Sartrean atheism and Marxism. The irony, of course, is that Badiou in his later years became fascinated in a more conspicuous way with Christian thought that any of his contemporaries. His book on St. Paul is a landmark in religious thought. In *St. Paul: The Foundation of Universalism* Badiou the philosophical formalist and apostle of set theory in mathematics becomes his own kind of apostle to the French intellectual community concerning the philosophical importance of Paul's message of salvation. Did Badiou have his own Damascus-road conversion?

There is no suggestion at all that Badiou underwent his own philosophical *metanoia* and suddenly acquired a Christian theological cast of mind. What does seem to have occurred is that Badiou, in both reading, and reading about, Paul, discovered a leverage point in the history of Western thought—as Heidegger did with the pre-Socratics—for his own take on philosophy as a whole. Badiou's contributions to contemporary philosophy at large are at this stage not as sizable perhaps as those of Derrida in the 1980s and Deleuze in the 1990s. Like Derrida,

Badiou sets out to establish a discourse that is postmodern because it is more "Jew-Greek" than "Greek-Jew" (as Hegel was). Whereas Greek discourse is that of the concept or *eidos*, "Jewish discourse," Badiou asserts, is "the discourse of the sign."[1]

The Discourse of the Sign

But Badiou's discourse is not merely that of the sign. The sign is an action or an indicator, but it is not in itself the basis for a philosophical operation. A Jew-Greek philosophy would find a means of adequating the concept to the sign in order to express the former through the latter rather than the other way around. We discern in this endeavor a willingness to take Deleuze further than Deleuze himself was able to go. Badiou makes clear in his homage to Deleuze that the latter exhibited "a great power of speculative dreaming," one that is "prophetic, although without promise."[2] Badiou believes he is himself carrying out the promise. He obviously reads Deleuze with a jaundiced eye, and not only are their two styles utterly incompatible, it is not obvious that what Badiou calls the latter's "tonality" can be transposed into his own philosophical register. Deleuze was a philosopher by trade and by ascription. Badiou seeks to restore philosophy from what he views as a stage of postmodernist disrepair into the grand mansion it supposedly once was. For Badiou, philosophy is concerned chiefly neither with the sign (although thought must be semiotically sensitive) nor with the concept (although it must attend to the general beyond the particular) but with the *event*. "Event" is the *bon mot* in all of Badiou's philosophy.

According to Badiou, Paul is the thinker of the event in this sense. "Paul's project is to show that a universal logic of salvation cannot be reconciled with any law, be it one that ties thought to the cosmos, or one that fixes the effects of an exceptional election. It is impossible that the starting point be the Whole, but just as impossible that it be an exception to the Whole. Neither totality nor the sign will do. One must proceed from the event as such, which is a-cosmic and illegal, refusing integration into any totality and signaling nothing."[3] Because Badiou does not rely on the familiar theological argot of Pauline Christianity, which has become the staple for orthodoxy, it is a bit mind-bending to attempt to understand how he unrolls his own theoretical discourse as a kind of parallel text to scripture itself. Greek and Jewish discourse, Badiou argues, "are both discourses of the Father," insofar as they "bind communities in a form of obedience (to the Cosmos, the Empire, God, or the Law)." Conversely, Paul's is "a discourse of the Son," which alone "has the potential to be universal."[4] What does Badiou mean by this sort of metonymic yet philosophical "apologetic" for what appears to be a religious position?

Badiou insists that Paul is somehow unique in the history of thought, even religious thought. Whereas the Gospel of John adapts an "exceptional" form of Jewish exceptionalism to the Greek mythopoetic philosophy of the Word, Paul's language of the Son as "Christ crucified" shatters this logocentrism. "The formula according to which God sent us his Son signifies primarily an intervention within History, one through which it is, as Nietzsche will put it, 'broken in two,' rather than governed by a transcending reckoning in conformity with the laws of an epoch."[5] If Nietzsche as the arch precursor and Deleuze as the apotheosis of the postmodern both militantly sought a "reversal of Platonism," then the *renversement* already occurred with the birth of Christianity. Christianity may be, as Nietzsche quipped, "Platonism for the mob," but that taunt does not apply to Paul. Paul's discourse of the son is neither Jewish nor Greek. It consists instead, according to Badiou, in a "diagonalization" of these discourses, by which he seems to mean that the discourse of *Christ incarnate* implies both a rupture and an unprecedented renewal. Christ is *une venue*, "a coming"; he "is what interrupts the previous regime of discourses. Christ is, in himself and for himself, *what happens to us*."[6] Christ is *pure event*, pure signifying event that inaugurates an infinite and rhizomic chain of future significations and signifying events. For Badiou, Paul's rhetoric of a slave becoming a son in Christ connotes that inequality and subjugation—the hierarchy of being from a cosmic perspective—is now "transvalued" (in Nietzsche's words) as equality and freedom. The resurrection event in which all of that is made plain must now be affirmed as a singularity—the *Christ singularity*—from which all universalistic claims about justice, human rights, and liberty must proceed. The event is "pure beginning." That is to say, "the real is identified as event."[7]

The real, which appears under the guise of a difference to all previous religious differences, shows itself correspondingly as an event that abolishes all religious differences. In Christ there is no Greek or Jew, and so forth. This reality—it is indeed an epicalic reality, one that breaks through as a *skandalon* with the shock of Žižek's Real and the incongruity of Levinas's Infinite—belongs neither to a "religious" nor to a "philosophical" tradition. It is more real that those histories ever were and ever shall be. The "real" of the Christ event "abolishes philosophy." Badiou notes that "this is probably what distinguishes Paul from contemporary anti-philosophers, who circumscribe the real-event within the realm of effective truth: 'grand politics' for Nietzsche; the arch-scientific analytic for Lacan; mystical aesthetics for Wittgenstein."[8] The *real event* that inaugurates Christianity has its reality in the fact that it is a "new beginning." We might want to say, with Tillich, that it is *ontologically inaugural* because Christ is the "new Being." But Badiou will have nothing of any new ontology of Heideggerian fundamental ontology, even a Christian ontology that can only be a theology in the broadest drift of the expression. Badiou's real is inaugural because it is a singular event. It is not a shift in worldviews. It is not a new cosmology. It is not even a "Christian" event, if we want to use some kind of generic designator from the taxonomy of recognized *religiones*. The event has more to do with the diagonality itself which, regarded from an overarching perspective, constitutes a transgression of the historically prevailing grammars of conveyance, classification, inference, and description, and can be seen as an *originary semiosis*, what in a vague way we might call the grand "deconstructive" moment for all the familiar Western codes of signification. Such a semiosis slices through the multidimensional schemas of propositionality, conceptuality, and meaningfulness that dominate our familiar discourse.

We must remind ourselves that Badiou calls himself the thinker of the "multiple," not of the unitary. Being is multiple for Badiou, who elaborates Deleuze's thesis of univocity. Being is a procession of singularities. The multiple is "not a part" but an "excess of itself," inasmuch as "superabundance cannot be assigned to any Whole."[9] Without indiscriminately trying to sound religious, Badiou through his theory of the event as singular event gives us the leverage we need to begin religious theory after postmodernism. The real event always "exceeds" its "contingent site." The local that has a strange kind of "illeity" invested within it—for example, watercourses, rock cairns, or black stones that become pilgrimage sites—is the beginning of the universal, which is where we begin to theorize the religious. "There is singularity only insofar as there is universality. Failing that, there is, outside of truth, only particularity."[10] Truth cannot be a particular truth, which would relativize it and thereby render it untruth. But it *can* be a truth that is broken open by the singular signifying event that opens up undelineated possibilities, "impossible possibilities," for universal truth. The singularity whom Kierkegaard named "the God-man" (or what in other religious traditions we might call an avatar) is the incarnation of truth. Incarnation is the universal made radically singular and the singular made radically universal. The relationship between the universal and the singular is not a dialectical one à la

Hegel, but an orthogonal one that constitutes the event. Moreover, there are two "truth-procedures," as Badiou would say, whereby this sort of truth can be prescinded. There is the event of resurrection, on which Badiou himself dwells as the beginning of the procedure. But there is also the event of incarnation, which cannot be discerned at the moment of inception, but only eschatologically with respect to the truth-procedure that prescinds from the inaugural "exception" to the laws of history, cosmos, community, and tradition in order to articulate the full spectrum of significant singularities and eventualities. That process of articulation we call theory.

If we follow Badiou, theory—and that includes religious theory—does not amount to a special instance that excludes general discourse. That modern positivism has created a brutal and triune system of "apartheid" between the religious, the scientific, and what Wittgenstein called *gewöhnliche Sprache,* or ordinary language, is testimony to the necessity of writing a new "manifesto for philosophy," in Badiou's parlance. The sanctions that force this apartheid to crumble, according to Badiou, come from a "revolution" in mathematics that transpired in the 1960s. It is not our business to explore the arcane byways of late twentieth-century mathematics, particularly set theory, which launched Badiou on his own discrete path. But Badiou's confidence that his often peculiar and metaphor-rich philosophical idiom is seated in a mathematical rigor that positivism never had at its disposal suggests that he is less "scientific" than what appears prima facie to be the case. For Badiou it is a natural transition from a *mathesis universalis* through a meditation on Deleuze and Plato's political critique to reflections on Paul's epistles. Each does not constitute a methodology, but a truth-procedure that arises from an evental engagement with the real.

Badiou's talk of Christ develops from his earlier efforts to rehabilitate Plato and ancient philosophy—not a philosophy of the idea, or *eidos,* but a philosophy of the singular that leads to a *truth-procedure.* In his chef-d'oeuvre, entitled *Being and Event,* Badiou challenges fundamentally the Derridean masking of the event as difference, or as *khōra.* Setting his face against Derrida and his ilk, Badiou denies any "ontology" of difference or of the negative. The problem of truth "is bound to the profound problem of the indiscernible, the unnameable, and the absolutely indeterminate." But Badiou argues that these "impossibles" or "undeconstructibles" can be discerned, named, and determined. The unpresentable is presentable. "It can be demonstrated that it may be thought."[11]

Badiou goes about presenting the presentable with respect to an ontology that departs from Platonism, neo-Platonism, Scholasticism, and even Heideggerianism. Ironically, it may be considered a return to what Heidegger denoted as the "ontic," but that does not imply any sort of revitalization of classical ontology. Classical ontology as laid out in Aristotle's *Metaphysics* is preoccupied with the question of Being as Being. In the evolution of ontology through neo-Platonism the question of Being (*to on*) accedes to a profound nescience in the contemplation of the One (*to hen*). However, Badiou wants to redirect the questioning of "what is" onto an entirely new track. To this end he rejects all formulations and permutations of metaphysics as well as apophatic thinking. Being, the One, or even the "Not" cannot be sufficient topics for consideration. All of these categories have the character of indiscernibility. "Strictly speaking, there is no unnameable."[12] In place of the One Badiou proposes the "multiple." The multiple is not the enumerated manifold, the many-ness. The notion of the multiple is the obverse of the principle of the singular, or of singular signification that produces further singularities. The multiple is the infinitely iterated singular, each of which in its own right constitutes a breakthrough for further iterations. This approach turns out to be Badiou's answer to Deleuze's transcendental empiricism. Philosophy is "empirical" to the extent that finite situations yield infinite elaborations. "Every *finite* multiple of presented multiples is a part which falls under knowledge, even if this only be by its enumeration."[13] Knowledge itself constitutes an "intervention" of the infinite into the finite multiple, which can then be teased out, directed, and universalized as a truth-procedure.

Saving the Names

Badiou wants to "save the names" (in Derrida's lingo) through a revolution in philosophy that takes the concern with truth beyond ontology, beyond Heidegger's understanding of truth as *aleitheia* or "unconcealing." The true arrives in the event, but truth itself is "post-evental," as Badiou says. "The process of a truth thus escapes ontology."[14] Throughout his career Badiou has been obsessed with the same question that entranced Heidegger—Parmenides' question of the identity of thought and being. Deleuze hit upon the solution of the singularity, Badiou contends, as a way to make signification something that does not require any "intentionality," as it has for phenomenology, on the part of the subject. But, for Badiou, Deleuze's resort to the

singular—an interpretation that is something of a misprision when
it comes to what Deleuze is really doing—amounts to "the ascetic
constraint of a case."[15] Deleuze's fixation on the case, and the site,
explains why he wrote such encyclopedic works that could only pro-
visionally be called "philosophical," ranging from treatises on the
aesthetic proprieties of literature and cinema to the kind of global
anthropology and linguistic experimentation that prove to be most
striking in *A Thousand Plateaus*. Deleuze offers us the possibility of
theory, but not theory itself, Badiou implies.

The undercurrents of Badiou's theorizing flow from his work in
set theory. Without delving into the details and density of set theory,
which is one of the foundational or "axiomatic" languages of most
mathematical formalism, we can attain a sense of where Badiou is
headed. It is worth a footnote that set theory has always been contro-
versial among mathematicians because of the importance it gives to
the idea of infinity. George Cantor, the nineteenth-century German
mathematician who invented set theory, assailed the basic assumption of mathematics, going all the way back to Euclid, that numbers
are eminently finite and computable. Cantor's suggestion that there
are "transfinite" numbers as well an "infinity of infinities"—a tacitly
theological locution that led one of his many harsh critics to dismiss
set theory as "God's mathematics" that only God could know—shook
up not only the world of numerics but over time the scientific establishment in general. Cantor did not help to allay suspicions by quip-
ping that he believed that set theory as a whole had been inspired
"by God." It was even more unsettling than Riemannian geometry,
which described the four dimensions, and perhaps beyond, as a con-
tinuation rather than a rupture in the classical metaphysical model
of space as "extension." Riemann paved the way for Einstein's theory
of relativity. But set theory has always been a thorn in the side of
philosophers and physicists who cling to a totalizing picture of the
scientific enterprise where legible and intelligible representations of
the universe have the final say. Even Wittgenstein, who put to rest
once and for all the correspondence theory of truth and propositions,
of an inherent collocation of words and things that undergirds the
philosophical dogma of language as reference, was appalled at Cantor's "discoveries" and dismissed set theory as a "joke."

In addition to transfinite numbers and the notion of an "infinity of
infinities," to which even Scholastic theologians objected because it
seemed more Protestant than Thomist, Cantor laid out the distress-
ing principle of the null set. While the null set is a basic presupposi-
tion in mathematics these days from algebra to calculus and beyond,

it remains troubling for any philosophy—which most "modernist" philosophies are—of establishing the finality of finitude. Mathematically, the null set plays some, though not all, of the same functions that the "not-God" of Angelus Silesius performs in negative theology and Derrida's program of saving the name. The null set is its own kind of "differend" that demonstrates at the base level the limitation, or boundary set, for all finite structures of inclusion, or what in set theory are called "well-ordered sets" built according to the rule of "cardinality." It is also key to Badiou's distinctive project of discerning the indiscernible and naming the unnameable.

One of the inveterate reasons for resistance on the part of mathematicians early on to set theory was that it did seem to be a sophisticated version of negative theology under the guise of number theory. Even though nullity and infinity had been employed as crucial terms in mathematics since ancient times, they were considered heurisms, useful abstractions with no positive content. When set theory seemed to make the case that these terms could no longer be regarded as heurisms, it was trashed as irredeemably "unmathematical." Cantor spoke, for instance, of an "actual infinity," an infinite set of "real" numbers with a "power" (*Mächtigkeit*) to control the set of finite numbers. That form of diction struck most of his contemporaries as raving God-talk. But Cantor was more interested in the mathematical productivity of generating sets of numbers than he was in "proving" what had previously been considered an abstraction. He was not so much trying to smuggle in some kind of late modern "ontological proof" for the existence of God as he was trying to make a case for a correlation between the dynamism of numbers and the dynamism of the natural order. It was a realization of the ultimate dynamism of nature (what the Greeks, especially the pre-Socratic Greeks, meant by *physis*, as Heidegger instructs us) energized by an "immanent" infinite that crystallized Deleuze's semiotics of the singular and informed his vocabulary concerning the interplay of the "virtual" and the "actual."

As Badiou points out, this particular "thesis of the infinity of being," which can be seen as opposed to the premise that only God is infinite, is necessarily "post-Christian" or "post-Galilean," though historically it is something that perhaps glimmers in Scotus, from whom the crowd of the radically orthodox claim postmodernism is derived. Actual or "effective" (Badiou's word) infinity "cannot be recognized according to the unique metaphysical punctuality of the substantial infinity of a supreme being."[16] That would be to confuse infinity, as Scholasticism did, with the one. "The mathematic ontologization of the infinite separates it absolutely from the one, which is not. If pure multiples are what must be recognized as infinite, it is ruled out that there may be some one-infinity."[17] The power of effective infinity resides in the activation of the "multiple" or, in our terminology, the power of the singular/multiple that can be considered an immanent or "incarnated" infinity.

Yet a thesis of an incarnated infinity demands that there be some "operator" (as one would say in mathematics) that "activates" the sign of infinity, that transmits it as a "signal" and transforms it into a signifying event. Badiou provides the argument for such an operator in what he terms "the theorem of the point of excess." Badiou's argument is rather technical. "The question," he writes, "is that of establishing that given a presented multiple the one-multiple composed from its subjects" happens to be "essentially 'larger' than the initial multiple." The comparison with the "larger" one is not an issue of "magnitude." Instead, "the 'passage' to the set of subsets is an operation in *absolute* excess of the situation itself." In addition, "the multiple of the subsets of a set necessarily contains at least one multiple which does not belong to the initial set."[18] The theorem—which for our purposes in the discourse of semiotics we shall dub the "principle"—of excess comes down to the fact that being must be reconsidered as *point-being,* as point-being that becomes in Deleuze's terminology an "active force."

What Heidegger criticizes as Nietzsche's "metaphysics" of the will to power was actually an effort to show how point-being must be rethought as *point-becoming.* For this task Nietzsche could only use the aphoristic style that segments systematic argument and concentrates on the power of the compact rhetorical fragment to disclose what has hitherto not been disclosed. Nietzsche's persistent trope of the *Überfluß* or "overflow," the key to unlocking the riddle of "overman," emphasizes this principle of excess. Zarathustra must come down from the mountain because he is "overrich," he embodies or incarnates everything that is "excess" in the *Allzumenschliche.* Zarathustra is the "operator" for the differential equation that signifies the passage from man to overman.

The principle of excess, as Badiou himself maintains, is initially found in Leibniz, from which Deleuze himself seems to have adduced the possibility of a dynamic singularity, whereby he could go on to be the "philosopher of the event." Badiou sees in Leibniz's theory of monads an ontological foreshadowing of the principle of excess and the thought of the event. The monadology is "an anticipation of set theory with atoms." Monads represent the "dissemination" of immanent infinity through "a network of *spiritual* punctualities that God continuously 'fulgurates.'" The monads as "metaphysical points" are "thus both quantitatively void" (the null set) and "qualitatively full" (an actual infinity). Monads "must be unities of quality," dynamic quality. Leibnizian monadology ultimately over generations, therefore, yields Deleuzean *nomadology*. Monads are, Badiou concludes, "in my eyes—pure names."[19]

Set theory gives us the conceptual apparatus to save the names—that is, recover the univocity of being without succumbing to Scotism or negative theology—while at the same time to loop around any structuralist, or poststructuralist, theory of signification the kind of *mathesis universalis* of which even Descartes and contemporary philosophers of science could only dream. Thus Badiou's theory is an incarnational theory. It does not trade off between finite and infinite in an ever oscillating notation of difference between the same and the not-same, the limited and the illimitable. It renders the real not as an "obscene" gesture (Žižek) but as an epiphany of the pure sign, the sign that is inseparable from event, the "I know not what" that is at the same time "I know what I never knew," an incision and an engrafting of the unnameable and undecidable onto the contingency of the natural with an output that has one expression—*it happened.*

Incarnated Infinity

Badiou's work is a conspectus for a religious theory that is at the same time an incarnational theory. But how would it apply more precisely to religious theory? Badiou does not deliberately or wittingly take us there. However, in extrapolating from his "hermeneutics" of the writings of St. Paul and cross-referencing it with his theory of the event as a continuum of procedures arising out of the expansion of the singular-multiple, we can begin to envision what religious theory after postmodernism might look like. Badiou is too bogged down in his own mathematicism to understand that the intervention of the infinite into the finite as the event that abolishes ontology has telling implications for religious theory. Badiou has only given us permission to do what we need to do. He has delivered us a warrant to become empowered with our own set of "procedures" that are not bound to the philosophy of language, as the phenomenologists, the poststructuralists, and the more "safe at home" varieties of postmodernists we read these days have tended to be.

One unexplored avenue for a theory of incarnate signification would be Julia Kristeva's conception of poetry, which is heavily encumbered by Lacanian psychoanalysis but which, if shorn of its Freudian instinctualism, may prove highly fruitful. Reading Deleuze and Badiou hypertextually alongside Kristeva can be useful. Kristeva's revisionist paradigm of semiotics, which she first advanced in the early 1970s, drew from a Lacanian or psychoanalytical redescription of how syntactical systems in language can generate semiotic singularities. Until that time semiotics had been understood since the days of Saussure to be a subdivision of formal linguistics. Besides Noam Chomsky, the leading theoretician of this formalistic semiotics was Louis Hjelmslev from the Copenhagen school, who proposed that signs mediate between "content" (concepts or psychological states) and their "expression" in perceptible or material performances. Deleuze's notion of "expressionism," not to mention his idea of signification as a "double articulation" as developed in *The Logic of Sense*, emanates directly from Hjelmslev's insight. Hjelmslev's guiding analogy was sign language, where formal structures of meaning can be communicated through nonphonetic gestures but still retain the same logical and grammatical regularities as spoken words. Hjelmslev's content/expression distinction was his refinement of Saussure's dyad of *langue* and *parole*. Hjelmslev referred to this refinement as "semiotics" only because the signs in the context where they operate have more theoretical value than their "content," even though, unlike in later semiotics, the content always conditioned, if not determined, the expression.

Kristeva on the other hand took her cue from the Prague school of linguistics, which rivaled the Copenhagen school in turning formalism against itself in its efforts to account for literary and aesthetic discourse as much as "natural language." It is possible to argue, although one must be careful in making too bold assertions, that Prague school semiotics, which considered itself formalist and eventually "structuralist" with its emphasis on the text as text, seeded the insights that led to the "poststructuralist" revolution in France in the 1960s, for which Kristeva, as a leader of the Tel Quel group that included Deleuze and Derrida, was perhaps the unsung motivation. One of the tenets of the Prague school is that language is capable of "literarization," meaning that there are certain strategies of signifying praxis that disrupt both communicative and interpretative routines that authors and poets—as well as critics—employ. The word the Prague school made famous in this regard was "defamiliarization," which may have been a conceptual forerunner of différance. The Prague school, following Marxism and countering the positivist biases of the Vienna and Copenhagen schools, focused on the historical or diachronic analysis of linguistic processes. Historically, signs always have a "political" or critical-theoretical function. The formalism of the Prague school became strangely both historicist and apodictic—as was Marxist Leninism—at the same time.

The secret of Prague school semiotics, Kristeva declares in an essay from 1967 that looks forward to Badiou, is that it deploys mathematic formalisms in a nonformalistic manner. "Mathematics and meta-mathematics [are] artificial languages that, due to the freedom of the signs they use, are more and more able to elude the constraints of a logic based on the Indo-European subject-predicate relation, and that as a consequence are better adapted to describing the poetic operations of language."[20] Kristeva gives only casual mention to set theory, but Badiou, in his bridging of mathematical formalism with poststructuralist rhetoric, makes much the same argument. Set theory always competed with the discipline of symbolic logic or the "predicative calculus" that had this white mythology in its foreground and exerted an hegemony over Western philosophy until the 1960s. But something of Badiou's program is implicit in her exposition. Her threefold "thesis" at this early stage of her work is as follows:

1. Poetic language is the only infinity of code.
2. The literary text is double: reading-writing.
3. The literary text is a network of construction.[21]

The last two statements are familiar as the principal theses of deconstruction. But the first cannot be found in deconstruction. It belongs to Badiou's semiology. Poetic language, Kristeva goes on to say, is a *"real infinity* that cannot be represented" and is therefore within the matrix of "semiology," not linguistics. "The task of the semiologist will be to try to read the finite in relation to an infinity by uncovering a signification that would result from modes of conjunction within the ordered system of poetic language."[22]

Later Kristeva labels this version of signification as the "thetic," taking a word from the theory of prosody that is difficult to render precisely into the philosophical syntax in which Kristeva first uses it. The thetic we may say, somewhat elliptically, is the operation of the sign outside the "law of the sign." That is why Kristeva's semiotics rejects the Saussurian model of "sign systems" and advances the view that we have only acts of significations and "signifying processes." Signs function not in accordance with laws of syntactical performances but as "moments of transgression" of these systematic codes—the Lacanian Symbolic. Lacanian analysis is concerned with the language of the "unconscious," which is structured like a language.

But Kristeva discards the Freudian construct of the unconscious—a ghostly metaphysical entity—and lays stress on the semiotic process whereby desire disrupts language and language blocks or reorients desire, what she dubs "semanalysis." Poetic language, which is the only real language, is the arch theme of semiotics. It reveals the "semiotic disposition" of all subjective speech, which as a voice of what is forbidden or unspeakable forces the "opening" in codified language to give words their signifying power and effective expression. Kristeva looks upon semanalysis as the heir to the failed dialectic. Kristeva notes that Peirce himself, the father of semiotics, had this succession in mind. He even called semiotics "Hegel in strange costume." There is no "heterogeneity" in Hegel, according to Kristeva. But semiotics compels this differentialism or heterogeneity in the specular moment which both the dialectic and psychoanalysis take as necessary to the development of consciousness. Kristeva describes what she calls the "unicity of the thetic," which cannot be "theologized" and serves as "the precondition for meaning and signification."[23]

The unicity of the thetic is comparable to Deleuze's understanding of signification as always "univocal" as well as Badiou's proposition concerning the multiple/singular. It also bears some resemblance to Žižek's irrepressibility of the real. The thetic depends on the fact that there are always "holes" in the code of language, what Kristeva names the "semiotic chora." Plato's *khōra* is largely a being-point (in Derrida's case a language-point or text-point) that allows for the *productivity of the negative.* But the semiotic chora is productive not because of its negativity but *because of its singularity.* The semiotic chora divulges to us that signification cannot be generalized in terms of protocols and rules of denotation, association, or contextualizaton. From Husserl through Frege, Kristeva insists, the singular was always subordinated to the general concept. Desire in the psychoanalytic medium disrupts, but it does not signify. Signification arises from the "thetic position" of the subject. Predication, or the "copulative" conjunction of subject and attribution, cannot express the thetic position. Language as the reciprocal system of generalization and particularization hides the thetic in its primacy. Thus semiotics both precedes and fulfils logic. But semiotics can never suffice for syntatics. It can only enlarge it—hence the necessity of "supplementing" grammatology with semiology. It is thoroughly "expressive," in Hjelmslev's sense. Poetry permits the "redistribution of the signifying order" and "the transposition of the thetic break into a homogeneous sign-system."[24] This transformation depends on the "infinity of code" inscribed in poetic expression.

Is religious expression a more complete example of this "infinity of code," perhaps something approximating Cantor's "infinity of infinities"? Clearly, Kristeva's identification of the Lacanian moment of ecstatic thesis, or *jouissance,* with poetic signification does not exhaust the realm of signifying eventualities that poetry incorporates. Our job here is not to lay out what a religious theory after postmodernism would include at length. That itself comes after this particular "prolegomenon." Badiou offers us a *mathesis* that can fruitfully transport us beyond mathematics. Kristeva with her theory of the semiotic chora tell us how the infinite as "operator" gives us recognizable resultants. Certainly the historical interdependence of poetry, the prophetic or oracular, and the theological—if not the metaphysical— should be an obvious guide wire for where we should be going.

But we want a theory, a theory that explains how the infinite becomes incarnate in the sign. That sort of "incarnational" principle is offered by theology, but is not wedded to it. The idea of the incarnational—as post-Nicene theology in the history of the Christian West makes clear—from what Willard Quine called the "logical point of view" always debouches in paradoxes, aporias, and putative absurdities. We must go beyond the logical to the semiotic and the rhetorical. Theory, if it is to serve as religious theory, must acquire the argot of the kinetics of singularities and what Deleuze calls "intensities." It must also draw inspiration from Žižek's (and to a certain extent Badiou's) later obsession with the "death of God" and what can loosely be designated as the *Christ event.*

Such renderings of the event are not theological, confessional, or triumphalistic, particularly since they are undertaken by philosophers who consciously disown all ideological "Christian" commitments. They are in fact ventures into a profound *semiological* reading of the infrastructure for the entirety of our Jew-Greek Western philosophical heritage. If Hegel had been a semiotician rather than an idealist philosopher, he might have made the connection as well. In a word, we need to discover, as Deleuze did, the dynamic disjunctiveness of all our propositions. We need a *theoretical rhetoric* (if by "rhetoric" we have in mind a manner of speaking that flows, that morphs, that constitutes a *rhetor*) that captures the sense of the transfinite, of actual infinity as well as the epicalic mutuality of the infinite as it engages the finite and the finite as it is activated by and responds to the infinite in every instance of singularity. We need to stop talking "about" religion while in the same breath refrain from "talking religiously."

Badiou's discussion of St. Paul can be a template for this project. But we need the power of Deleuze's "semiotic anthropology" and tropic linguistics that disclose the movement of territorialization and deterritorialization as it affects the "history of religions" as a whole. Badiou, as we have seen, has undertaken a "formalization" of Deleuze's argument for immanence. But Deleuze's argument—or more precisely his rhetoric—has often been misunderstood and subtly disfigured because of the inveterate bias of our white mythological discourse toward predicative logic, even if it is a "fuzzy" predicative logic. One of the challenges in deploying Deleuze's myriad writings along a focused, theoretical trajectory, especially in order to make sense out of the "religious," is that those works with which we are most familiar and which have given us a unique "Deleuzian" vocabulary are the least helpful in crafting the philosophical scaffolding for such an enterprise. The collaboration with Guattari was most momentous in radicalizing Deleuze's core philosophical project, but it also deprives us of a set of middle terms by which we might move beyond our inveterate Hellenism—and by implication our preference for various Orientalisms—which even Derrida's suggestion of a new kind of "Jew-Greekness" cannot get a grip on.

The Fourth Specter

Ironically, it is Deleuze's last conventionally "philosophical" work concerning Spinoza that may offer those middle terms, those terms that provide the transition from the concept to the sign. Spinoza is indeed the fourth specter that stalks postmodernism, as Nietzsche's barely conscious use of the former's religious thought underscores. But Spinoza, or perhaps Deleuze's reinterpretation of Spinoza, is what can begin to define the era "after postmodernism." It is not our business here to work as carefully as possible through Deleuze's reading of Spinoza. Spinoza is often regarded by ontotheological thinkers as an anomaly of sorts within the tradition of "Continental rationalism" who has about him a whiff of unpardonable heresy. Spinoza is as much of a "heretic" within modern philosophical orthodoxy as he is in the ambit of classical Judeo-Christian theism. While theologians since his first publications have derided him as a "pantheist," conventional philosophers have regarded him as some sort of arcane metaphysician speaking with an unfamiliar diction. Those who mutter about Deleuze's own strange kind of diction tend not to recognize that it is Spinozistic all the way down. In his book on Spinoza, Deleuze credits him with making the kinds of signal conceptual breakthroughs that he himself touts as the "new image of thought." In terms of its ramifications for religious theory, the semiotic richness of Deleuze/Spinoza has far more fruitful implications than the thought-image of Badiou, which is tethered to a mathematical formalism he cannot escape. The difference is that Badiou's thought-image, despite its formalism, is more intuitively obvious, while Deleuze's must be teased out.

Deleuze and Spinoza in their own unique way—the former incidentally throws in Leibniz as well, who as a mathematician and occasional experimental scientist tried to resolve what he perceived to be methodological inconsistencies in the latter—offer the thought-image of religious theory as the theory of *infinite expressive signification*. Prior to Spinoza, the theory of signification—or of signs in general, what today in the argot of poststructuralism we dub *semiotique*—was bundled inseparably with the Platonic model of a hierarchy of being identified with mimesis and varied gradations of adequate representation. Nominalism had changed the equation slightly, especially when it sought to relativize the object signified, and in formulating a theology relied fatefully no longer on the Platonic doctrine of *methexis*, or participation, but on the principle of divine power. It is Spinoza who performs a catachrestic operation on the Platonic notion of participation through his critique of the Aristotelian and Scholastic idea of substance with the result that he is no longer talking about *methexis*, but *dynamis* and *potestas*. That is Deleuze's fundamental discovery.

Deleuze, however, concentrates on what he calls the "expressive" character of Spinoza's metaphysics, refined by Leibniz. Thus Spinoza and Leibniz count for a quiet revolution against Cartesianism and by implication all of the Western philosophical tradition. For the first time, in Spinoza, a "de-Platonized" philosophy becomes self-consciously "expressionistic," anticipating Nietzsche's (and Deleuze's) *renversement* of the Platonic legacy. What does Deleuze mean by "expressionism"? Deleuze's employment of the term has some of the connotations of the word as it is more familiarly mobilized to discuss the movement of the arts at the turn of the twentieth century from representation to subjective response. But Deleuze gives the word certain technical overtones that betray Spinoza's own distinctive approach to thinking. Philosophy is expressionistic to the extent that the infinite capacity of thought, implicated in Spinoza's dictum of *Deus sive natura* ("God, that is, nature"), iterates itself through finite sequences of signifying operations.

Deleuze discovers this process of iteration in Spinoza's modalism wherein there is no such thing as a mind-body, or a thought-matter, duality, but such terms constitute merely "ideas" derived from co-equal attributes of the *simpliciter* singular, yet infinite, Deity as parallel sequences of signification. These sorts of signification are neither the sign-constellations of medieval theology, which approximate and consist in various levels of adequation to the infinite reality of God, nor the sign-differentials of Saussurean linguistics from which the notion of the deconstruction of texts emerges. They are not signs per se, nor are they signifying instances. They are momenta or signifying processes that ceaselessly "express" the creativity and productivity of the infinite itself. Oddly, Levinas's God and Spinoza's God line up as the strangest of bedfellows in this context. The apparent *Ganz Anderssein* of Levinas's Old Testament Deity and Spinoza's "heretical," modernist, thoroughly immanent Deity still occupy the "Jew" side of the fundamental Derridean aporia. Spinoza's *Deus sive natura* ("God or immanence"), the putative pantheistic principle, is easily rendered as *Vi naturae invenitur in Deo* ("God as force encountered within immanence"), the broad Levinasian principle of "otherwise than Being," especially if we take into account that God in both instances is utterly what Deleuze would term "virtual," the source of events as well as The Event. According to Deleuze, Spinoza considers the immanent awareness of these infinite sign-momenta and signifying sequences as a "third kind of knowledge," which he associates with *revelation*. Or, more precisely, the infinite "God" reveals himself through infinite signifying processes with respect to finite minds and artistry. It questions "the transcendence of a One above Being along with the transcendence of a Being above Creation. Every concept has in it a virtual apparatus of metaphor."[25]

But the "revelation" of God through semiosis, which is always tropic and "metaphorical," is not at all what in theological terms would be designated as "general revelation," or the signifying complexity of the divine design. It is, strictly speaking, a "special revelation" of the kind that is similar in form, if not in content, to the Christian one. In other words, the infinite becomes finite, that is, *incarnate*, insofar as it tends toward an infinity of what Deleuze dubs "singular essences," comparable to Leibnizian monads, or what we have named "signifying singularities." The special revelation of Deleuzian semiosis can in principle apply to all religions, and thus it is not the sort of Niceanism camouflaged as Hegelianism that historians of religion attuned to Western "philosophical" theories of religion are always flagging for subtexts. "So there is in Spinoza," Deleuze writes, "no metaphysics of essences, no dynamic of forces, no mechanics of phenomena. Everything in Nature is . . . a physics of extensive quantity, that is, a mechanism through which modes themselves come into existence; a physics of force, that is, a dynamism through which essence asserts itself in existence, espousing the variations of the power of action."[26] There are no "things," which therefore are not predicable. Quality is taken as intensity, and names turn out to be always fleeting simulacra for the production of these intensities in the flux of what Deleuze terms "assemblages." We have only what later in Nietzsche would be called valuations and affirmation. We can conceive of the "metaphoricity" of countless and diverse forms of religious expression: the notions of the *dharma-kaya* of "dependent co-origination" in Buddhism, the monitory "signs" which a Qur'anic revelation as "recitation" yields in Islam, or even the cosmic Christ of Colossians by whom "all things were created—things in heaven and on earth, visible and invisible, whether thrones or powers or rulers or authorities . . . and in him all things hold together."[27]

Philosophical expressionism is tacit in neo-Platonism with its doctrine of emanations, according to Deleuze. But it also furnishes a lingua franca for an incarnational theory of language. The concept of expression, Deleuze states, has "two sources: one of them ontological, relating to the *expression of God*, and born within the traditions of emanation and creation, but bringing these profoundly into question; the other logical, relating to *what is expressed by propositions*, born within Aristotelian logic, but questioning and shaking it. Both meet in the problem of divine Names, of the Logos or Word."[28] The problem of propositions at this level of course comes down to what more recently has arisen as the problem of "religious language." But the "religious" is not a stratum of language; it is the key to language itself in the measure that directs us toward the infinite generativity of language—not merely grammar—that has its source in the divine itself. This generativity works two ways: back to the infinite source and forward to the specificity and the pure situationalism of the singular word or phrase. Religious language itself works both ways, and religious theory thus has to work with word not merely as text but as a strange "donation" (as Deleuze would say) of sense and the singularity of evocation and address.

Expression is the movement of territorialization and deterritorialization when it comes to language. A theory of expressive signification constitutes the linchpin for religious theory *tout ensemble*. The religious is a "territory" that is always deterritorializing itself, while becoming deterritorialized and reterritorialized by its own relentless dynamism. The religious figure forever rambles at the rough and blurred boundaries of the empire of signs. At the same time, the same figure "incarnates" this process of infinite, expressive signification through his, or her, life and the odyssey of open-ended interpretation, "deconstructive" appropriation and memory, and conceptual intervention

beyond the religious event *ab initio*. The so-called Abrahamic traditions testify to this universality of expansive, *rhizomic* signification
that bursts forth within the horizon of temporal events, yet hides
the event itself. An erupting volcano is not the *event itself*, but an
"eventuality" that indicates the horizon of all future and past, virtual and actual, "conscious" and "unconscious," parallactic chains of
signifying moments that reach back into both the depths of mysterious subterranean forces and the breadth of possible effects, implications, and repercussions. Similarly, Abraham's encounter at the Oaks
of Mamre is the eventuality that harbors the event that can only be
vaguely summarized as historical monotheism. The same would be
true of Gautama's instant of self-realized consciousness under the
Bodhi tree, or even that peculiar, storied moment when a merchant
named Mohammed, while meditating in a cave on Mount Hira in the
Arabian peninsula, was told by the angel to "recite."

As Deleuze writes in *The Logic of Sense*, such "events" are "singularities" that remain at the same time "turning points and points
of inflection." The singularity "belongs to another dimension than
that of denotation, manifestation, or signification."[29] The religious
singularity is determinative in such a manner. It is not merely the
visible event but the "undeconstructible" source of all these religious
eventualities, spinning out all the complex filigrees of signification
that give the history of religion its textual, ritual, and commemora-
tive richness. It is the *event horizon*—the true nameable name for the
Singularity of singularities—of all those things that are "sacrally" and
even profanely nameable.

CONCLUSION

TOWARD A REVIVAL OF RELIGIOUS THEORY

■

> She tore a hole in our universe, a gateway to another dimen-
> sion. A dimension of pure chaos. Pure [. . .] evil. When she
> crossed over, she was just a ship. But when she came back [. . .]
> she was alive! Look at her, Miller. Isn't she beautiful?
>
> —Dr. Weir, in the movie *Event Horizon*

BUT IF IN considering the religious we find ourselves in such a
strange "place," seeking to peer over the generative rim of events, we
must ask the question: how do we think at, and across, this horizon?
How do we theorize the *infinite, or illimitable, horizon of the event*
that Spinoza's God, Deleuze's "expressive" semiosis, Levinas's face,
Derrida's "friendship," and Žižek's singular materiality pose to us. The
horizon, or "place of religion," is only the site for this infinite *indica-
tivity* within our own time-space continuum. Spinoza himself said the
infinite continuum of God allowed for an infinity of divine attributes,
only two of which we are capable of thinking God. A human being is
limited to thinking God through the attributes of mind and matter.

There are of course now other means of thinking the infinite. String
theory in physics, for example, has supplied a mathematic apparatus
for thinking n dimensions beyond what we can conceive, perceive, or
measure, even though we can characterize the sense of that generativity of a multidimensional universe and a transdimensional God by
certain empirical procedures. Mathematics is one signifying series on
which we can rely. But ultimately the infinite, or the transfinite, cannot be thought simply in the manner of Spinoza. If we are conscious
(or "sentient," as Buddhists would say) entities, then our thinking is a
response, and a response to an "address" by the transfinite. Religious

theory must take one step beyond Heidegger/Derrida, Deleuze/Badiou, and Lacan/Žižek, all of whom, as energetic, binary stars in the galaxy of modern philosophy, have in their own fashion sought to de-reify Western ontology and respond in different but provocative vernaculars to the *question of the sign,* or more precisely to the question of the relation between the singularity and the sign. The next step must be to consider the possibility of a *transversal of the finite signifier* that Levinas bequeaths to us and is entailed in any "incarnational" theory. Mathematics can give us the sign of the incarnate—Isaiah's sign of *Emmanuel*—but it cannot address the thetic source of signification, nor be the addressee.

The Infinite as Signification

Kierkegaard's "paradox" of the infinite singularity of the "God-man" (that is, the infinite singularity that meets us in our finite singularity that requires a response) will continue to haunt us, the last and least exorcizable of specters. Though not all "religions" encompass an explicit language of infinite address, they contain the elements of the vocative and of the invoked. It is the vocative that separates religious language from poetic language and religious theory from aesthetics. A theory of the vocative is barely in its infancy. It can be teased to a certain extent out of Kristeva and Lacan, though all forms of psychoanalysis are in the last synopsis *theories of the subject.* Religious theory is a theory of the infinite intersubjective, or the infinity of the interpersonal. The infinite intersubjective is what "translocates" the singular location we designate as the religious. The kind of naming that saves the names depends on the open-endedness of the intersubjective relation. The infinite or divine, as Luther said, is always "*für uns.*" It is neither "in itself" nor "for itself," but "for us." This for-us is more than a relationality; it is the relativization of all logical and tangential relations in a singular moment of orthogonality. Yet this orthogonality constitutes a time of the full penetration of Badiou's multiplicity by the singularity of infinite dwelling as event, as the impossibility of a reduction within the horizon of signification. That event can be called an *eschatological event,* which means it is not an event at all. It is the event that is exceptional, that pulls toward itself all moments and eventualities, that annihilates and affirms. Eschatology is not an event within *some* religions; it is the cipher of the religious singularity.

If postmodernism has declared the end of all comprehensive histories, grand narratives, and dialectical philosophies, *it must declare its own end as well.* And postmodernism as we understand it is ending. The language of "endings," as few contemporary commentators recognize, has its roots in Heidegger's declaration of the end of metaphysics. The "end" of the postmodern does not have quite the same grandiose implications, however. The end of the postmodern reflects the fact that postmodernism now, as Tim Woods observes, "has developed a history."[1] This history coincides with the intellectual ferment that proceeded from the cultural revolutionary movements in the West in the late 1960s and 1970s as well as with the collapse of militant socialism in the late 1980s and early 1990s and the acceleration of a global market economy. The 1990s was both the golden age and fin de siècle for consumerist, or what some Marxist theorists termed "late," capitalism. But it is also a period when the push for democratic capitalism around the globe and the massive commodification of desire in the form of popular entertainment, media culture, and image-based advertising acquired a planetary reach, fostering a sense that the "postmodern" world had assumed the status of historic inevitability.

That giddy consensus, of course, was savaged by the events of 9/11. While the production of much sentimental and patriotic fluff along with professional pontificating has been spawned by the terrorist attacks on New York and Washington that day, it is becoming obvious that the date signals a distinct, if not obvious, oscillation of the historical pendulum. The day now known as 9/11 revealed the presence of a force that had not succumbed—as even Marxism, a Western phenomenon in its own right, ironically did—to the steamroller of globalization, or "globo-Latinization." That force was dimly perceived as a recrudescent Islamism, which has never in a millennium and a half made accommodation with the West and was mislabeled a "clash of civilizations." But the trends run much deeper.

The trend was also misidentified as some global "revival" of religion, which had never gone away during an epoch of celebratory secularity. Religion is the ineradicable ground cover for human culture that persists throughout history. What was overlooked was the relentless mobilization of these forces into a social and political explosion of religion as the "deeper" exceptionality that defies simple cultural-historical analysis, as the introduction of a transcendent—and frequently disconcerting—imperative into the Enlightenment consensus and the ideological sphere of social democracy. This development has been erroneously labeled "fundamentalism." The postmodern era has been the sunset rather than the rejection of the Enlightenment. What comes after postmodernism remains difficult to anticipate overall.

But we are already witnessing the auguries of the transition. Religion is not "reviving." It is instead beginning to overshadow in numerous venues the *saeculum* while at the same time divulging its more abysmal, and let us dare say *darker,* impulses. This eruption of the exceptionality has strange parallels to what Karl Jaspers termed the "axial" age when collectivist mythologies of tribe and nation suddenly began to dissipate into prophetic or mystical symbols of interiority, when morality replaced magic and a great age of salvation spread from China to the Levant, and the now historic faiths that modernity challenged appeared throughout the known world like so many exotic mushrooms in a damp meadow. The accession to the axial results from the delegitimation of parochial cosmologies wrought by the spread of empire and exchange along with the intellectual and spiritual anomie that development engenders.

The transition out of the modern—and postmodernism has always been a transitional rather than a teleological term—is almost finished as the commercial and technological unification of the planet nears its completion. The uniquely European idols of predicative rationality and pragmatic negotiation are tumbling. Postmodernism did not undermine them or pull them down like the statue of Saddam Hussein; it merely captured their demise. Postmodernism has left a somewhat confused field with revanchists clamoring for the reinstatement of a regimen of monolithic rationality, liberationists constantly widening the borderlands of the self and redefining the gravity of oppression, and cultural revolutionaries engaged in new forms of aesthetic and behavioral dissent as well as utopian experimentation.

But these sorts of statements are really the last twinges of modernist civilization, which also signal the end of the European era. A better analogy to the present time might be the *Wandervölkung* of the late Roman empire when "barbarians" overwhelmed not only the physical frontiers but the dying civic religiosity contained within those frontiers. So-called fundamentalism is a global wave that expresses the profound transcendental yearnings of those unassimilated to Western cosmopolitan rationality, who were previously marginalized, not just in the economic sense, but also from a cultural vantage point. Hence the rise of a new patriarchalism and antilibertinism among Islamic radicals, "Red State" conservatives, and third world religious devotees alike. This kind of fervor has been misnamed "fundamentalism." It has been leveraged politically by "theocrats" or religious authoritarians, at least for the time being, because democratic liberalism has often failed to allow adequate historical expression for the passions that fuel such movements. Our interest is not, however, in the relation between fundamentalism and politics, which generally colors the public understanding of the phenomenon. Instead it centers on the semiotic process by which postmodernity has stripped the religious signifier of its correlative, or "representational," content and forced Western philosophy to gaze upon a boundless and roiling ocean of imaginal possibilities, possibilities that approximate Bataille's—and Derrida's—*impossible*. Levinasian personalism, Derridean apophaticism, and Deleuzian immanentism communicate in entirely different idioms the decline of the metaphysical legend of *adequation*.

Signifiers are no longer "adequate" to what they signify. On the contrary, signification is a "machine"—to use Deleuze's trope—for producing a multitude of "senses." An open, multisignifying process in the religious realm compels the detotalizing of all sacral icons and representations, yet it is also conducive as well to a new totalism that expresses the power of the infinite as negation in a political and violent guise. By misstating the power of the negative in religion as mere anti-intellectualism, or textual literalism, theory fails to comprehend both the past and future of religion.

Religion as Active Force

As the biblical saw goes, "God is not mocked." Religious thought mocks God—that is, the singular that claims and overwhelms us—when it refuses to acknowledge that the force of the religious is more than a psychological, social, or political indicator. Ultimately the force of the religious is Deleuze's "active force," a concept he reinscribes over Nietzsche's enigmatic notion of the "will to power" and the subsequent psychoanalytical construct of the "unconscious." "Consciousness merely expresses the relation of certain reactive forces to the active forces which dominate them," Deleuze writes. "Consciousness is essentially reactive. . . . It is inevitable that consciousness sees the organism from its own point of view and understands it in its own way; that is to say, reactively. What happens is that science follows the paths of consciousness, relying entirely on *other reactive forces.*"[2] Religion is an active force; it is a force that wells up from the organism itself and generates the "reactivity" that we know as rational understanding, or *Aufklärung*. Religious theory can penetrate the activity that prompts the reactivity of thought by deciphering the very sign processes whereby thinking and reflection emerge from the nomadism of desire.

But something far greater is perhaps at stake here. Heidegger may have sensed something of this eventuality in the late 1930s at the height of the parabolic and frightful Nazi coming to power when he named what he called "the last god" (*der letzte Gott*) and what we have named the "after" of postmodernism. He called this moment in which "it is no longer a case of talking 'about' something, but rather of being owned [*ereignet*]." It is "the crossing to the other beginning, into which Western thinking is now entering."[3] This "event" (*Er-eignis*) is "singular" (*eigen*); it is our own, and through it we are *owned* by it. This singularity (*Eigenschaft*) is brought to a completion, as the German prefix "er-" connotes, through this singularity that draws into itself all episodes and signifying events. If we are "owned" by the last god, called as its own, then what we ourselves "own" is nothing in itself. We do not even own our language, as Heidegger reminds us. Dare we designate this "crossing to the other beginning" the crossing from the syntagmata of the proposition to the *semiotique* of the religious? The last god both calls and commands. The "god" calls and commands within a safe and resonating space of language profusions and expressivities that seem to be talking "about" something, particularly the religious. "In the age of infinite needing that originates according to the hidden *distress of no-distress-at-all*, this question necessarily has to appear as the most useless jabbering—beyond which one has already and duly gone. Nevertheless the task remains: *to restore being from within the truth of be-ing*."[4]

We do not need to "Heideggerize" our own task through injecting the language of ontology into the deconstruction of the theories that have gone before. But the question of truth remains essential for our task, as it was for Heidegger. The question of religion is consonant on Heidegger's own terms with the question of truth. It is a question of our own *enownment* by the "ownmost" (Heidegger's word) *singularity* that we call the religious. The question of truth cannot be settled "propositionally," *only* this way. Truth, as Nancy propounds in his own "ownership" of Heidegger's enownment, is a kind of "sovereign majesty" before whom we register an *awe-ful* reverence. The religious as enownment is our ultimate *revenant*. For Heidegger, truth must "hold sway." But, for Nancy, it holds sway as what he calls "dis-enclosure," the opening of space and the quest for the farthest limits of sense and reference that approximate the last god, what Heidegger dubs *der Wink* (literally, a "wink" that calls or beckons while it merely hints and multiplies allusions). "From the genius of one language to that of another there can be nothing but winks, blinks, and scintillations in the universe of sense, in which truth is the black hole into which all these glimmers are absorbed." In addition, "a *Wink* departs from the established order of communication and signification by opening up a zone of allusion and suggestion, a free space for invitation, address, seduction, or waywardness. But that departure beckons toward the ultimate sense of sense, or the truth of sense."[5] In the truth of sense we find the something familiar to us as the "religious." In the truth of sense we find an incarnate "supersensibility." All incarnations are dangerous "landings" of divine impossibilities. They bring not peace but a sword, and of course fire upon the earth.

As Victor Taylor propounds in his discussion of the recent historic relationship between postmodern religious thought—or "postmodern theology"—and religious studies in addition to what has loosely been taken as "religious theory," the changeover to theory itself can be even more painful and disruptive than the impact Derrida originally had upon the field.

> "Religious theory" from "postmodernism" is a religious studies set against itself, beside itself, a para-religious study. This runs contrary to the standard organization of religion into "subject regions" that replace the theoretical with "data," thus defining religious studies as merely an intuitive, observational, and verificational form of "final" analysis. In the wake of "postmodernism" and the fundamental re-examination of the Western theo-philosophical tradition that it entailed, scholarly work and disciplinary boundaries have undergone significant redefinition, a re-definition that pre-empts any closure to boundary or discourse.[6]

There is no such thing as a "postmodern religious theory" per se, since postmodernism almost by definition commits constant acts of sedition when it is applied to what has previously been known as "religious theory." That is not necessarily true of theory in other fields. "Theory" has more recently prevailed over "criticism" in literary studies because the latter has never for the most part had any pretension to do anything materially distinct from what has conventionally been profiled as "theoretical" exercises. The so-called New Criticism, which overshadowed literary studies from the 1920s to the early 1960s, was not formally distinct from deconstruction and "reader response" theory, which in the 1980s established themselves as the central trajectory of the field. Both New Criticism and post-structuralist readings never went "outside the text." Hence Derrida's notorious dictum only continued the tradition of a literary formalism and was only shocking to fields like religious studies with a crypto-theological pedigree of the kind that Eliade among others institutionalized, which assumed they there was some sort of objective correlativity with such pseudo-theoretical terms like "the holy," the "sacred," or the "divine."

Philosophy has never needed theory, because it is theory of a kind by its own nature. It was Rorty's scandalous suggestion, after he read Derrida in the late 1970s, that philosophy could no longer consider itself a "mirror of nature" (i.e., some sort of correlative or descriptive mode of theorizing) that drove his field in an antitheoretical direction. The same can be said of Paul Feyerabend's *Against Method*, which called for something akin to "scientific anarchism." Feyerabend contended that scientific theory and the "methodological" presuppositions that purport to make it uniformly consistent and universally reliable in the quest for knowledge are not all they are cracked up to be.[7] The same goes with those other disciplines in the humanities— political theory, cultural studies, and even musicology—that have been affected by postmodernism.

Postmodernism has undermined, except perhaps in the investigation of literature, what has been the status of theory. The rhetoric of difference can only remotely be termed theory. It is a theory that in reality simulates what we have called the "science of the negative." The science of the negative is prototheoretical, but it must still be built into a "positive" theory that is self-consciously *nonpositivistic*. The "not-ness" of religious transcendence lends the illusion of theory (like the mathematical theory of irrational numbers), and that is why we have been stalled lately with the post-Derridean apophaticism that has found its way into theological thinking.

But if we take Kristeva seriously, we must begin to see how the "not" as "semiotic chora" can be productive of boundless signification. We must inquire into what is really going on in, for instance, Buddhist meditation (not Madhyamika *skepsis*), Jewish suspension of naming in worship, Sufi ecstasy and Sunni veneration of sharia as an expression of Shahada, or perhaps the late Hellenistic form of différance that marked the debates over the meaning of an "iota" in the Christian formulation of Nicea or the confusion of the significations of *prosopa* in the condemnation of both Nestorianism and Monophysitism. In other words, our religious semiology, or theory of religious signs, must deal with contextualized signification as it occurs in history and culture. But it must be anchored in the type of formalism that calls into question all those logical formalisms that have prevented the "human sciences" from taking religion seriously at all. Religious theory, when animated by this kind of formalism, can become a kind of metatheory that shines over all the other human sciences. The theoretical and the "theological" therefore converge, and are in many ways indistinguishable from each other. As Christian Danz in his investigation of the transformation of the theological idiom by the long history of religious theory notes, the problem of "religious pluralism" can only be attacked in this day and age by rediscovering in a post-Hegelian and nondialectical manner the embeddedness of the universal in the particular, rather than the other way around. The problem of religion remains ungeneralizable in the broad sense that nineteenth-century theorists imagined, but it cannot be addressed merely by drawing up a laundry list of topical and methodological particulars. The singularity of the theological signifier is what makes religious theory possible in the first place.[8] If there is any feasible means of characterizing "religion" within this framework, we can say perhaps that *the religious is the event horizon of the signifying webwork; it is the singularity that exceeds all signs.* It is Nancy's "black hole" where sense and non-sense disappear and crystallize "eventually" in a deep space supernova of semiotic creativity.

Postmodernism has shown how the word became a sign, how both sense and signification (Frege's *Sinn* and *Bedeutung*) are collapsed into a semiotic singularity that is at once theological and religious. The semiotic singularity "transcends"—perhaps we should say "inhabits" or indwells—Derrida's transcendental signified. It transcends by way of Deleuze's "transcendental empiricism," wherein the purely localized expresses the ungeneralizable force of what philosophically is known as the universal but is in reality the immanent infinity of the signifying moment itself. God is ultimately and eminently immanent, not because God "derives" from immanence, but because God is the *singularly singular* intersection of infinite intensity with finite possibility, the pure virtual in its activation that reveals itself as *autrement*, "otherwise" than any ontological instantiation of "meaningfulness." That is taking Hegel's principle of incarnate Spirit to the far horizon of imaginability, or conceivability.

After postmodernism we must explore how the sign directs us toward the illimitable engines of signification itself in every direction toward which this discovery ramifies. We must understand the sign in its "fourfold" activation of such a divine intensity, as its deposition in the movement that characterizes textual deconstruction (Derrida), in the self-generating assemblages of active and passive forces (Deleuze), in the incarnate or embodied singularity (Badiou), and the vocative as the orthogonality of the infinite (Levinas)—a "call," as it were.

The religious is not a subject matter, a phenomenon, a "region" of being to delight the new phenomenologists, a *topos*. The religious, the totally deterritorialized territory populated by those curious singularities first characterized as the different *religiones*, is the very condition of the event of language, which Heidegger dimly but fatefully understood. Nor is it an "event," or series of "events," in the way many self-proclaimed "postmodern theologians" currently employ the term. The religious can only be regarded as the *event horizon* of those events, even the most "terrifying," which philosophy is able to identify and interpret. The event of the religious—the "angel"—occurs in a world that is indeed *overinterpreted*, as Rilke suggests.

> Every single angel is frightful.
> And thus I restrain myself and drink down the siren song of my own dark sobbing. Alas, whom are we then able to need? Not angels, not human beings, for the resourceful animals already realize that we are not really at ease in the interpreted world.[9]

In our unstinting efforts to compress our signifying arabesques—our "interpretations"—into plain cloth, we miss not only the forest for the trees but the event for the horizon. We are blinded to the very density and obscurity of our origins.

We forget the fire.

NOTES

■

Introduction

1. Olivier Roy, *Holy Ignorance: When Religion and Culture Part Ways*, trans. Ros Schwartz (New York: Columbia University Press, 2010), 5.
2. Jacques Derrida, *Writing and Difference*, trans. Alan Bass (Chicago: University of Chicago Press, 1978), 3. The quotation is from the essay "Force and Signification," originally published as "Force et signification," *Critique*, nos. 193–94 (June–July 1963).
3. Gilles Deleuze, *The Logic of Sense*, trans. Mark Lester (New York: Columbia University Press, 1990), 22. Earlier in his career Deleuze characterizes the virtual as "real without being present." The virtual is the "principle of localization, rather than of individuation. It appears *as local essence.*" Deleuze, *Proust and Signs*, trans. Richard Howard (New York: George Braziller, 1972), 60.

1. Religion and the Semiotic Revolution

1. Charles S. Peirce, *The Essential Peirce: Selected Philosophical Writings*, ed. Nathan Houser and Christian Kloesel (Bloomington: Indiana University Press, 1992), 281.
2. Jonathan Z. Smith, *To Take Place: Toward Theory in Ritual* (Chicago: University of Chicago Press), 101.
3. Jean Baudrillard, *The Transparency of Evil: Essays on Extreme Phenomena*, trans. James Benedict (New York: New Left Books, 1993), 132.
4. See my article "*A-dieu* to Derrida," in *Secular Theology: American Radical Theological Thought*, ed. Clayton Crockett (London: Routledge, 2001), 37–50.
5. Perry Anderson, *The Origins of Postmodernity* (New York: Verso, 1998), 62.
6. Max Horkheimer and Theodor W. Adorno, *Dialectic of Enlightenment: Philosophical Fragments*, trans. Edmund Jephcott (Stanford: Stanford University Press), 131.
7. Richard Murphy, *Theorizing the Avant-Garde: Modernism, Expressionism, and the Problem of Postmodernity* (Cambridge: Cambridge University Press, 1999), 272.

8. See Gary Genosko, *Undisciplined Theory* (London: Sage Publications, 1998).
9. For a good discussion of Peirce's semiotics as analysis of the human "sign" that establishes the sign, see Jorgen Dines Johansen, *Dialogic Semiosis: An Essay on Signs and Meaning* (Bloomington: Indiana University Press, 1993).
10. See Jack Goody, *Representations and Contradictions: Ambivalence towards Images, Theatre, Fictions, Relics, and Sexuality* (London: Blackwell, 1997).
11. This insight was actually discovered by Durkheim. In the *Elementary Forms of Religious Life,* Durkheim notes that the synecdochal relationship between part and whole is the basis of the sense of "sacrality." "A mere fragment of the flag represents the Motherland just as well as the flag itself. Therefore, it is sacred in the same way and to the same degree." Émile Durkheim, *Durkheim on Religion,* ed. W. S. F. Pickering (Atlanta: Scholars Press, 1994), 139.
12. Genosko actually uses the term "representation" instead of "mimesis," but he employs it in a special sense, which I am avoiding in order not to confuse the reader with "representational" kinds of epistemology that stem from Plato's epistemology of truth as the original versus its "copy."
13. Genosko, *Undisciplined Theory,* 151.
14. See Stephen Gersh, *Concord in Discourse: Harmonics and Semiotics in Late Classical and Early Medieval Platonism* (Berlin: Mouton de Gruyter, 1996).
15. Derrida works out the beginnings of this argument in *Of Spirit: Heidegger and the Question,* trans. Geoffrey Bennington and Rachel Bowlby (Chicago: University of Chicago Press, 1991), a transitional work to what is usually considered the "middle" or "later" Derrida.
16. Jacques Derrida, *On the Name,* trans. David Wood, John P. Leavy, and Ian McLeod (Stanford: Stanford University Press, 1995), 121.
17. Ibid., 120.

2. Theory and the *Deus Evanescens*

1. The word *religiones* was frequently used by Roman writers to describe the secret ceremonies and guarded mysteries of the Druids. For works that discuss the Roman view of *religiones* as shadowy activities that go on in impenetrable woods, see Peter B. Ellis, *The Druids* (Grand Rapids, MI: William B. Eerdmans, 1995), 58–59. See also Nora Chadwick, *The Celts* (Cardiff: University of Wales Press, 1966).
2. Victor Taylor, *Para/Inquiry* (New York: Routledge, 2000), 3.
3. Ibid., 17.
4. Jacques Derrida, "Of an Apocalyptic Tone Newly Adopted in Philosophy," trans. John P. Leavey Jr., in *Derrida and Negative Theology,* ed. Harold Coward and Toby Foshay (Albany: State University of New York Press, 1992), 36.
5. Ibid., 53.
6. Jacques Derrida, "Post-Scriptum: Aporias, Ways and Voices," in *Derrida and Negative Theology,* 289.
7. Ibid., 299.
8. Mark C. Taylor, "nO nOt nO," in *Derrida and Negative Theology,* 175.

9. Mark C. Taylor, *About Religion* (Chicago: University of Chicago Press, 1999), 40–41.
10. Mark C. Taylor, "Paralectics," in *On the Other: Dialogue and/or Dialectics,* ed. Robert P. Scharlemann (Lanham, MD: University Press of America, 1991), 29.
11. Ibid., 30.
12. See Russ McCutcheon, *Manufacturing Religion: The Discourse on Sui Generis Religion and the Politics of Nostalgia* (New York: Oxford University Press, 1997).
13. Smith, *To Take Place,* 101–2.
14. Ibid., 110.
15. Ibid., 105.
16. Jonathan Z. Smith, *Imagining Religion: From Babylon to Jonestown* (Chicago: University of Chicago Press, 1982), 43.
17. Slavoj Žižek, *The Fragile Absolute—or, Why Is the Christian Legacy Worth Fighting For?* (New York: Verso, 2000), 86.
18. Slavoj Žižek, *Looking Awry: An Introduction to Jacques Lacan through Popular Culture* (Cambridge, MA: MIT Press, 1992), 38.
19. Slavoj Žižek, "The Spectre of Ideology," in *The Žižek Reader,* ed. Elizabeth Wright and Edmond Wright (Oxford: Wiley-Blackwell, 1999), 79.
20. Jean-Luc Nancy, *Dis-Enclosure: The Deconstruction of Christianity,* trans. Bettina Bergo, Gabriel Malenfant, and Michael B. Smith (New York: Fordham University Press, 2008), 23.

3. Postmodernism and the Return of the "Religious"

1. Richard Kearney, "Deconstruction, God, and the Possible," in *Derrida and Religion: Other Testaments,* ed. Yvonne Sherwood and Kevin Hart (New York: Routledge, 2005), 304.
2. Jacques Derrida, *Specters of Marx: The State of Debt, the Work of Mourning and the New International,* trans. Peggy Kamuf (New York: Routledge, 1994), 221.
3. Jacques Derrida, *Acts of Religion,* ed. Gil Anidjar (London: Routledge, 2002), 79.
4. Ibid., 79.
5. Ibid., 82.
6. Ibid., 92.
7. Derrida, *Specters of Marx,* 219.
8. Derrida, *Acts of Religion,* 78.
9. According to Bertens, postmodernism is impossible because the phrase has an illimitable extension. In effect, there are multiple "postmodernisms." Postmodernism, he argues, "is several things at once." Bertens distinguishes as many as four "postmodernisms." The word "refers, first of all, to a complex of anti-modernist artistic strategies which emerged in the 1950s and developed momentum in the course of the 1960s." These developments and

strategies are confusing enough. But "at a second level of conceptualization we find similar confusions. Here postmodernism has been defined as the 'attitude' of the 'new sensibility' of the 1960s social and artistic avant-garde," a sensibility that is "eclectic" and "radically democratic," rejecting "the exclusivist and repressive character of liberal humanism and the institutions with which it identifies that humanism." According to Bertens, we may identify this phenomenon as a type of "political" postmodernism that was first identified in the mid-1960s by the literary critic Leslie Fiedler. Then in the 1970s postmodernism was absorbed into the stream of French poststructuralism. Bertens names this movement "poststructuralist postmodernism," which in itself has two phases. The first "derives from Barthes and Derrida and is linguistic, that is, textual in its orientation," concentrating an attack on "foundationalist notions of language, representation, and the subject."

The second "moment," Bertens maintains, is poststructuralist postmodernism, which "derives from Foucault and, to a much lesser extent, Lacan. It belongs to the 1980s rather than to the 1970s, although it is difficult to pinpoint its appearance." The focus of the second phase was on the "workings of power" and its relationship to the production and maintenance of knowledge. At this level much of the neo-Marxist or "cultural Marxist" rhetoric of political postmodernism in the 1960s, particularly its unmasking of ideological postures and formations, became fused with the more "theoretical" innovations of French conceptual postmodernism. The longstanding domestic partnership between Marxist activism and the French intelligentsia reinforced this trend. "Postmodernism," Bertens writes, "means and has meant different things to different people at different conceptual levels, rising from humble literary-critical origins in the 1950s to a level of global conceptualization in the 1980s." See Hans Bertens, *The Idea of the Postmodern: A History* (London: Routledge, 1995), 3ff.

10. Derrida, *Acts of Religion*, 44.
11. Bertens, *The Idea of the Postmodern*, 244.
12. Ibid., 245.
13. Charles H. Long, *Significations: Signs, Symbols, and Images in the Interpretation of Religion* (Aurora, CO: Davies Group, 1999), 85.
14. Ibid., 22.
15. Žižek, *Looking Awry*, 39.
16. Ibid., 39.
17. Ibid., 144. For Žižek's investigation of this theme in terms of concrete, cultural analysis, see his chapter "'The Wound Is Healed Only by the Spear That Smote You,'" in *Tarrying with the Negative: Kant, Hegel, and the Critique of Ideology* (Durham, NC: Duke University Press, 1993), 165–99.
18. Slavoj Žižek, *The Parallax View* (Cambridge, MA: MIT University Press, 2006), 17.
19. André Patsalides and Kareen Ror Malone, "Jouissance in the Cure," in *The Subject of Lacan: A Lacanian Reader for Psychologists*, ed. Kareen Ror

Malone and Stephen R. Friedlander (Albany: State University of New York Press, 2000), 130.

20. Hägglund's basic argument that the entirety of Derrida's work, even the "later" Derrida, follows a "radically atheist logic" that privileges the "trace" as a irreducible marker of finitude and temporality, thereby rendering all talk of "faith," "messianicity," etc., as simply rhetorical camouflage for the latter's authentic lifelong position, fails to convince because it tries to (1) formalize and domesticate the experimental venture of Derrida's early work, and (2) deploy it as a template to read the same into the whole of his writings, as if there were some kind of obvious, transparent thread to what he calls the "logic" of deconstruction. See Martin Hägglund, *Radical Atheism: Derrida and the Time of Life* (Stanford: Stanford University Press, 2008). Hägglund is apparently clueless about the particular philosophy of language—what I here term the "semiotic revolution"—that drives Derrida from beginning to end. Deconstruction was never a "logic," but a whole new take on the philosophy of language from the very beginning. In his book Hägglund assails Caputo, who pushes back by insisting that the former has clumsily overread him, which seems to be the case. Caputo maintains that Hägglund fails to grasp how one can be an "atheist" or even a "materialist" while still asserting some kind of meaningful concept of religion (i.e., a "religion without religion"). See Jack Caputo, "The Return of Anti-Religion: From Radical Atheism to Radical Theology," *Journal for Cultural and Religious Theory* 11, no. 2 (Spring 2011): 32–125. If he is correct about Hägglund's reading of Derrida, Caputo still adheres to the idea that Derrida has somehow facilitated the persistence of a "radical theology," to which Caputo seems to want to conflate any theory of religion.

21. Derrida, *Acts of Religion*, 77.

22. Ibid., 77.

23. Ibid., 81.

24. Ibid., 82.

25. Jacques Derrida, *The Gift of Death*, trans. David Wills (Chicago: University of Chicago Press, 1995), 49.

26. See John Caputo, *The Prayers and Tears of Jacques Derrida: Religion without Religion* (Bloomington: Indiana University Press, 1997).

27. Derrida, *The Gift of Death*, 80.

4. Radical Religion in the "Desert of the Real"

1. See Slavoj Žižek, *Welcome to the Desert of the Real* (New York: Verso, 2002).

2. Derrida, *Acts of Religion*, 46.

3. Edward Said, *Orientalism* (New York: Random House, 1979), 347.

4. Ian Almond, *The New Orientalists: Postmodern Representations of Islam from Foucault to Baudrillard* (London: I. B. Tauris, 2007), 4.

5. Ibid., 61.

6. Ibid., 60.
7. Gianni Vattimo, *After Christianity*, trans. Luca D'Isanto (New York: Columbia University Press, 2001).
8. Derrida, *Acts of Religion*, 306.
9. Olivier Roy, *Globalized Islam: The Search for a New Ummah* (New York: Columbia University Press, 2004), 233.
10. Ibid., 331.
11. Ibid., 332.
12. Gianni Vattimo, *Nihilism and Emancipation: Ethics, Politics, and Law*, trans. William McCuaig (New York: Columbia University Press, 2003), 81.
13. Ibid., 83–84.
14. Mark C. Taylor, ed., *Critical Terms for Religious Studies* (Chicago: University of Chicago Press, 1998), 12.
15. Jean-François Lyotard, *The Postmodern Condition: A Report on Knowledge*, trans. Geoff Bennington, Brian Massumi, and Fredric Jameson (Minneapolis: University of Minnesota Press, 1984), 82.
16. Derrida, *On the Name*, 65–66.

5. Bataille and Altizer

1. Georges Bataille, *Guilty*, trans. Bruce Boone (Venice, CA: Lapis Press, 1988), 11.
2. Ibid., 12.
3. Ibid., 16.
4. Ibid., 37.
5. Ibid., 42, italics mine.
6. Georges Bataille, *Lascaux, or, The Birth of Art: Prehistoric Painting*, trans. Austryn Wainhouse (Lausanne: Skira, 1955), 38–39.
7. Georges Bataille, *Theory of Religion*, trans. Robert Hurley (New York: Zone Books, 1992), 44.
8. Bataille, *Lascaux*, 130.
9. Friedrich Nietzsche, *Philosophy in the Tragic Age of the Greeks*, trans. Marianne Cowan (Chicago: Henry Regnery, 1962), 40.
10. See Georges Bataille, "The Cruel Practice of Art," trans. Supervert 32C Inc. (1993), http://supervert.com/elibrary/ georges_bataille/; originally published as *L'Art, Exercise de la cruauté*, in *Médicine de France* (1949).
11. Jean-François Lyotard, *Lessons on the Analytic of the Sublime* (Palo Alto: Stanford University Press, 1994), 1.
12. Immanuel Kant, *Critique of the Power of Judgment*, trans. Paul Guyer and Eric Matthew (Cambridge: Cambridge University Press, 2001), 146.
13. Clayton Crockett, *Interstices of the Sublime: Theology and Psychoanalytic Theory* (New York: Fordham University Press, 2007), 63.
14. Thomas J. J. Altizer, *The Gospel of Christian Atheism* (Philadelphia: Westminster Press, 1966), 41.

15. See, for example, the following statement: "History is moving toward the ultimate dissolution of the distinction between God and man and a merging of the two in the new godmanhood of the eschatology age." Theodore Runyan Jr., "Thomas Altizer and the Future of Theology", in *The Theology of Altizer: Critique and Response,* ed. John Cobb Jr. (Philadelphia: Westminster Press, 1970), 49.

16. Hebrews 2:14 (NIV).

17. Hebrews 9:20 (NIV).

18. Thomas J. J. Altizer, *The Self-Embodiment of God* (New York: Harper & Row, 1977), 96.

6. Levinas and the Final À-dieu to Theology

1. "The proper name 'Sinai' is thus just as enigmatic as the name 'face.' In the singular and the plural, retaining the memory of its Hebraic synonym, what is here called 'face' also starts to resemble some untranslatable proper name." Jacques Derrida, *Adieu to Emmanuel Levinas,* trans. Pascale-Anne Brault and Michael Naas (Stanford: Stanford University Press, 1999), 119.

2. Consider Derrida's famous remark, announcing the aporia that gives rise to deconstruction: "Are we Jews? Are we Greeks? We live in the difference between the Jew and the Greek, which is perhaps the unity of what is called history. We live in and of difference, that is, in *hypocrisy,* about which Levinas so profoundly says that it is 'not only a base contingent defect of man, but the underlying rending of a world attached to both the philosophers and the prophets.'" Jacques Derrida, *Writing and Difference,* trans. Alan Bass (Chicago: University of Chicago Press, 1978), 153.

3. Derrida, *Writing and Difference,* 141.

4. This argument essentially follows the analysis of Peter Sloterdijk in his provocative little book on Derrida written upon the latter's death in 2004. See Sloterdijk, *Derrida, an Egyptian: On the Problem of the Jewish Pyramid,* trans. Wieland Hoban (Malden, MA: Polity Press, 2009).

5. Derrida, *Adieu to Levinas,* 10.

6. Derrida, *Of Spirit,* 1.

7. Ibid., 112–13.

8. *Emmanuel Levinas: Basic Philosophical Writings,* ed. Adriann T. Peperzak, Simon Critchley, and Robert Bernasconi (Bloomington: Indiana University Press, 1996), 25.

9. Ibid., 86.

10. Emmanuel Levinas, *Ethics and Infinity: Conversations with Philippe Nemo,* trans. Richard A. Cohen (Pittsburgh: Duquesne University Press, 1985), 24–25.

11. It is significant that the movement of radical orthodoxy does not accede to the Levinasian reading of Descartes, though it is certainly aware of it. Such an accession would, in effect, undermine its systematic critique of

postmodernism as the culmination of modernist metaphysic. In a recent article Jean-Luc Marion seeks to refute the notion that there is a Cartesian "argument to the other" by insisting that the position Descartes develops in the third meditation belongs within the sphere of metaphysics and is not an implicit critique of ontotheology. The Cartesian argument is actually, according to Marion, "the thought of the cause completing the principle. Cartesian thought thus belongs strictly to metaphysics since it twice fulfills its onto-theo-logical constitution." That dyadic fulfillment, for Marion, derives from the Scholastic ideal of "sufficient reason," which is an onto-logical principle, not an opening to the "otherwise," as it is for Levinas. See Marion, "Descartes and Onto-Theology," in *Post-Secular Philosophy*, ed. Philip Blond (London: Routledge, 1998), 96.

12. Jacques Derrida, "Faith and Knowledge," in *Religion*, ed. Derrida and Gianni Vattimo (Stanford: Stanford University Press, 1996), 48.

13. In one important sense radical orthodoxy simply follows the "Christian" line of Israelite salvation, replacing the Derridean messianism of the *ganz Andere* with the liturgical community of faith. Both radical orthodoxy and deconstruction are involved in spectral conversations. As John Caputo says of Derrida, "Deconstruction talks with (*s'entretenir avec*) ghosts, with a spectral messianic figure, a figure of the impossible, of a *tout autre* whose comings we can only invoke but cannot foresee." See John D. Caputo, *The Prayers and Tears of Jacques Derrida: Religion without Religion* (Bloomington: University of Indiana Press, 1997), 149.

14. Emmanuel Levinas, *On Thinking-of-the-Other Entre Nous*, trans. Michael B. Smith and Barbara Harshav (New York: Columbia University Press, 1998), 73.

15. Emmanuel Levinas, *Otherwise than Being, or Beyond Essence* (The Hague: Martinus Nijhoff, 1981), 1.

16. See Levinas's discussion of being as "apophansis," the verbalization of the nominative that points us in the direction of the *autrement*. "In a predicative proposition, an apophansis, an entity can make itself be understood verbally, as a 'way' of essence, as the *fruitio essendi* itself, as a *how*, a modality of this essence or this temporalization." Levinas, *Otherwise than Being*, 38. Tracing back the temporalization into the "otherwise" is a "reading before" to the moment we call Sinai.

17. Levinas, *Otherwise than Being*, 43.

18. Ibid., 178.

19. Jacques Derrida, *The Politics of Friendship*, trans. George Collins (London: Verso, 1997), 188.

20. Ibid., 224.

21. Derrida, *The Gift of Death*, 47.

22. Ibid., 51.

23. Ibid., 50.

24. Ibid., 53.

25. Ibid., 56.

26. Ibid., 63.
27. Ibid., 84.
28. Ibid., 109.
29. For an extended discussion of how Kant makes this move, see my own *Moral Action, God, and History in the Thought of Immanuel Kant* (Missoula, MT: Scholars Press, 1973).
30. See Quentin Meillassoux, *After Finitude: An Essay on the Necessity of Contingency* (New York: Continuum, 2008).
31. There is a story that has circulated in recent years among those who studied with Levinas in France that once in a seminar the Jewish philosopher rejected any final insinuation that his phenomenology was ethical at all in the strict philosophical sense. "I'm not interested in ethics," he is reported to have fumed, "only holiness."
32. Emmanuel Levinas, *Collected Philosophical Papers*, trans. Alphonso Lingis (Amsterdam: Springer, 2008), 53.
33. Ibid., 54.
34. Emmanuel Levinas, *Beyond the Verse: Talmudic Readings and Lectures* (Bloomington: Indiana University Press, 1994), 149.
35. This point is emphasized by Hans-Dieter Gondek, "Cogito and Separation: Lacan/Levinas," in *Levinas and Lacan: The Missed Encounter*, ed. Sarah Harsym (Albany: State University of New York Press, 1998), 30.
36. Saint Augustine, *Confessions*, trans. R. S. Pine-Coffin (New York: Penguin Books, 1985), 207.
37. Emmanuel Levinas, *Totality and Infinity: An Essay on Exteriority*, 4th ed. (Amsterdam: Springer, 1980), 253.
38. Ibid., 253.
39. Jacques Lacan, *Écrits: A Selection*, trans. Bruce Fink (New York: W. W. Norton, 1966), 86.
40. Levinas, *Collected Philosophical Papers*, 43. For a collection of essays on the relationship between these two thinkers, see Harasym, *Levinas and Lacan*.
41. Gilles Deleuze, *Pure Immanence: Essays on a Life*, trans. Anne Boyman (New York: Zone Books, 2001), 67.
42. Ibid., 86.
43. Gilles Deleuze, *Expressionism in Philosophy: Spinoza* (New York: Zone Books, 1992), 49.
44. Gilles Deleuze, *The Logic of Sense*, trans. Constantin Boundas, Mark Lester, and Charles Stivale (New York: Columbia University Press, 1990), 179.
45. Levinas, *Beyond the Verse*, 129.
46. See, for example, Carl Olsen, *Zen and the Art of Postmodern Philosophy: Two Paths of Liberation from the Mode of Representational Thinking* (Albany: State University of New York Press, 2000); Steve Odin, "Derrida and the Decentered Universe of Chan/Zen Buddhism," *Journal of Chinese Philosophy* 17 (1990): 61–86; David Loy, "The Deconstruction of Buddhism," in *Derrida and Negative Theology*, ed. Harold Coward and Toby Foshay (Albany: State University of New York Press, 1992), 227–53. The book that launched these

sorts of discussions is Robert Magliola's *Derrida on the Mend* (West Lafayette, IN: Purdue University Press, 1984).

47. Keiji Nishitani, *Religion and Nothingness*, trans. Jan Van Bragt (Berkeley: University of California Press, 1982), 71.
48. Ibid., 71.
49. Ibid., 149.
50. Ibid., 150.
51. Deleuze, *Expressionism in Philosophy*, 27.
52. Jacques Derrida, *Of Grammatology*, trans. Gayatri Spivak, corrected ed. (Baltimore: Johns Hopkins University Press, 1998), 11.

7. Deleuze and Nomadology

1. Gilles Deleuze and Félix Guattari, *A Thousand Plateaus: Capitalism and Schizophrenia*, trans. Brian Massumi (Minneapolis: University of Minnesota Press, 1987), 374.
2. Gilles Deleuze, *Nietzsche and Philosophy*, trans. Hugh Tomlinson (New York: Columbia University Press, 1983), 3.
3. Ibid., 108.
4. Ibid., 75.
5. Ibid., 78.
6. Ibid., 104.
7. Ibid., 108.
8. Ibid., 195.
9. G. W. F. Hegel, *Phenomenology of Spirit*, trans. A. V. Miller (Oxford: Oxford University Press, 1977), 482.
10. Deleuze and Guattari, *A Thousand Plateaus*, 374–75.
11. Ibid., 351.
12. Mark C. Taylor, "GNICART TRACING," in *New Dimensions in Philosophical Theology*, ed. Carl Raschke (Chico, CA: Scholars Press, 1982), 85–108.
13. Deleuze and Guattari, *Nietzsche and Philosophy*, 197.
14. Jacques Derrida, *The Work of Mourning*, ed. Pascale-Anne Brault and Michael Nass (Chicago: University of Chicago Press, 2001), 192.
15. Jean-Luc Nancy, *Being Singular Plural*, trans. Robert D. Richardson and Anne E. O'Byrne (Stanford: Stanford University Press, 2000), 39.
16. Nancy, *Being Singular Plural*, 84.
17. "There is a simple general formula for the signifying regime of the sign (the signifying sign): every sign refers to another sign, and only to another sign, ad infinitum. That is why, at the limit, one can forgo the notion of the sign, for what is retained is not principally the sign's relation to a state of things it designates, or to an entity it signifies, but only the formal relation of sign to sign insofar as it defines a so-called signifying chain. The limitlessness of signifiance replaces the sign." Deleuze and Guattari, *A Thousand Plateaus*, 112, italics mine.
18. Nancy, *Being Singular Plural*, 85.

19. Ibid., 86.
20. Ibid., 165.
21. Ibid., 171.
22. Deleuze and Guattari, *A Thousand Plateaus*, 261.
23. Ibid., 263.
24. Ibid., 263.
25. Ibid., 264.
26. David Hale, *Of Nomadology: Religion and the War Machine* (Berlin: VDM Verlag, 2008), 105.
27. Deleuze and Guattari, *A Thousand Plateaus*, 266.
28. Ibid., 270.
29. Ibid., 271.
30. Ibid., 289.
31. Gilles Deleuze and Felix Guattari, *What Is Philosophy?*, trans. Hugh Tomlinson and Graham Burchell (New York: Columbia University Press, 1996), 208.
32. Deleuze and Guattari, *A Thousand Plateaus*, 318.
33. Ibid., 322.
34. Ibid., 350.
35. Deleuze and Guattari, *What Is Philosophy?*, 110.
36. Deleuze and Guattari, *A Thousand Plateaus*, 321.
37. Deleuze develops the notion of "conceptual personae" in *What Is Philosophy?*, which he wrote with Guattari toward the end of his career. The "conceptual personae" is the real concept that can only be disclosed in its relationality, its interassembly, and its dynamism and creativity. Deleuze argues, in effect, that there is no such thing as an "intellectual history" of concepts, or such a thing as a history of philosophy per se. The Greek "tradition" of philosophy begins with a collegial friendship of sages and disciples that has a life of its own. In other words, philosophy is always interpersonal, and genetically so. "The friend who appears in philosophy no longer stands for an extrinsic persona, an example or empirical circumstance, but rather a presence that is intrinsic to thought, a condition of possibility of thought itself, a living category, a transcendental lived reality." It is this "vital relationship with the Other," whether a friend or an enemy, whereby philosophy becomes "the discipline that involves creating concepts." *What Is Philosophy?*, 3, 5.
38. Derrida, "Faith and Knowledge," 60.
39. Ibid., 66.
40. Ibid., 66.
41. Ibid., 51.
42. Deleuze, *The Logic of Sense*, 271.
43. Gilles Deleuze, *Difference and Repetition*, trans. Paul Patton (New York: Columbia University Press, 1994), 202.
44. Ibid., 205.
45. Ibid., 216.

46. Ibid., 139.
47. Deleuze and Guattari, *What Is Philosophy?*, 85.
48. Ibid., 85.
49. Ibid., 21.
50. Ibid., 88.
51. Ibid., 89.
52. Ibid., 89, italics mine.
53. Ibid., 90.
54. Ibid., 97.
55. Ibid., 101.

8. Žižek and the Failure of the Subject

1. See the video clip on the web at http://vimeo.com/7732119.
2. For a brilliant tour of how all this comes about in Žižek, see Adrian Johnson, *Žižek's Ontology: A Transcendental Materialist Theory of Subjectivity* (Evanston: Northwestern University Press, 2008).
3. Schelling's importance for postmodern philosophy, which Žižek brings to the fore, is encapsulated in this well-known statement. So much of postmodern philosophy, particularly the work of Deleuze, can be viewed as a reaction against Hegel, who in turn developed his own dialectic as a reaction to Schelling. Hegel could not bear the thought that philosophy could intuit the "ground," the primal identity, of what is in the cosmos. While identity cannot be philosophically posited or presupposed, as far as Hegel is concerned, neither can it be deduced metaphysically by invoking the law of noncontradiction. There must be a temporal process to its development, the "labor of the negative"—hence the dialectic. "The issue between Schelling and Hegel," as Andrew Bowie observes, is "whether the Absolute can, as Hegel thinks, be grasped by the process of reflection." Bowie, *Schelling and Modern European Philosophy: An Introduction* (London: Routledge, 1993), 56. For a further and closer reading concerning the controversy between Schelling and Hegel, see John Laughland, *Schelling versus Hegel: From German Idealism to Christian Metaphysics* (Burlington, VT: Ashgate, 2007).
4. Bruce Fink, *The Lacanian Subject: Between Language and* Jouissance (Princeton: Princeton University Press, 1995), 45.
5. Ibid., 52.
6. Žižek, *The Ticklish Subject: The Absent Centre of Political Ontology* (New York: Verso, 1999), 184–85.
7. Ibid., 483.
8. Slavoj Žižek, *The Indivisible Remainder* (New York: Verso, 1996), 48.
9. Žižek, *The Indivisible Remainder*, 110.
10. Žižek, *The Ticklish Subject*, xxiii.
11. Ibid., 36.
12. Ibid., 37.
13. Deleuze and Guattari, *What Is Philosophy?*, 156.

14. Deleuze, *Expressionism in Philosophy*, 28.
15. Ibid., 28.
16. Slavoj Žižek, *Organs without Bodies: On Deleuze and Consequences* (New York: Routledge, 2004), 20.
17. Ibid., 53.
18. Ibid., 61.
19. Ibid., 69.
20. Slavoj Žižek, *The Puppet and the Dwarf: The Perverse Core of Christianity* (Boston: MIT Press, 2003), 17.
21. Slavoj Žižek, *The Fragile Absolute, or Why Is the Christian Legacy Worth Fighting For?* (New York: Verso, 2000), 86.
22. Ibid., 92.
23. Slavoj Žižek and John Milbank, *The Monstrosity of Christ* (Cambridge, MA: MIT Press, 2009), 117.
24. Ibid., 169.
25. Ibid., 81.
26. Ibid., 80.
27. Ibid., 80.
28. Ibid., 257.
29. Ibid., 260.

9. Badiou and the Prospects for Theory

1. Alain Badiou, *St. Paul: The Foundations of Universalism*, trans. Ray Brassier (Stanford: Stanford University Press, 2003), 40.
2. Alain Badiou, *Deleuze: The Clamor of Being*, trans. Louise Burchill (Minneapolis: University of Minnesota Press, 2000), 101.
3. Badiou, *St. Paul*, 42.
4. Ibid., 42.
5. Ibid., 43.
6. Ibid., 48.
7. Ibid., 57.
8. Ibid., 58.
9. Ibid., 78.
10. Ibid., 97.
11. Alain Badiou, *Being and Event*, trans. Oliver Feltham (New York: Continuum, 2005), 16.
12. Ibid., 331.
13. Ibid., 331.
14. Ibid., 355.
15. Badiou, *Deleuze: The Clamor of Being*, 79.
16. Badiou, *Being and Event*, 143.
17. Ibid., 145.
18. Ibid., 84.
19. Ibid., 322.

20. Julia Kristeva, "Toward a Semiology of Paragrams," in *The Tel Quel Reader*, ed. Patrick Ffrench and Roland-François Lack (London: Routledge, 1998), 25.
21. Ibid., 26.
22. Ibid., 29.
23. Julia Kristeva, "Revolution in Poetic Language," in *The Kristeva Reader*, ed. Toril Moi (New York: Columbia University Press, 1986), 112. See a careful exposition of Kristeva's views (despite its Freudianism) in Calvin Bedient, "Kristeva and Poetry as Shattered Signification," *Critical Inquiry* 16 (Summer 1990): 807–29.
24. Kristeva, "Revolution in Poetic Language," 108.
25. Deleuze, *Expressionism in Philosophy*, 322.
26. Ibid., 233.
27. Colossians 1:16–17.
28. Deleuze, *Expressionism in Philosophy*, 323.
29. Deleuze, *The Logic of Sense*, 52.

Conclusion

1. Tim Woods, *Beginning Postmodernism* (Manchester: Manchester University Press, 1999), 257.
2. Deleuze, *Nietzsche and Philosophy*, 41.
3. Martin Heidegger, *Contributions to Philosophy (From Enowning)*, trans. Parvis Emad and Kenneth Maly (Bloomington: Indiana University Press, 1999), 3.
4. Ibid., 8.
5. Nancy, *Dis-Enclosure*, 107.
6. Victor Taylor, "Disfiguring Postmodern Theology," *Bulletin of the Council of Societies for the Study of Religion* 37 (April 2008): 43. Taylor's perspective on the connection between postmodern religious thought and religious studies is first sketched in his groundbreaking book *Para/Inquiry*. He develops this argument in a somewhat different way in his *Religion after Postmodernism: Retheorizing Myth and Literature* (Charlottesville: University of Virginia Press, 2008).
7. See, for example, Feyerabend's profession that "not only are facts and theories in constant disharmony, they are never as neatly separated as everyone makes them out to be." Paul Feyerabend, *Against Method* (New York: Verso, 1993), 51.
8. "Religionsverständnis ist ohne religiöse Bildung nicht möglich. In dessen Bildung darf eine der Hauptaufgabe der Theologie in der Gegenwart gesehen werden. Um diese Aufgabewahrnehmen zu können, muss sich die Theologie religionstheoretischen und kulturhermeneutischen Fragestellungen und Methoden öffnen und *sich also normative Religionswissenschaft verstehen.*" (The understanding of religion apart from its development is not possible. In the development of religion can one of the main tasks of theology today be seen. In order to be able to conceive of this task, theology must unravel the

question and methods of the theory of religion and cultural hermeneutics, and it must therefore understand itself as a normative science.) Christian Danz, *Die Deutung der Religion in der Kultur* (Koblenz: Neukirchner Verlag, 2008), 145, italics mine.

9. . . . Ein jeder Engel ist schrecklich.
Und so verhalt ich mich denn und verschlucke den Lockruf
dunkelen Schluchzens. Ach, wen vermögen
wir denn zu brauchen? Engel nicht, Menschen nicht,
und die findigen Tiere merken es schon,
daß wir nicht sehr verläßlich zu Haus sind
in der gedeuteten Welt. . . .

> Rainier Marie Rilke, *Duino Elegies*, First Elegy, translation mine.

INDEX

■

234   INDEX

sacrifice, concept of, 68–69, 73, 90,
   93–96, 98, 102–5, 110–11, 118, 158,
   174, 177
Schelling, Friedrich Wilhelm Joseph
   von, 166, 169–72, 174, 176, 224n3
science, 9, 15–16, 21–22, 26–27, 29, 31,
   34, 40, 54, 63–64, 67, 82, 85, 106, 113,
   117, 133, 137, 142, 161–62, 181–82,
   193, 207, 210; "human sciences,"
   22, 66, 83, 115–16, 163, 210, 226n8;
   of religion, 14, 34, 36–38, 46–51, 60,
   83; social sciences, 14, 21–22, 38, 46,
   65, 82
semiosis, 27, 29–30, 39, 41, 49, 58, 100,
   106, 110, 122, 149, 152, 154, 187, 200,
   203
semiotics, theory of, 6, 16, 25–29,
   31–33, 50, 64–65, 82, 102–4, 106–7,
   116, 123, 128, 131, 133, 137, 142, 147,
   149, 152, 154, 158, 162–64, 168, 183,
   191, 194, 214n0; immanent, 130, 161;
   semiotic chora, 196–97, 210; semiotic
   revolution, 4–5, 85; semiotic turn, 26.
   See also Prague school of semiotics
set theory, 184, 188, 190–93, 195. See
   also Badiou, Alain
sign, concept of the, 4–6, 9, 14–20,
   22, 24–28, 30, 32, 36, 38–40, 42–44,
   46–48, 50–51, 54, 56, 58–62, 64, 66,
   68–69, 72, 74, 76, 78, 80, 82, 84–85,
   89, 92, 95–96, 99, 109–10, 114–15,
   118, 126, 131–33, 137–39, 141–43,
   147–48, 150–51, 154–55, 158, 162,
   185, 192–95, 197–99, 201, 204,
   210–11; negative, 125; religious,
   47, 162, 210; sign-differentials, 200;
   sign-events, 139; sign-functions, 26,
   33; sign of signs, 137–39, 162; sign-
   singularity, 115
signification, 8, 16, 18, 20, 25, 27, 30,
   32, 39–42, 55, 57–58, 62, 64, 71, 92,
   95, 99–101, 110, 115–16, 122–23, 126,
   128–32, 136–37, 139, 144, 147–48,
   150–54, 160, 163, 166, 175, 180,
   186–87, 189, 193–97, 199, 202, 204,
   207–8, 210–11, 216; force of, 125, 140;
   order of, 45, 50; postmodernist theory
   of, 91; religious, 104, 139; signature
   as, 49, 89, 92, 95, 109, 113, 116, 153;
   singular, 143, 189; theological, 131;
   theory of, 128, 193
signifier, idea of the, 16, 27, 30, 50,
   57–58, 62, 100, 137, 140, 158, 179,
   207; theological notion of the, 211;
   religious, 51, 207

Sinai, 108–11, 113–14, 132, 219–20
singularity, 5–9, 37, 51, 54, 56, 65, 75,
   83–85, 99–101, 105–7, 109, 114–15,
   121, 124, 135, 142, 147–49, 155,
   174–76, 180–81, 187, 189, 196–97,
   201–2, 204, 208, 211–12; infinite, 204;
   semiotic, 194, 211; signifying, 9, 140,
   149, 188; religious, 181, 202, 204
site, 7, 29, 56, 72, 103, 110, 113, 124,
   128, 155, 158–59, 174–75, 181, 190,
   203
Smith, Jonathan Z., 17, 28, 47–48, 82
space, smooth (in Deleuze), 51, 139, 163
specter, Derrida's notion of the, 40,
   49–50, 53, 55, 71–72, 81, 108, 110,
   114, 117, 139, 170, 178–79, 198, 204
Spinoza, Baruch, 119, 130, 137, 173,
   198–200, 203
spirit, philosophical concept of, 59,
   93–94, 96, 101, 103, 108, 111–13, 132,
   144–45, 181, 211
state, Deleuze's theory of the, 142–46
subject, theory of the, 24, 39, 50, 63–64,
   67, 93, 116–17, 119, 123–24, 127–28,
   130, 134, 143, 151–54, 158, 160,
   164, 166–73, 175, 177, 179–80, 183,
   189, 192, 196, 204, 215n9; barred
   (in Žižek), 116, 166, 168; sovereign,
   92; split, 166–67, 169–70, 175.
   See also Cartesian subject
subjectivity, 75, 113, 116, 119, 128, 134,
   164, 167–69, 171–72, 175, 180
sublime, concept of the, 37, 49, 76,
   99–100, 106
supplement, the philosophical, 19, 50,
   53, 69, 95, 125, 158, 169, 179, 196. See
   also Derrida, Jacques
symptom, philosophical notion of the,
   69, 142, 178. See also Deleuze, Gilles;
   Lacan, Jacques

Taylor, Mark C., 43–44, 82, 97, 106
Taylor, Victor, 39, 209
territorialization, 7, 53, 57, 83, 154–57,
   198, 201. See also deterritorialization
territory, Deleuzian notion of, 7, 33,
   136, 139, 154–56, 160, 163, 172, 201,
   211
text, philosophical treatment of the, 3,
   16, 26, 31–32, 39, 44, 47, 65, 69, 74,
   76, 84, 90, 99, 109–11, 113–14, 122,
   125, 133–34, 136, 146–48, 150, 178,
   194, 201. See also Derrida, Jacques
theology, 5, 9, 18–20, 28–29, 31, 41,
   43–44, 46, 60, 65–66, 69, 76, 81, 84,

RECENT BOOKS IN THE STUDIES IN RELIGION AND CULTURE SERIES